CW00671953

Martin Robson is a member of the Corbett Centre for Maritime Policy Studies, Defence Studies Department, King's College London, at the Joint Services Command and Staff College. He is a specialist in British grand strategy, maritime global conflict and the Royal Navy during the age of sail. He holds a PhD from the Department of War Studies, King's College London, and is a former Caird Senior Research Fellow at the National Maritime Museum. His books include *Britain, Portugal and South America in the Napoleonic Wars: Alliances and Diplomacy in Economic Maritime Conflict* (I.B.Tauris) and *The Battle of Trafalgar.*

A History of the Royal Navy: The Age of Sail
Andrew Baines (ISBN: 978 1 78076 992 9)

A History of the Royal Navy: Air Power and British Naval Aviation
Ben Jones (ISBN: 978 1 78076 993 6)

A History of the Royal Navy: The American Revolutionary War
Martin Robson (ISBN: 978 1 78076 994 3)

A History of the Royal Navy: Empire and Imperialism
Daniel Owen Spence (ISBN: 978 1 78076 543 3)

A History of the Royal Navy: The Napoleonic Wars
Martin Robson (ISBN 978 1 78076 544 0)

A History of the Royal Navy: The Nuclear Age
Philip D. Grove (ISBN: 978 1 78076 995 0)

A History of the Royal Navy: The Royal Marines
Britt Zerbe (ISBN: 978 1 78076 765 9)

A History of the Royal Navy: The Seven Years' War
Martin Robson (ISBN: 978 1 78076 545 7)

A History of the Royal Navy: The Submarine
Duncan Redford (ISBN: 978 1 78076 546 4)

A History of the Royal Navy: The Victorian Age
Andrew Baines (ISBN: 978 1 78076 749 9)

A History of the Royal Navy: Women and the Royal Navy
Jo Stanley (ISBN: 978 1 78076 756 7)

A History of the Royal Navy: World War I
Mike Farquharson-Roberts (ISBN: 978 1 78076 838 0)

A History of the Royal Navy: World War II
Duncan Redford (ISBN: 978 1 78076 546 4)

The Royal Navy: A History Since 1900
Duncan Redford and Philip D. Grove (ISBN: 978 1 78076 782 6)

A HISTORY OF THE
ROYAL NAVY
The Napoleonic Wars

Martin Robson

in association with

Published in 2014 by I.B.Tauris & Co. Ltd
6 Salem Road, London W2 4BU
175 Fifth Avenue, New York NY 10010
www.ibtauris.com

Distributed in the United States and Canada Exclusively by
Palgrave Macmillan, 175 Fifth Avenue, New York NY 10010

ISBN: 978 1 78076 544 0
eISBN: 978 0 85773 508 9

A full CIP record for this book is available from the British Library
A full CIP record is available from the Library of Congress

Library of Congress Catalog Card Number: available

Typeset in Perpetua by A. & D. Worthington, Newmarket, Suffolk
Printed and bound in Great Britain by T.J. International, Padstow,
Cornwall

Contents

List of Tables, Figures and Maps		vii
List of Colour Plates		xi
Series Foreword		xiii
Acknowledgements		xv
Preface: 'The ever to be lamented death of Vice Admiral Lord Viscount Nelson'		xvii
	Introduction: 'Wherever there is water to float a ship, we are sure to find you in our way'	1
1.	'Never was a more hard fought action in the Seas': Home Waters, 1793–1802	7
2.	'Nelson's Patent Bridge for Boarding First Rates': The Mediterranean, 1793–1802	39
3.	'The first point to make perfectly certain': The Global War, 1793–1802	75
4.	'I do not say they cannot come, I merely say they cannot come by sea': The Invasion Threat, 1802–05	101
5.	'Engage the Enemy more closely': The Battle of Trafalgar, 1805	121
6.	'I cannot too much lament not to have arrived a few days sooner': Home Waters and the Baltic, 1805–15	145
7.	'Our maritime superiority': The Mediterranean and the Peninsular War, 1805–15	163
8.	'The carrier of the commerce of the continent of Europe': Economic Warfare, 1805–15	183

9.   'A complete stop to all trade and intercourse by Sea':
     The War of 1812   201
     Epilogue: 'That will do [...] Fire, my fine fellows':
     Algiers, 1816   227
     Conclusion: 'Lords of the sea'   231

     Notes   235
     Bibliography   251
     Index   259

Tables, Figures and Maps

Tables

4.1.	State of the opposing forces at the start of March 1805	110
6.1.	The European navies, 1805–10	147

Figures

P.1.	Fruit bowl depicting a somewhat romantic view of the death of Nelson (NMRN)	xviii
P.2.	*The Death of Nelson, 21 October 1805* by Arthur William Devis, 1807 (NMRN)	xviii
P.3.	The surgeon's table aboard HMS *Victory* (NMRN)	xxi
I.1.	Napoleon being transferred from the *Bellerophon* to the *Northumberland* for his final voyage to St Helena (NMRN)	2
I.2.	*A View of the Royal Navy of Great Britain*, 1804 (NMM)	5
1.1.	The Glorious First of June. Plans for the fleet's 'order of sailing' in three or two lines (NMRN)	13
1.2.	The Glorious First of June, 1794	15
1.3.	Lord Howe on the quarterdeck of the *Queen Charlotte* receiving a ceremonial sword from King George III (NMRN)	17
1.4.	The 'French Cap of Liberty' taken from the French frigate *Unité* by HMS *Revolutionaire* on 12 April 1796 (NMRN)	18

1.5.	A sailor's description of a chase and capture (NMRN)	19
1.6.	The battle of Camperdown, 11 October 1797	24
1.7.	John Jervis, 1st Earl of St Vincent, after Abbott (NMRN)	28
1.8.	The battle of Copenhagen, 2 April 1801	31
1.9.	The battle of Copenhagen, 1801 (NMRN)	33
1.10.	Sword broken in the hand of Captain John Stuart on board HMS *Medusa* (NMRN)	37
2.1.	The battle of Cape St Vincent, 14 February 1797	50
2.2.	The battle of the Nile, 1 August 1798	58
2.3.	*Extirpation of the Plagues of Egypt* (NMRN)	61
2.4.	Nelson and the 'Victors of the Nile' (NMRN)	61
2.5.	Admiral Sir William Sidney Smith defending the ramparts of Acre (UK government art collection)	64
2.6.	Nelson's plans (1799) to use two divisions (weather and lee) to attack an enemy fleet (NMRN)	67
2.7.	Saumarez's action of 12 July 1801 (NMRN)	69
2.8.	The successful amphibious assault by British forces on 8 March 1801 (NMRN)	73
3.1.	Captain Faulkner's HMS *Zebra* assaults and captures Fort Louis, Martinique, 20 March 1794 (NMM)	81
3.2.	Thomas Byam Martin's soup tureen, presented by a merchant of Antigua, 1797 (NMRN)	83
3.3.	Recapture of the *Hermione* by Captain Edward Hamilton's HMS *Surprise*, 25 October 1799 (NMRN)	84
3.4.	Sir Edward Hamilton (NMRN)	85
3.5.	Sir Home Riggs Popham (NMRN)	96
4.1.	*The Plum Pudding in Danger* (NMRN)	103
4.2.	*Let them boast of invasion* (NMRN)	106
4.3.	Nelson's pursuit of Villeneuve across the Atlantic (NMRN)	112
4.4.	Admiral Charles Middleton, Lord Barham (NMRN)	113

5.1.   Nelson explaining his plan of attack to his officers
       (NMRN)   123
5.2.   The battle of Trafalgar, 21 October 1805   127
5.3.   Captain Charles Adair (Royal Marines Museum)   134
5.4.   HMS *Victory*'s gundeck (NMRN)   135
5.5.   *The Battle of Trafalgar* by Thomas Luny (NMRN)   138
5.6.   *Britannia Triumphant* (NMRN)   141
6.1.   Lloyd's Patriotic Fund £50 sword presented to
       Lieutenant John Haswell of HMS *Pallas* (NMRN)   146
6.2.   British tars towing the Danish fleet into harbour
       (NMRN)   149
6.3.   Admiral Sir James Saumarez (NMM)   151
6.4.   Destruction of the French fleet in Basque Roads, 12
       April 1809 (NMM)   160
7.1.   Vice Admiral Cuthbert Collingwood (NMRN)   165
7.2.   *A large First Rate, said to be HMS 'Victory', lying off the*
       mouth of the Tagus (T. Buttersworth)   176
7.3.   Naval General Service Medals awarded in 1847 to
       men who participated in Hoste's action at Lissa, 13
       March 1811 (NMRN)   182
8.1.   *The Continental Dockyard* (NMRN)   184
8.2.   Lieutenant William Coombe's presentation sword
       for a boat action on 21 January 1807 (NMRN)   191
8.3.   1847 Naval General Service Medal for the *Galatea*'s
       boat action with the *Lynx* (NMRN)   192
8.4.   Île de France. View from the deck of the *Upton*
       Castle (NMM)   195
8.5.   Banda Neira Silver Vase, 1812 (NMRN)   198
9.1.   HMS *Shannon* taking the USS *Chesapeake* in just 11
       minutes, 1 June 1813 (NMM)   208
9.2.   The shallow draft of the 102-gun first rate HMS *St*
       Lawrence (NMM)   217
9.3.   Rear Admiral George Cockburn (NMM)   222

9.4.	Sword presented to Captain John Richard Lumley of the 38-gun frigate *Pomone* (NMRN)	224
E.1.	Presentation sword of Sir Edward Pellew, Lord Exmouth, for his action against the Dey of Algiers, 27 August 1816 (NMRN)	229
C.1.	'Nappy in tow' by Cruickshank, 24 August 1803 (NMRN)	233

Maps

1.	The Atlantic	xxii
2.	The Caribbean	xxiii
3.	Europe	xxiv
4.	The Mediterranean	xxv
5.	The Far East	xxvi

Colour Plates

1. Model of HMS *Kent* (NMRN)
2. Boat action involving Nelson off Cadiz in 1797 (NMRN)
3. *The Destruction of 'L'Orient' at the Battle of the Nile, 1 August 1798* by George Arnald (NMM)
4. *The Battle of Trafalgar, 21 October 1805* by Nicholas Pocock (NMRN)
5. *The Battle of Trafalgar, 2.30pm* by W.L. Wyllie (NMRN)
6. HMS *Victory*, sailors' messing facilities and hammocks slung between guns (NMRN)
7. HMS *Victory*'s dining cabin (NMRN)
8. HMS *Victory* pictured in 2011 (NMRN)

Series Foreword

The Royal Navy has for centuries played a vital if sometimes misunderstood or even at times unsung part in Britain's history. Often it has been the principal, sometimes the only means of defending British interests around the world. In peacetime the Royal Navy carries out a multitude of tasks as part of government policy – showing the flag, or naval diplomacy as it is now often called. In wartime, as the senior service of Britain's armed forces, the Navy has taken the war to the enemy, by battle, by economic blockade or by attacking hostile territory from the sea. Adversaries have changed over the centuries. Old rivals have become today's alliance partners; the types of ship, the weapons within them and the technology – the 'how' of naval combat – have also changed. But fundamentally what the Navy does has not changed. It exists to serve Britain's government and its people, to protect them and their interests wherever they might be threatened in the world.

This series, through the numerous individual books within it, throws new light on almost every aspect of Britain's Royal Navy: its ships, its people, the technology, the wars and peacetime operations too, from the birth of the modern navy following the restoration of Charles II to the throne in the late seventeenth century to the war on terror in the early twenty-first century.

The series consists of three chronologically themed books covering the sailing navy from the 1660s until 1815, the Navy in the nineteenth century from the end of the Napoleonic Wars, and the Navy since 1900. These are complemented by a number of slightly shorter books which examine the Navy's part in particular wars, such as the Seven Years' War, the American Revolution, the Napoleonic Wars, World War I, World War II and the Cold War, or particular aspects of the service: the Navy and empire, the Women's Royal Naval Service, the Royal Marines, naval aviation and the submarine service. The books are standalone works in their own right, but when taken as a series present the most comprehensive and readable history of the Royal Navy.

Duncan Redford
National Museum of the Royal Navy

'The role in Britain's history of the Royal Navy is all too easily and too often overlooked; this series will go a long way to redressing the balance. Anyone with an interest in British history in general or the Royal Navy in particular will find this series an invaluable and enjoyable resource.'

Tim Benbow
Defence Studies Department,
King's College London at the
Defence Academy of the UK

Acknowledgements

I will always be indebted to a number of people who have helped me in my chosen career. Professor Andrew Lambert at the Department of War Studies, King's College London was my PhD supervisor and remains a source of much inspiration. Conversations many moons ago with Dr Thomas Munch-Petersen provided much useful information relating to the Copenhagen expedition of 1807 and the transfer of the secret intelligence from Tilsit in 1807.

My colleagues at King's College London's Defence Studies Department at the Joint Services Command and Staff College, Defence Academy of the UK have provided a constant source of inspiration, expertise and advice. By the time this book is published I will have left for pastures new but I remain very much in their debt. Conversations about naval history with Professor Geoffrey Till across our respective desks have provided a welcome distraction from more day-to-day matters. I am also thankful to fellow 'Corbettians', notably the Director of the Corbett Centre for Maritime Policy Studies, Professor Greg Kennedy, and to Drs Jon Robb-Webb, Andrew Gordon, Tim Benbow, Harry Dickinson and Huw Davies. Our candid and wide-ranging conversations over coffee or lunch have provided me with much food for thought about the Royal Navy during the Napoleonic era.

I would also like to thank the staff at a number of archives and libraries for their helpful assistance in my research: the Joint Services Command and Staff College, The National Archives, the British Library, the National Maritime Museum, Cambridge County Record Office, the Institute of Historical Research and the West Yorkshire Archive Service. I am grateful to the estate of Lord Harewood for permission to quote from the George Canning Papers. I am also grateful to the copyright holders for permission to reproduce the images contained in this book; their contributions are mentioned at the appropriate place. The help provided by picture archive staff at the National Museum of the Royal Navy, the Royal Marines Museum and the National Maritime Museum has greatly assisted me in sourcing the images for the book.

Yet again, Jo Godfrey at I.B.Tauris has displayed much patience during the writing process. Covering 22 years of conflict in 70,000 words is no easy matter, and the comments of my series editor, Dr Duncan Redford, have contributed greatly to achieving the impossible of actually pouring a quart into a pint pot as well as providing a sounding board for ideas. Of course, any errors that remain in the work are entirely my own.

It is far too easy to become immersed in the minutiae of seapower, naval history and the Royal Navy, and Charlotte, Horatio and Lysander have provided a much loved and very welcome distraction from the brutal business of war at sea in the age of sail.

Martin Robson, Ide, Devon, 2014

'The ever to be lamented death of Vice Admiral Lord Viscount Nelson'

Mention of the Royal Navy of the French Revolutionary and Napoleonic Wars inevitably leads to three subjects: the battle of Trafalgar of 21 October 1805, Nelson's death at that battle and his famous ship HMS *Victory*. The history of the Royal Navy during these years is far richer and far more important than just these three subjects, yet it is impossible for a book like this to escape fully from the shadow of the most decisive battle in the Royal Navy's history, the most important naval officer ever to serve and the tangible link to the age of the sailing man of war which can still be explored at the National Museum of the Royal Navy, Portsmouth.

By the time of his death, Nelson's career had marked him out as the greatest exponent of naval warfare of his time. He was the first real popular celebrity, even possessing the obligatory controversial private life. With typical drama, the nature of his personal suffering at the time of his greatest victory came to overshadow the wider strategic achievements of the Royal Navy on 21 October 1805. For Nelson's death was not instantaneous. He was not truncated or decapitated by roundshot, nor did he suffer an immediately fatal musket shot. Instead his was a lingering death. He did not die on his quarterdeck, but below in the gruesome, dark and cramped confines of HMS *Victory*'s cockpit. This was where the surgeons went about their grisly business; wounded men lay in every inch of

Fig. P.1. Fruit bowl depicting a somewhat romantic
view of the death of Nelson.

Fig. P.2. Painted in 1807, *The Death of Nelson, 21 October 1805* by Arthur
William Devis was a careful, if highly inaccurate, study, lifting Nelson
from the realm of mortal men into a quasi-religious icon.

deck space. It was a nauseating, hellish place and *Victory*'s chaplain, Alexander Scott, one of the key eyewitnesses to the last few hours of Nelson's life, had nightmares about it for the rest of his life. In all his remaining years Scott could only bring himself to talk about it once, when he referred to the scene: 'it was like a butchers shambles!' Nelson was examined by *Victory*'s surgeon, William Beatty, who recognized that the wound was mortal. Beatty was also responsible for preserving Nelson's remains, which he placed in a large cask filled with brandy. The musket ball that killed him had been fired from the tops of the *Redoubtable* and was recovered by Beatty during the autopsy. It was presented to Beatty by King William IV, who knighted him in 1831.

Nelson's death was recorded for posterity by key eyewitnesses and was immediately portrayed in quasi-religious imagery. Beatty himself wrote a detailed account entitled *An Authentic Narrative of the Death of Lord Nelson*. Admiral Cuthbert Collingwood, Nelson's second in command, began his post-battle report with the words, 'The ever to be lamented death of Vice Admiral Lord Viscount Nelson, who, in the late conflict with the enemy, fell in the hour of victory'. The battle and his death raised Nelson from the ranks of normal humanity into an immortal figure revered as a demigod. For a society which was being transformed by the wars against France, moving away from the age of Enlightenment through to the Romantic movement of post-war peace, Nelson's demise was legendary: 'it was the ideal romantic death'.[1]

This contrasts starkly with the log of HMS *Victory* for Tuesday 22 October which describes the action of the battle of Trafalgar fought the previous day:

ModtWd at 11.40 the action commenced between the Ry Sovereign and the rear of the enemy's line, at 11.50 the van of the enemy's line opened their fire on us, all sail set, at 12.12 opened our fire, at 12.20 in attempting to break through the enemy's line fell on board the 10th and 11th ships, the action became general with the van ships of both columns, at 1.15 the Right Honble Lord Viscount Nelson was wounded, at 1.30 the Redoutable having struck ceased firing our starboard guns, the action continued larboard side with the San Tissima Trinidada and some other ships, at 3.0 all the enemy's ships near us having struck ceased firing, observed the Royal Sovereign had lost her main and mizen mast, and several dismasted prizes around her, at 3.10 4 of the enemy's van tack'd and stood along our line and engaged us in passing, at 3.40 made the signl for our own ships to keep their wind, for the purpose of attacking the enemy's van, at 4.45 the Spanish Rear Adm struck and one of the enemy's ships blew up, the Right Honble Lord Viscount Nelson departed this life [...]

This is an impersonal, unemotional account of *Victory*'s role in the battle and the death of Nelson. What is more enlightening was what happened over the course of the next few hours:

at 5 the mizzen mast fell, our ships employd in taking possession of the prizes, Vice Admiral Collingwood hoisted his flag on board the Euryalus, employd securing the masts and bowsprit, sounded occasionally from 19 to 13 fathoms, observed 14 sail of the enemy standing to the northward and three to the southward AM struck the fore top mast to fish the fore masts at noon the fleet and prizes in company but not having communication of any of our ships remain ignorant of the no. taken our loss on board the Victory is as follows
6 Officers and 48 Seamen and Marines killed
7 Officers and 74 Seamen and Marines wounded

Nelson and others on board were dead and he would be mourned and sorely missed, but the sailors and officers of HMS *Victory* and the wider Royal Navy still had a job to get on with. By the time of Trafalgar they had been getting on with it for the best part of 12 years and would continue to do so for another ten until peace came in 1815. And when peace did come for Britain, it was a successful peace largely due to the activities of the Royal Navy over the course of a period of conflict longer than the duration of the world wars of the twentieth century combined – and then doubled.[2]

While the story of Nelson and the battle of Trafalgar inevitably form a natural centrepiece to this book, for they are crucially important, they are not the be all and end all of the history of the Navy

Fig. P.3. The surgeon's table aboard HMS *Victory* where William Beatty undertook ten limb amputations on men wounded at Trafalgar. Compare the cramped conditions between decks with Devis's painting (Fig. P.2.).

during this time. Fought on a global scale with a cast of millions, it was much, much more than 'Nelson's war'. Having begun the story of the Royal Navy in the heat of battle it is time to broaden the view. For to understand not just what the Royal Navy did, but why it was important to British success, the first step is to understand what exactly the wars were and were not about for Britain.

Map 1. The Atlantic

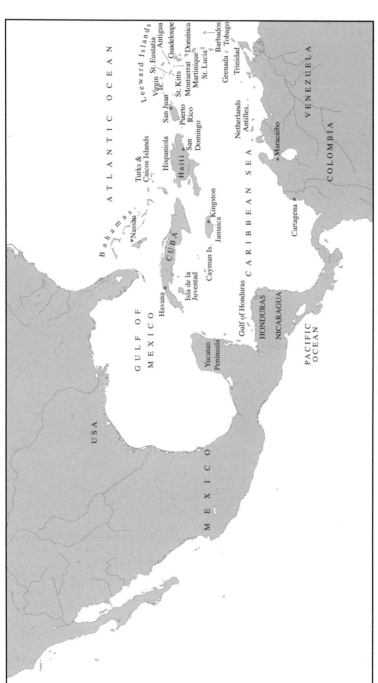

Map 2. The Caribbean

Map 3. Europe

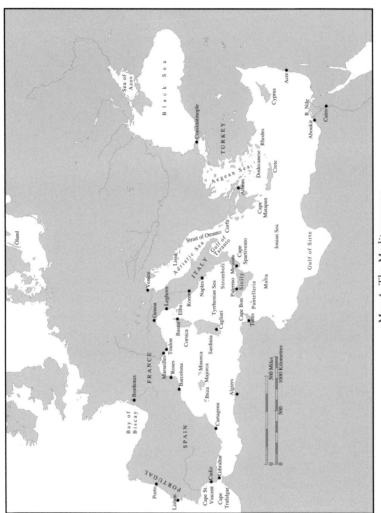

Map 4. The Mediterranean

Map 5, The Far East

'Wherever there is water to float a ship, we are sure to find you in our way'

On 1 February 1793 the French Revolutionary Government declared war on Great Britain and the United Netherlands. In fact the first shots of the war had already been fired. On 2 January the brig-sloop HMS *Childers* had been hit by shot fired from the batteries at the French naval base of Brest – one of the French cannonballs was later presented to the Admiralty. Over 22 years later, between 6 and 7 o'clock on the morning of 15 July 1815 a barge came alongside HMS *Bellerophon*, then off the French port of Rochefort. *Bellerophon*, a veteran of the battles of 'The Glorious First of June' in 1794, the Nile in 1798 and Trafalgar in 1805, had seen much active service. She had also been involved in blockade duties and patrolling in the western approaches and had been stationed in home waters, in the Baltic, the Mediterranean and the West Indies. If the Royal Navy had begun British involvement in the wars with France, on 15 July 1815 *Bellerophon*'s Captain, Frederick Lewis Maitland, RN, would end that involvement. For the barge carried Napoleon Bonaparte who, once on the quartedeck of the British man of war, declared to Maitland, 'I am come to throw myself on the protection of your Prince and your laws.' He would later declare, 'If it had not been for you English, I should have been Emperor of the east. But wherever there is water to float a ship, we are sure to find you in our way.' [1]

Fig. I.1. Napoleon being transferred from the *Bellerophon* to the
Northumberland for his final voyage to St Helena.

While much that Napoleon said has to be taken with a pinch of
salt, there is a grain of truth here, for the Royal Navy was responsible for Napoleon's downfall in that it made possible Britain's ultimate success in the wars. To judge success one needs to compare
the outcome with British war aims. The French Revolutionary Wars
began in April 1792 when France declared war on Austria. Britain
did not respond to the French declaration of war by attempting to
grab territory in Europe, restore the Bourbon monarchy in Paris,
defeat the French militarily or restore order in France. Many factors
played a part in defining British war objectives, but the prime one
was essentially defensive: French expansion into the Low Countries
directly threatened British maritime security. Opposite the River
Thames, Britain's main commercial artery, and the open flat coun-
tryside of Essex, are the Scheldt, Rhine and Maas estuaries and
the shipbuilding ports of Antwerp and Flushing. This was the ideal
location from which to launch an invasion of mainland Britain and
would negate the traditional British strategy of stationing a fleet
in the western approaches to watch over the major French fleet

base at Brest. Antwerp in French hands was 'a standing menace to England's safety', and an independent Low Countries, or at least one free of French influence, was the prime British war aim in Europe.[2]

There were two other areas of British interest in Europe and the object in both cases was free access for British ships. First in importance was the Baltic, the principal source of British naval stores, such as iron, tar, timber for masts, planking and decks, pitch, tallow, linseed and hemp. In 1794 1,011 British ships left Russian ports. The River Elbe was a major artery into Central Europe for British trade and in return a conduit for important grain shipments from Prussia. To the south, in the Mediterranean, British maritime trade was less important; here the main interests were political – supporting Austria and Russia – and strategic – blockading the French fleet base at Toulon.[3]

How could Britain secure her interests? With a small army unable to defeat a major continental power, diplomacy was vital in order to organize continental alliances against France. As the war progressed it became clear that Austria could not be relied upon to help achieve British aims, and it was Russia who became the single most important country in British diplomacy. Diplomacy would be underwritten with British cash in the form of subsidies, but these were forthcoming only as long as British maritime trade continued to fuel the British economy.[4]

This is critical for understanding Britain's role, and that of the Royal Navy, in the wars. Britain was not part of the European system; it was on the periphery – only marginally a European country. But it *was* at the centre of an Atlantic empire, encompassing possessions in the West Indies, East Indies and Canada. This empire was based on maritime commerce and protected by the Royal Navy. It was only natural that in fighting Napoleon Britain should rely on those advantages granted to her by this position at the centre of the global maritime economic system. For Britain 'there was no decisive theatre anywhere within reach of the enemy's main forces, except the sea'. Consequently, the successful outcome of the wars was largely built on her maritime power, *vis-à-vis* her two main rivals in economic maritime conflict, Spain and France. To use an ends, ways and means framework, British war aims (ends) would be achieved by a maritime war (ways) using the Navy (means). It was the Royal Navy that prevented France invading the British Isles, and, by negating French and Spanish naval power, protected and fostered maritime trade, thereby providing the vital economic strength necessary for subsidizing allies.[5]

In this sense it is useful to view the war at sea for the Navy as falling into two interrelated but distinctly different periods. The first, lengthier, period lasted from 1793 to 1805 and can be seen as the Navy's attempt to obtain command of the seas over its enemies, largely France and Spain. While there were a number of battles fought between fleets, it was the blockade of enemy ports, particularly Brest, that was of prime importance:

> the blockade of Brest consequently came to complement the great expeditions to the West Indies that characterised the Revolutionary War. After 1795 the principle of maintaining the blockade was consistently applied. Even though the resources that could be devoted to it were at times limited by deployments to other stations, there was full recognition that the blockade was indispensable to the maintenance of the British war effort in other theatres.

That security would allow for a maritime war overseas. France had territory and possessions susceptible to the exercise of maritime power in many areas of the globe. It was only natural that Britain would attack enemy commerce while protecting British trade. The object was for Britain to stay fighting.[6]

The second period, after Trafalgar in October 1805, was more to do with the Royal Navy exercising the command of the sea obtained by a succession of fleet battles, the maintenance of blockades and numerous other actions. This was about shaping what demands Britain could make in any peace settlement, in other words ensuring that British interests were achieved. Wars were (and still are) not the same for all the protagonists:

> wars tend to take certain forms each with a marked idiosyncrasy; that these forms are normally related to the object of the war and to its

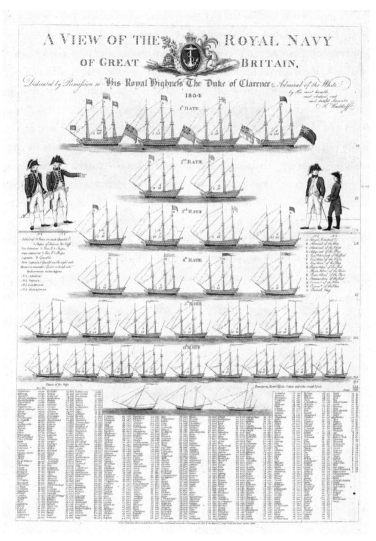

Fig. I.2. *A View of the Royal Navy of Great Britain*. Produced in 1804, it is a useful guide as to how ships were rated, but the underlying message is clear: set against a potential invasion by Napoleon, it is the Royal Navy that protects the British Isles.

value to one or both belligerents; that a system of operations which suits one form may not be that best suited to another.[7]

So while France fought an aggressive, territorial war for chunks of land, Britain fought to preserve her maritime security and trading interests in Europe and overseas. Maritime trade was at the heart of the system providing the money and credit which allowed for long-term fiscal planning: 'British naval power ensured that Britain gained this wealth and her opponents lost it, and this was vital to the ability of the British state to finance its actions in peace and war.'[8]

While many aspects of this period, such as developments in ship design, changing social conditions and administrative reform, are of great interest, they cannot be covered in this volume (for more information see *A History of the Royal Navy: The Age of Sail* by **Andrew Baines**). Even with regard to the operations of the Royal Navy and their impact on the strategic and political outcome of the war, it is impossible to cover everything the Navy did during these years. Instead the clear and overriding focus of this book is the Royal Navy's contribution to Britain's rise to global superpower status in 1815.

CHAPTER 1

'Never was a more hard fought action in the Seas'

Home Waters, 1793–1802

Given the importance of the Low Countries in British thinking, it is not surprising that British involvement in the wars against France began in that theatre. With France at war with Austria then Prussia in April 1792, it was not until 1 February 1793 that France declared war on Britain. In response, British troops were transported from Greenwich to Helvoetsluis in the Republic of the United Provinces. The naval part of the expedition was under the command of Captain John Manley in the 32-gun frigate HMS *Syren*. The night of 15 March was calm and foggy, perfect for an attack by gunboats under the command of Lieutenant John Western. This little force succeeded in driving the enemy out of five forts constructed to bombard Willemstadt. On the 21st, while laying a 12pdr cannon in his gunboat, Western was shot through the head. He was the first Royal Navy officer casualty of the war, lost not in a great battle but during an inshore gunboat action providing fire support to allied forces ashore.[1]

On 29 May a brigade of cavalry arrived in Ostend carried in 40 transports, and further reinforcements continued to arrive during the autumn of 1793. Royal Naval assistance to the forces ashore was evident in the army's failed attempt to capture Dunkirk in August and September 1793. On 27 August transports arrived with gunners for the siege (but no heavy artillery) and on the 29th the frigate HMS

Brilliant and a number of armed cutters were off the coast. Taking command of the naval forces the following day was Admiral John MacBride. Given the nature of his task, support to the army ashore and the importance of cordial relations between the services, he was to operate under the direct command of Henry Dundas, from 1794 Secretary of State for War, rather than the Admiralty.

The army was critical of the Navy's lack of apparent support leading to the failure of the siege. This was replicated at the highest levels, with the army's commander, the Duke of York, criticizing Lord Chatham, the First Lord of the Admiralty, for not providing gunboats. York's view also overlooked the role of the Navy in supplying stores, provisions and guns to the army, for between 4 August and 18 September a number of storeships laden with ordnance and stores arrived in Flanders. In fact the apparent lack of naval support was a smokescreen; in reality it was far too late in the year for the army to mount a successful siege.[2]

MacBride's flotilla had been temporarily blown off station only three days after arriving at Dunkirk, highlighting the perennial problem of bad weather interfering with naval operations. With land operations winding down in October 1793, MacBride was given a wide-ranging role, though still under the command of Dundas, whose prime concern at that time was a French invasion attempt. By 31 October MacBride's squadron consisted of his flagship, the 32-gun *Quebec*, a further frigate, a sloop and a floating battery as he cooperated with British forces ashore in removing the French from Ostend and Nieuport. In November the army asked the Navy to provide a hundred sailors to man the artillery batteries at Nieuport.[3]

The naval officer who received this request was Lieutenant Home Riggs Popham. In September 1793 Popham had been appointed as Agent for Transport to the British Army. Operating out of Ostend, which would serve as the major logistical port until evacuated in June 1794, he was in familiar territory, as he had lived in the town for the previous five years. Alongside his core duty of organizing the stream of inward and outbound transport ships and disembarking and embarking troops and stores for the army, he organized local fishermen into a Sea Fencibles force to defend the town. With the army wintering in the Low Countries in late December 1793 the *Experiment* transport was typical of the traffic Popham had to deal with. She was made ready at Deptford with a quantity of naval stores for use by the battalions of Foot Guards serving in York's army, as well as transporting a number of officers, their baggage and servants. Such tasking required immense organizational skills, attention to detail and experience of shipping, and it is important to note that the army relied on a naval officer to supply this expertise.[4]

Popham was so successful in his supply role that in March 1794, in preparation for the coming campaigning season in a country-side criss-crossed by waterways, the Duke of York requested that Popham command the army's inland navigation. This was approved, but Popham and the duke could do little to stem the French advance in June and July 1794 leading to the loss of Ostend. In all this the Duke of York noted Popham's 'unremitting zeal and active talents' which saved much British property and stores during the British retreat, which by November had reached the River Waal at Nijmegen. Here a hundred sailors working under Popham main-tained a key pontoon bridge.[5]

The campaign of 1794 had been a disaster and the Duke of York returned to England in December leaving behind an army with an increasing sick list, in constant retreat and harried by the zeal of French Revolutionary forces. As the army infrastructure disinte-grated, Popham assisted as best he could, getting the army across waterways and organizing gunboats to patrol. In January 1795 French cavalry rode across the frozen Zuiderzee to capture the Dutch fleet. Popham continued sourcing, arming and manning gunboats, embarking the wounded and sick, as well as piloting ships and purchasing hammocks for transports that had arrived in a wholly unfit state to evacuate British troops back to England. Embarking the formed troops and the ragtag stragglers was a continuous duty throughout the autumn of 1795: 'I was never so fag'd with Dogs and Devils,' Popham wrote on 23 October. 'I wish the business was at an end, and if I ever have anything more to do with Transports, you may Transport me to Botany Bay.' Popham, never one to play down his role, estimated that in 1795 he had been responsible for the safe evacuation of 40,000 infantry and 6,000 cavalry. In January 1796 he left the continent, promoted to post captain and possessing the moniker of 'The Duke of York's Admiral'. Yet he had never commanded a naval ship. Instead he had used his expert seamanship and hydrographic skills to become a specialist in joint amphibious power projection; a role which he would continue to perform during the next 19 years of conflict.[6]

The Channel Fleet

The safety and security of British home waters was the job of the Channel Fleet and it was entrusted to the Royal Navy's most experienced officer, Admiral Richard Howe, 1st Lord Howe. Keeping watch over the French fleet base at Brest, he preferred an open blockade, stationing his main fleet towards Spithead and using frigate and light squadrons to keep close watch on enemy ports. While this seemed contrary to the British tradition of the 'Western Squadron' positioned off Ushant, there was strategic rationale. As far back as 1784 Howe had thought that stationing a fleet directly off the French coast was 'a very improper and hazardous measure'. Ships would be damaged and crews would become sick; keeping a close blockade of Brest was 'a dangerous situation, and should never be taken but upon great emergencies'.[7]

There were other factors at play in 1793 which justified Howe favouring an open blockade, primarily the apparent naval superiority of Britain over France. Until 1795 Spain was an ally of Britain and her ships need not be factored into the equation. France was still embroiled in internal and external land campaigns which reduced the likelihood of an invasion against Britain or an expansionist colonial policy. Crucially the French naval officer class, which had tasted success during the American War, had suffered from republican purges and emigration, while there were problems sourcing and maintaining sufficient manpower. (For French successes against the Royal Navy in the American War see *A History of the Royal Navy: The American Revolutionary War* by **Martin Robson**.) In March 1793 a small French squadron had put to sea but its commander,

Vice Admiral Morard de Galles, found his crews, although driven by republican fervour, unwilling to go aloft in a gale; 'nothing can make them attend to their duties,' he lamented. When news of a counter-revolution in Toulon reached the Brest fleet on 13 September 1793 they mutinied. The situation was only brought back under control by the replacement of Galles with Rear Admiral Louis-Thomas Villaret-Joyeuse and a new code of naval discipline enforced by *Madame Guillotine*. The French navy 'was reduced to virtual impotence by the political conflicts on shore'.[8]

With Howe using the Channel Fleet to fulfil his mission of protecting British trade and troop convoys while annoying that of the enemy, he undertook a number of cruises in 1793 off the Scilly Isles, skirmishing with a French squadron on 18 October. By December Howe had 22 sail of the line under his command, though most of his ships rode out the winter storms at Spithead or Plymouth until he sailed again in early May 1794 leading to the first major fleet engagement of the war.

The Glorious First of June

In 1793 one of the Royal Navy's less well-known officers, Sir Charles Knowles, was sent to North America in the *Daedalus* frigate. His job was to watch a French convoy preparing to sail from America and to report on general French movements in North American waters. He warned the British forces in the West Indies of the size and lucrative value (around £2 million) of the French convoy and the arrival of a number of French warships to provide an escort. He also noted that the Americans displayed 'treachery and implacable hatred [...] to the British Nation'. Knowles noted that the convoy sailed on 19 April.[9]

Across the Atlantic the French fleet at Brest under Villaret-Joyeuse had been ordered to put to sea and escort this convoy, carrying much needed grain safely into Brest for transport on to Paris. The resulting engagement with Howe's fleet, known as the 'Glorious First of June', is rather unique. Most naval battles take place in the littoral – coastal waters – whereas this one occurred in open waters about 400 nautical miles west of Ushant. Over the course of several days a number of engagements were fought between Villaret-Joyeuse's fleet of 26 sail of the line and Howe's fleet, now numbering 25 sail of the line.

The Admiralty had informed Howe on 17 April of the 'very large and valuable Fleet of Merchant ships [...] shortly expected from America'. Intercepting that convoy 'is an object of the most urgent importance to the success of the present war'. Howe sailed from Spithead on 2 May escorting outward-bound British convoys before taking up station in the western approaches off Ushant. He initially found the French fleet still in Brest, but Villaret-Joyeuse slipped out in a fog on 16/17 May. Howe gave chase and made contact with the French on 28 May. This was a partial action with both sides attempting to gain favourable positions, during which the 74-gun HMS *Audacious* suffered much damage in combat with the larger 110-gun *Révolutionnaire*. Both ships headed for their respective ports to repair.

Next day Howe attempted to gain the weather gauge on the French fleet, but Villaret-Joyeuse stuck to his task of frustrating the Royal Navy's attempts to intercept the convoy. On the 29th there were further brushes between the fleets, with some British ships suffering damage to their rigging and masts, but this was more than compensated for by Howe's seamanship which allowed him to finally take up the weather gauge. This would allow him to choose exactly when and where to attack the French fleet. Two days of thick fog frustrated his plan but the weather cleared early on the morning of 1 June.[10]

By now the fleets were about five miles apart and at 07:16 Howe's flagship, the 100-gun three-decked *Queen Charlotte*, signalled his intent to attack the centre of the French fleet. The next signal, at 07:25, was for his fleet to pass through the French line and engage the enemy from the leeward side. After the British crews had breakfasted, Howe directed *Queen Charlotte* to bear down upon the French while signalling that each of his ships should engage its opposite number. In effect, instead of attacking in line ahead formation, his ships would turn and attack line abreast; each Royal Navy warship

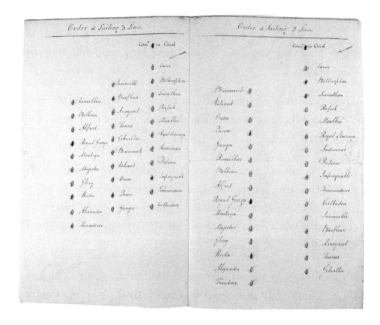

Fig. 1.1. The Glorious First of June. Plans for the fleet's 'order of sailing' in three or two lines.

would cut the French line astern of an opponent before engaging them on the leeward side, thereby preventing their escape.

The French opened fire at 09:24 with the *Queen Charlotte* responding at 09:52. HMS *Defence*, captained by James Gambier, was the first British ship though the French line. Midshipman William Henry Dillon later recalled:

> We retained our fire till in the act of passing under the Frenchman's stern, then, throwing all our topsails aback, luffed up and poured in a destructive broadside. We heard most distinctly our shot striking the hull of the enemy.

Defence shattered the stern of the 74-gun *Mucius* before drawing up close alongside. *Defence* also found herself engaged by the *Tourville*. Dillon continues:

> The lower deck was at times so completely filled with smoke that we could scarcely distinguish each other, and the guns were so heated

that, when fired, they nearly kicked the upper deck beams. The metal became so hot that fearing some accident, we reduced the quantity of powder, allowing also more time to elapse between the loading and firing of them.

Regarding the fate of John Polly, a tar of 'very short stature' who had remarked 'he was so small the shot would pass over him', Dillon relates a grisly tale:

> The words had not been long out of his mouth when a shot cut his head right in two, leaving the tip of each ear remaining on the lower part of the cheek. [...] The head of this unfortunate seamen was cut so horizontally that anyone looking at it would have supposed it has been done by the blow of an axe.

Polly's body was, as was usual, 'committed to the deep'. The *Defence* would be completely dismasted by French fire. Over the course of the battles of 28 and 29 of May and 1 June she lost 18 killed and 39 wounded.[11]

The battle now descended into a number of smaller duels as each British ship sought out its opponent. Some of Howe's captains clearly did not understand what he had intended, coming up short and engaging the enemy in a more conventional manner from the windward side. Captain Molloy of the *Caesar* would later be court martialled and dismissed from his ship for failing to do his utmost to follow Howe's orders. There was little that Howe could do about this; even if he could see his ships through the gun smoke there would be even less chance of signals being seen and understood. The engagement was sharp and short, with much of the hard fighting over by 11:30, though mopping up damaged French ships would take most of the afternoon. One French ship sank and six more were captured; French losses were around 4,200 men killed and 3,300 captured – in the region of 10 per cent of the total available French naval manpower.[12]

It had been a hard fight, evidenced by the significant British casualties of around 1,200. As one Royal Navy lieutenant who observed the fighting from the *Phateon* frigate remarked, 'It is allowed on all

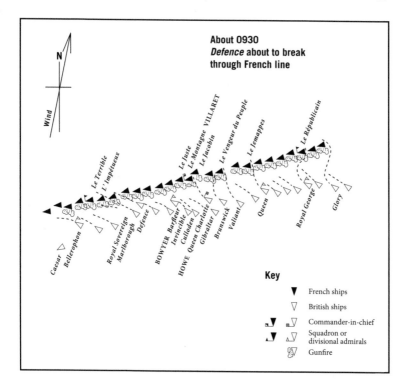

Fig. 1.2. The Glorious First of June, 1794.

sides that there never was a more hard fought action in the Seas.'
It was a striking tactical and operational victory for Howe, yet the
French had still achieved their strategic objective, for the convoy
eventually arrived in Brest supplying much needed flour to placate
the Parisian mob's need for bread. Although the French had been
strategically successful, and the French navy, ripped apart by the
Revolution, had stood toe to toe with the Royal Navy, many thought
that apart from the loss of valuable seamen the French navy had
suffered a severe blow to its morale. 'Although the French fought
desperately,' the lieutenant on the *Phateon* wrote, 'I am convinced
that they will not stand such close fighting as on this day.' So in fact,
while the short-term strategic effects were beneficial to France, in
the long term the battle seriously dented French naval capabilities.
The loss of experienced seamen was both chronic and acute and

while revolutionary fervour might work wonders on land, at sea it was no replacement for skill and experience. Dealing heavy blows against French naval power was fundamental to maritime security in home waters, which would allow Dundas to direct British efforts overseas.[13]

The battle would also have a further effect on the Royal Navy and therefore British success in the wars. Howe's plan was ambitious and built upon Admiral George Rodney's victory at the battle of the Saintes in 1782. While it was not wholly successful, enough of his captains understood his intentions for Howe's fleet to achieve the most important British naval victory for over a hundred years. The key factors were superior British seamanship, fleet discipline and close-range gunnery. Howe's tactics, of bringing on a pellmell battle, and the superiority of the British fleet in close action would also inspire the next generation of naval commanders. Howe later received a visit from King George III, who presented him with a bejewelled sword on the quarterdeck of the Queen Charlotte.

Following his victory, Howe's fleet spent a considerable portion of the remainder of 1794 in port. The stresses of sea life and declining health led to Howe's request to be relieved of command. As a compromise he was allowed to exercise command from Bath when the fleet was in port awaiting intelligence of French fleet movements that could then be acted upon. He repeated the request in December 1794 around the same time the Brest fleet put to sea again. The French winter cruise of 1794–95 was, despite the rare taking of the British 74-gun Alexander, a disaster: six French ships were lost to shipwreck, comparable to battle losses at the First of June.

British strategy towards Brest changed during the summer of 1794 with the arrival of Sir Charles Middleton at the Board of Admiralty. He looked to the Seven Years' War, when a western squadron had kept the French bottled up in their Atlantic ports allowing for the projection of British expeditions overseas; ships on blockade duty would be rotated to allow repair (for more information see *A History of the Royal Navy: The Seven Years' War* by **Martin Robson**). Yet problems remained, including a mutiny on

Fig. 1.3. Lord Howe on the quarterdeck of the *Queen Charlotte*
receiving a ceremonial sword from King George III.

board the *Culloden* in December 1794 leading to the execution of
eight sailors. While the grievances related to the unfit state of the
ship the authorities expressed concerns over the possible spread of
revolutionary ideals from France. Also worrying was the reappear-
ance of the debilitating disease of scurvy, and while lemon juice
would be distributed as a cure, it was not until 1800 that it became
part of the daily ration for sailors in the Channel Feet.

All this had the potential to impact on the Channel Fleet and
on the revived Western Squadron that Middleton now considered
as the prime Royal Navy deployment. Problems remained over its
command, however, and with Howe ashore it was left to his deputy
Alexander Hood, Lord Bridport, to command at sea. Brest remained
notoriously difficult to keep under constant blockade and a further
French incursion into the Channel occurred in January 1795. The
French fleet undertook a 34-day cruise capturing over a hundred
British merchant and naval ships, but the key danger was that French
squadrons might escape and provide local naval superiority in the

Fig. 1.4. During the revolutionary war period French ships carried caps at their mastheads as symbols of their liberty. This 'French Cap of Liberty' was taken from the French frigate *Unité* by HMS *Revolutionaire* on 12 April 1796. The cap was made from moulded metal, painted red and black with attached star in red, black and white. The tassel is formed from pieces of metal and painted yellow, the attachment at the top (broken) was for hanging from the masthead.

Mediterranean or the West Indies; this occurred when six French sail of the line reinforced their Toulon squadron in February 1795.[14]

Channel frigate squadrons

Integral to British strategy was the deployment of frigate squadrons in the Channel to protect British trade, keep watch on French ports and annoy them wherever possible, while the big ships of the Channel Fleet remained in port. The exploits of Sir Sidney Smith on 3 January 1795, when he took the frigate HMS *Diamond*, flying the *tricolore*, into Brest harbour to reconnoitre the French fleet and spoke

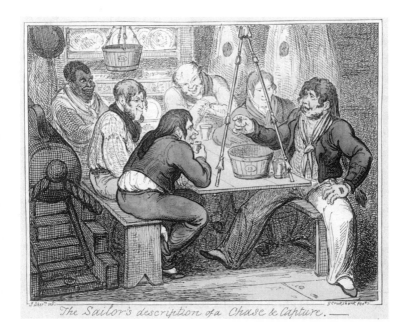

The Sailor's description of a Chase & Capture.

Fig. 1.5. While a sailor's description of a chase and capture would make an entertaining story, what he was really interested in was a share of the prize money.

to several French ships thereby collecting useful intelligence, was one of the most celebrated. Smith's remark to Lord George Spencer, First Lord of the Admiralty, that 'the frontier of Great Britain is high water mark in France' summed up his attitude. Of particular note was a frigate squadron of five ships commanded by capable and aggressive captains under the command of Commodore Sir John Borlase Warren operating out of Falmouth. Further south, Sir James Saumarez operated from the Channel Islands in the *Crescent*.

Serving under Warren in the *Flora* was perhaps the most famous naval officer of the early years of the war, Sir Edward Pellew, in the *Arethusa*. Previously on 18 June 1793 while commanding the *Nymphe* Pellew had, in a much celebrated action for which he was knighted, made the first capture of a French frigate in the war, *La Cléopâtre*. Combining the newer heavy 18pdr and 24pdr frigates with the cream of the up and coming naval talent operating independently of the battlefleet, such frigate squadrons wreaked havoc on French shipping, privateers and smaller warships in the English Channel. In 1793 Sir Andrew Snape in the 18pdr *Phaeton* took prizes valued at £300,000. In April 1794 Warren became the first captain in the wars to take a French 24pdr ship, *La Pomone*, a valuable prize herself and which became the model for the Royal Navy's *Endymion* frigate. Pellew in the *Arethusa* took the 22-gun *Babet* in this action. A year later Captain Lord Henry Powlett in the *Astrea* captured *La Gloire* 'after a close action of 58 minutes'. His report points to a key factor in British success in these engagements. While *Astrea*'s crew suffered three men seriously wounded and five less so, Powlett reported, in stark contrast, that 'the slaughter on board the enemy has been considerable', with 40 killed and wounded, including her captain who suffered a head wound, out of a crew of 275.[15]

French attempt to invade Ireland

On 16 June 1795 Vice Admiral Sir William Cornwallis, commanding a detachment from the Channel Fleet, fought an engagement against a superior French force. Cornwallis, in the 100-gun *Royal Sovereign*, went to assist the 74-gun *Mars*, assailed by the van of a French fleet of 12 sail of the line, including one 120-gun ship and 11 frigates. The success of 'Cornwallis's Retreat', a rightly celebrated example of the Royal Navy's aggressive spirit, was also due to French timidity, helped somewhat by the British frigate *Phaeton* signalling to an imaginary relief fleet, causing the French to break off the action. Along with the First of June, 'Cornwallis's Retreat' was a highly visible early example of a crucial factor in British success at sea during the wars: a generally aggressive, confident spirit amongst a cadre of naval officers that was often lacking in their enemies.

Just over a week later on 22 June Bridport was covering an amphibious landing of French royalists in Quiberon Bay to assist an anti-republican insurgency in the Vendée, when he sighted the French fleet under Villaret-Joyeuse. Bridport chased him down for most of the day, with only his van entering serious action against the French during the early hours of 23 June off the Isle de Groix.

In doing so the Royal Navy recaptured the *Alexander*, along with two new French 74-gun ships, the *Formidable* and *Tigre*. Both were added to the Navy, the former as the *Belleisle*. Bridport had won a victory, but with a number of French ships within his grasp, he signalled to call off the action, losing the opportunity to strike a more decisive blow to French naval power.

With Prussia making peace with France, the prospect of a French invasion of the British Isles loomed large, so keeping a careful eye on the French invasion flotilla assembling at Dunkirk was crucial. Moreover, the French conquest of the Low Countries meant that the Royal Navy now had to watch over Dutch ports as well. The threat, however, would finally be manifested further south where the royalist émigrés landed by Bridport in 1795 were crushed by republican forces led by General Lazare Hoche in July. By the time he had mopped up lingering resistance, General Bonaparte had used his 'whiff of grapeshot' to suppress a royalist revolt in Paris, leading to the centralization of power in the French Directory established on 2 November 1795. Enhanced security on land allowed Hoche's forces to prepare for an overseas expedition, and greater direction of the war from Paris led to the political imperative to provide direct support to the Irish nationalist movement. Plans were hatched between Hoche and the Irish nationalist Wolf Tone for the Brest fleet, now under Admiral Morard de Galles, to avoid engaging the Royal Navy and instead cover the landing of Hoche's force at Bantry Bay. Hoche would then march to seize the Royal Navy's major victualling establishment at Cork, undermining its ability to keep the Channel Fleet at sea.

British intelligence indicated that the French were preparing for a major expedition but could not be sure of its destination. In response, the open blockade of Brest favoured by Howe was tightened, with 15 sail of the line from the Channel Fleet under the command of Vice Admiral Sir John Colpoys stationed off Ushant. The *Indefatigable*, a former third-rate 64-gun ship, now razeed down to a 38-gun frigate and under the command of the formidable Captain Edward Pellew, was keeping watch over Brest with two other frigates. By December 1796 Colpoys' ships were suffering

from the inevitable wear and tear of 'seakeeping', as recognized by
Spencer at the Admiralty, who wrote to instruct Bridport to be
ready to take out a squadron to relieve the worst of them.[16]

This was the situation on 16 December when the French fleet
of 17 ships of the line, 13 frigates, six corvettes and transports, put
to sea carrying around 18,000 troops. Things went badly from the
start; the *Séduisant* was wrecked on rocks with the loss of around
680 lives. This was symptomatic of the problems facing the French,
as was political interference from the Directory and inter-service
rivalry, Hoche himself stating 'Our hateful navy cannot and will
not do anything'; he thought the officers 'chaotic and divided' and
suffering from 'arrogance, ignorance, vanity and folly'. It was Hoche
who had made the decision to leave Brest by the Raz de Sein which
directly led to the loss of the *Séduisant*. The French fleet was ill
provisioned (carrying enough food for only two weeks) and, lacking
adequate sea time, suffered from poor seamanship. Admiral Galles
and Hoche were on board the *Fraternité* frigate which was separated
from the rest of the fleet which, when it arrived off Bantry Bay in a
snow storm on 22 December, lacked decisive leadership to take the
opportunity to land the troops.[17]

Pellew had sent a warning to Colpoys before heading for
Falmouth. Colpoys himself was not aware of the French fleet sailing
until 18 December by which time he had been blown off station and
headed for Spithead to undertake repairs to his battered ships, arriving there on 31 December. Bridport could not leave Spithead until 3
January owing to contrary winds and tides which caused a number
of accidental collisions. In the meantime, Vice Admiral Sir Robert
Kingsmill, commander in chief off the Irish coast, had notified the
Admiralty of the arrival of the French fleet in Irish waters. Bridport
arrived off Bantry Bay on 9 January to find the French gone, so
headed for Ushant, arriving on station on 13 January, by which
time the French fleet was back in Brest 'without having landed its
army and having lost about a quarter of its ships through foundering,
grounding or capture'.[18]

One of those ships lost was the 74-gun *Droits de l'Homme*, engaged
in a gale by Pellew in the 38-gun *Indefatigable* on 13–14 January.

Accompanied by the 36-gun *Amazon*, Pellew fought a gruelling night-time action in hard weather. *Droits de l'Homme* was laden with troops and stores and in the heavy seas could not open her lower gun ports; she was also damaged aloft which affected her handling, allowing Pellew and the *Amazon* to position themselves off her bow. All three ships suffered in the bad weather; in the *Indefatigable* guns broke free, on the main deck men were up to their waists in water and she had suffered damage to her masts. Saved by a Breton pilot, Pellew managed to just avoid the dangerous lee shore. The *Amazon* and *Droits de l'Homme* were not as fortunate. The former ran aground with the majority of her crew making it ashore where they were captured. Those on board the overloaded French ship were less fortunate: she was wrecked on the coast with the loss of up to a thousand sailors and soldiers out of the 1,300 souls on board; it took rescuers four days to reach the survivors. As per the norm with the loss of a Royal Navy ship, Captain Robert Reynolds and his crew were tried for the *Amazon*'s loss and honourably acquitted.[19]

The French invasion was not defeated by the Royal Navy but by poor French decision making, poor seamanship and bad weather. Further British embarrassment was to come with a French force which was to mount a diversionary attack on Bristol while the main force headed for Ireland. Also hampered by bad weather, this second force actually managed to land troops in Wales at Fishguard on 22 February 1797. While the 1,500 or so poorly motivated troops that were landed were quickly captured, the shock led to a financial crisis for the British government which in the short term raised questions over the British ability to finance the war. Also raising concerns about the Royal Navy were the mutinies in April and May 1797 at Spithead and the Nore over pay and conditions (for more information see **A History of the Royal Navy: The Age of Sail by Andrew Baines**).

The battle of Camperdown, 11 October 1797

Set against invasion attempts and naval mutinies, Admiral Adam Duncan, operating off the Texel, provided a much needed tonic to

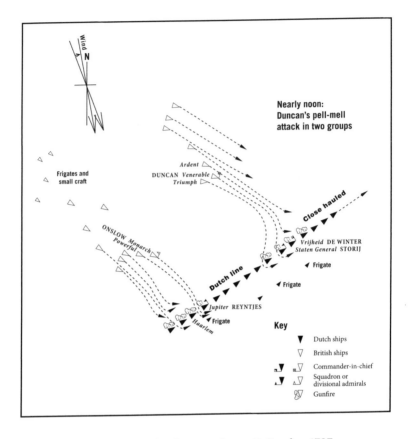

Fig. 1.6. The battle of Camperdown, 11 October 1797.

British spirits in October 1797. It was originally envisaged that the pro-French Dutch fleet under Admiral de Winter would convey a landing force to the east coast of England, but he was prevented by poor weather. Perhaps this would also have taken advantage of discord in the British fleet following the 1797 mutinies; if so, de Winter was more than fashionably late. More likely he sailed in response to political pressure to contribute something to the war effort that could be seen as 'Dutch' rather than inspired by the French. This could be traced back to internal Dutch politics where there was a clear divide between the 'Orangist' faction who supported their exiled family and the more radical revolutionary elements whose abortive revolution had presaged that of the French. With the majority of Duncan's fleet victualling at Yarmouth, de Winter, rather unwillingly, weighed anchor and put to sea on 6 October.

While Duncan had used his personality and presence to limit some of the effects of the 1797 mutinies, many of his ships had been affected, for his command was generally composed of older, leaky ships. It is not surprising that along with the monotony of block-ade and the usual weather conditions off the Dutch coast, morale was generally low in Duncan's fleet. Yet once the mutinies had been dealt with, the British seamen, so one informed Duncan himself, were keen to prove that the 'unhappy event which has stained the character of the British tar' could be redeemed by 'bravery [...] loyalty to our King [...] and our personal regard for the best of Commanders'. What was needed was a victory.[20]

Duncan had 16 ships under his command, and while his seven 74s could be considered as suited to the line of battle, his seven 64s were less so and his two 50-gun ships certainly not. It was thought that Duncan's ships could be kept serviceable by the short distance to a home port, but he was given smaller ships than usual due to the nature of the enemy and his theatre of operations. The Dutch fleet was configured to take into account the shallows of the coast-line and hence tended to be small for their ratings. In this context, Duncan's fleet would be more than adequate to deal with them.

De Winter was trying to re-enter the Texel with his 16 sail of the line, five frigates and five brigs on 11 October when Duncan caught sight of him. Duncan had, in fact, purposely placed his fleet between de Winter and the Texel so as to ensure there would be an engagement. Manoeuvring in poor weather among the sandbanks and shallows of the Dutch coast, Duncan's fleet was in two divi-sions. He commanded the Weather Division in the *Venerable*, with Vice Admiral Richard Onslow in the *Monarch* commanding the Lee Division. Upon sighting de Winter he immediately hoisted 'General Chase', and once the distance had been closed abandoned his orig-inal intention to form line of battle. Instead Onslow attacked the Dutch rear with Duncan going for the enemy van. Duncan made the signal for each ship to bear up, break the enemy line and engage her opponent from leeward, which also placed the British between the Dutch and the land. He was, in effect, recreating Howe's tactics from the First of June.

Onslow cut the Dutch line first with his nine ships taking on and crushing five Dutch. Duncan's *Venerable* raked the *States General* before coming alongside de Winter's *Vrijheid*. With *Venerable* outnumbered, support came in the form of the *Triumph*, *Ardent* (whose captain Burges was killed in the action) and *Director*, the latter captained by William Bligh, formerly of the *Bounty*. De Winter surrendered and was brought on board the *Venerable* to offer his sword; Duncan refused to take it and shook hands with him instead. Duncan scored a resounding victory, capturing seven ships of the line, two of the Dutch 56-gun ships (though one was later wrecked) and two frigates (one ran ashore and one was later recaptured). Along with de Winter two other Dutch admirals were taken prisoner. Amongst the 'British Spirit', Duncan noted one sour point, Captain John Williamson of the *Agincourt*, who failed to bring his ship into action. Williamson was court martialled for negligence and never served at sea again, his career, justifiably, in tatters.[21]

As well as dealing a severe though not yet fatal blow to Dutch seapower in the North Sea and easing the pressure on the resources of the Royal Navy, when added to John Jervis's victory in February 1797 (see Chapter 2) and set against the mutinies of the summer, it was another astounding success for the Royal Navy, which had now racked up three victories over Britain's enemies. In December 1797 George III attended a service of Thanksgiving at St Paul's Cathedral for the victories of The Glorious First of June, St Vincent and Camperdown.

Ireland and the Channel

Offensive measures to deal with a potential French invasion of the British Isles or Ireland had to be undertaken and here the ever inventive mind of Captain Popham had come up with a plan to attack the Saas Lock at Ostend. Disabling it would prevent the French from using the waterway to securely move invasion barges built inland. Instead they would have to move by sea and hence be open to attack. Popham's plan involved a joint army–navy attack from a flotilla of old warships armed *enflute*, bomb-vessels, gunboats with special sliding keels along with sloops and a lugger carrying the mines to blow up the lock. The force arrived off Ostend on 19 May 1798. The land commander, Major General Eyre Coote, keen to take advantage of the surprise gained, insisted his force was put ashore despite Popham's concerns about the heavy surf. Popham was correct, for despite the *Biter*, *Hecla* and *Tartarus* bomb-vessels pounding Ostend and setting fire to buildings and the land force succeeding in blowing the lock, Coote's force of 1,100 men was surrounded by the enemy and forced to surrender. Popham was confident from information received that the 'works destroyed [...] had taken the States of Bruges five years to finish'. The operation was well planned, showing great attention to detail, and well executed but, as Popham rued, 'I cannot contend against the elements.' [22]

Given the importance of an independent Low Countries to Britain, in 1799 an Anglo-Russian invasion of the Netherlands was launched to open up another front in the war against France while Russian and Austrian forces pushed the French back in Italy and Germany. For the British it was also an opportunity to seize remaining Dutch warships in the Texel. Conceived in late 1798 and with detailed planning commencing in April 1799, the expedition was, like many amphibious operations, delayed until it finally sailed in August 1799. The British landing at Den Helder on 27 August was organized by Sir Ralph Abercromby and was fortunately unopposed, as Admiral Andrew Mitchell had deposited the troops ashore in a terrible jumble with brigades and battalions mixed up together. It took a considerable time to assemble a fighting formation.

Mitchell found 13 disabled Dutch warships which he seized before passing into the Zuiderzee. A joint Anglo-Russian naval attack on the Dutch fleet in the Texel on 30 August 1799 succeeded in taking a total of eight Dutch ships of the line. On land initial progress was good, but a hoped for Dutch uprising against the French never materialized. With reinforcements bringing the total

Fig. 1.7. John Jervis, 1st Earl of St Vincent, after Abbott.

number of British troops to 30,000 under overall command of the Duke of York, the campaign bogged down as the allies could not break out of the narrow Den Helder peninsula. Again Popham was involved, organizing a flotilla of gunboats, and seamen fulfilled their usual roles of hauling supplies to the army. When news arrived of French success against the Austrians in Italy, York obtained favourable terms from the French and successfully evacuated the British army which was now suffering from sickness in the poor weather conditions. Mitchell could not continue to operate in the Zuiderzee without land forces to secure the shoreline and so withdrew. The whole complex, allied, amphibious operation ended in recriminations as Tsar Paul I blamed the British for not supporting the expedition. Russia would shortly turn from ally to enemy.[23]

Meanwhile Bridport's open blockade of Brest had allowed Admiral Étienne Bruix to sea in 1799 and led to a change in command, for in April 1800 John Jervis, now ennobled as the Earl of St Vincent, was given the task of knocking the Channel Fleet into shape. Discipline was always a problem during monotonous blockade duty and St Vincent brought with him a strict regime. He also implemented a much more aggressive blockade, not only to keep captains and crew occupied but to keep enemy ships bottled up in port, thereby denying them sea room for training and manoeuvre.

In order to negate the concentration of enemy naval force at Brest, St Vincent's ships were victualled at sea with fresh provisions and for the first time lemon juice was issued as a preventive to scurvy. Repairs to ships were undertaken on station unless the services of a dockyard were truly necessary. All this allowed him to keep his men healthy and his ships on station, having an operational and strategic impact by imposing a close blockade. Ships of the line were kept close inshore to close the port of Brest completely. Crucial was the dangerous work of frigates and cutters plying the waters off the port riddled with uncharted rocks. In bad weather the main fleet might shelter in Torbay, but St Vincent demanded the inshore squadron remain off Ushant, ready to close the port the instant the weather permitted. It was brutal and relentless work, but it was critical, for plans could now be laid for British overseas expeditions safe in the knowledge that the enemy ships in Brest were, at least in theory, in no position to interfere.[24]

The fact that the French fleets could not interfere was no guarantee of success, however. On 4 June 1800 Sir Edward Pellew with five sail of the line covered the landing of 5,000 troops to assist French royalists at Quiberon Bay before attacking the important island of Belle Isle but the troops were evacuated and sent on to the

Mediterranean. Similarly, on 25 August an attack was made on the four Spanish sail of the line sheltering at Ferrol. Troops were landed to attack the shore defences but were withdrawn and shipped to Gibraltar.

As was often the case, the blockade was not completely infallible, as on 23 January 1801 Rear Admiral Honoré Ganteaume escaped from Brest with six sail of the line heading for the eastern Mediterranean to assist a French army cut off in Egypt. On the way he received intelligence that a British expedition had in all probability already landed there and he instead headed for Toulon before arriving off Egypt in early June. He then headed west, landing some troops at Benghazi before heading back to Toulon, entering the harbour on 22 July. In all this he had just avoided being caught near Minorca by a squadron under Sir John Borlase Warren in March, then off Egypt by Lord Keith in June. Ganteaume's only real achievement during the six-month cruise was the capture of Captain Sir Benjamin Hallowell's 74-gun *Swiftsure* on 24 June.

The battle of Copenhagen, 2 April 1801

While Ganteaume was on the loose, problems were growing with the northern nations. The background to the British attack on Copenhagen on 2 April 1801 was the need to ensure free access for British trade in the region, particularly the importation of vital naval stores and grain. Denying naval stores to the enemy was a further consideration, as prime minister William Pitt stated to parliament: 'Shall we allow her [France] to receive naval stores undisturbed and to rebuild and refit that navy which the valour of our seamen has destroyed.' In other words, all that had been achieved at sea since 1793 as part of British strategy to crush French seapower, was now threatened.[25]

Anglo-Russian relations were already degenerating after Den Helder and worsened over the fate of Malta, as Tsar Paul wanted Russian forces to capture the island and hand it back to the Knights of St John. Horatio Nelson, blockading the French garrison on the island, refused to have anything to do with such a scheme and on 22

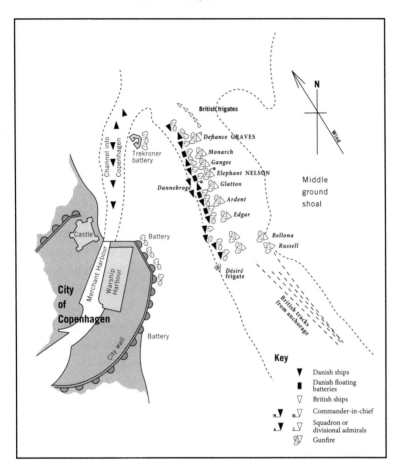

Fig. 1.8. The battle of Copenhagen, 2 April 1801.

December 1799 Paul ordered the Russian fleet in the Mediterranean to return to the Black Sea. With France bowling over British allies on land, Napoleon, in a move designed to sow further discord between his enemies, symbolically gifted Malta to Paul.[26]

British claims of 'right to search' neutral shipping was the final straw for Tsar Paul who snapped and ordered the seizure of all British shipping in Russian ports and joined Prussia, Sweden and Denmark in the League of Armed Neutrality designed to prevent British access to the Baltic. Although a step short of outright war, such a policy was clearly hostile to British interests. The reaction was swift and violent. Although Pitt's government was in its death throes over Catholic emancipation, an embargo was declared on Russian, Swedish and Danish shipping and the First Lord of the Admiralty, Lord Spencer, before handing the post over to St Vincent, dispatched Admirals Hyde Parker and Nelson to the Baltic with a fleet of 18 ships of the line and 35 other vessels.

Their object was to defeat the League of Armed Neutrality and open the Baltic to British trade, ideally through diplomacy but if that failed then crushing the naval forces opposed to British free passage. That was primarily the Russian fleet, but defeat of the Danish fleet at the entrance to the Baltic was a more immediately achievable object. Instructions to Parker noted that if conciliation failed he should 'destroy the port of Copenhagen with the whole of the shipping'. Once matters at Copenhagen had been brought to a conclusion, he was to proceed to attack the Russian fleet at Reval (modern-day Tallinn). The 61-year-old newly wed Parker loitered at Great Yarmouth for two weeks, entertained by his 25-year-old wife, until prodded by St Vincent, the fleet sailing on 11 March. After passing the Sound under fire from Danish forts, Parker's fleet anchored within sight of Copenhagen on 30 March.[27]

On board Captain Edward Riou's *Amazon*, Parker, Nelson, Admiral Graves and Captains Foley and Fremantle assessed the Danish defences. The Danes had used Parker's delay to strengthen their positions. Copenhagen Sound is split in two by the Middle Ground, giving two passages, the Outer Deep and the King's Channel, the latter giving direct access to the port. The Royal Navy had not been in Baltic waters for many years, and both passages presented navigational dangers. After assessing the prospects of attacking via the northern entrance to the King's Deep, where the Danes had the powerful Trekroner and Crown batteries, with their fleet of 18 vessels including some hulks stretching down the passage from north to south, Nelson offered to take ten sail of the line and navigate the Outer Deep, to attack the weaker southern end of the Danish line. Parker would lead the remaining eight sail of the line down from the north. The Outer Deep was marked by navi-

Fig. 1.9. The battle of Copenhagen, 1801, which portrays a relatively
orderly scene rather than the more chaotic events which
required Nelson to micro-manage his fleet.

gational buoys from Nelson's fleet (the Danes having removed the
usual navigational aids) and by 20:00 on 1 April he was anchored in
position at the southern end of the Danish position. At this point,
flying his flag in the 74-gun *Elephant* (he had switched to this shal-
lower draft vessel from the three-decked *St George* on 29 March),
Nelson called his captains to a conference and issued verbal orders.
Now the task was to sound the King's Deep, which was undertaken
during the hours of darkness.

There was no respite for Nelson, who, using the opportunity
presented by a passive defence, spent the night composing meticulous orders to his captains, including directing ships to specific
opponents in the Danish line. Early on 2 April Nelson's squadron of
seven 74s, two 64s, a 50-gun ship, a 56-gun converted merchantman, four frigates and a sloop was led into battle by the 74-gun
Edgar. She was to position herself alongside the *Jylland*, the fifth
Danish ship. Two successive ships would take on the next two ships
in the enemy line, while the next two would attack the rearmost
Danish ships, which would now have been pounded by three British
sail of the line. The rest of Nelson's fleet would pass up and attack

the van of the Danish line. Bomb-vessels would rain down fire upon the Danish ships and the arsenal while the frigates would attack the enemy van with the *Désirée* appointed to place herself to rake the massive *Prøvestenen*, the rearmost enemy ship. It was thought that the Danes were moored too close to the shallows to allow their line to be doubled.[28]

Things quickly started to unravel. With *Edgar* in position and firing on the *Jylland* around 11:00, as successive British ships moved up, and with the *Agamemnon* already stuck on the Middle Ground playing no part in the battle, *Bellona* and *Russell* now also ran aground. The pilots in Nelson's fleet were, incorrectly, convinced that the deeper water was nearer the Middle Ground. Sensing that to follow his plan for successive ships to pass on the unengaged side of *Bellona* and *Russell* would lead to the rest of the fleet sharing their fate, Nelson took the *Elephant* between them and the Danish line before anchoring to fire upon the *Dannebrog*, *Aggershus* and Floating Battery No. 1. The rest of the fleet followed and a disaster had been averted. With his plan going awry, a succession of orders were signalled from the *Elephant* as Nelson, in his high-pitched Norfolk accent, hailed passing ships to personally supervise the revised placing of his ships to cover gaps in the line and to maximize his firepower. By 11:50 those British ships that had navigated the waters were all in action and starting to pound their respective enemies. But it was not all one way, as Nelson later wrote, 'Here was no manoeuvring; it was downright fighting.'[29]

The caution of the pilots caused Nelson's *Elephant* and the rest of his fleet to be placed 500 yards from the enemy line, doubling the range he had wished and thereby diffusing the dreadful effect of British gunnery. Moreover, the Danish floating batteries were hard targets to hit and Danish resistance was far more effective and spirited than Nelson counted on. 'Well Stewart,' he remarked to Lieutenant Colonel William Stewart commanding a detachment of the rifles on board *Elephant*:

> those fellows hold us a better Jug than I expected, however we are keeping them up a noble fire, & I'll be answerable that we shall bole

them out in four if we cannot do it in three hours, at least I'll give it them till they are sick of it.[30]

Viewing the unfolding drama with a growing sense of unease, Parker hoisted his famous signal 39: 'Discontinue the engagement'. The frigates at the head of the British line adhered, Riou's *Amazon* being the last to turn away. 'What will Nelson think of us?,' he remarked moments before he was truncated by a Danish round-shot. Nelson certainly did not adhere, and his comments as related by Surgeon Ferguson have entered naval folklore: 'Then damn the signal; take no notice of it and hoist mine for closer action: that is the way I answer such signals [...] Now nail mine to the mast!' He then turned to his flag captain: 'Foley, you know I have lost an eye and have a right to be blind when I like; and damn me if I'll see that signal.' In directly disobeying the orders of a superior, Nelson was clearly running immense risk, but as the man on the spot he judged correctly, for to have followed Parker's order before the Danes had surrendered would have involved Nelson's ships passing the Trekroner fort and uncharted shallows. As Admiral Graves later recalled, if Nelson had followed orders 'we should all have got aground and been destroyed'.

There was another reason: between 12:30 and 13:10 five Danish ships had begun to disengage from the action while *Elephant*'s enemy, the *Dannebrog*, was in flames largely caused by incendiary devices fired by the *Glatton*. On board the *Dannebrog* one eyewitness recalled, 'the lower gundeck was so full of dead that you could hardly avoid treading on them'. Her flag would be hauled down at 14:30 and two hours later she was destroyed when the flames reached her magazines. The *Glatton* was captained by William Bligh, formerly of the *Bounty*, and the poor handling ship was an experimental close-range smasher, equipped with 28 68pdr carronades and 28 48pdr carronades.[31]

Nelson would have seen the Danish fire subsiding, a point borne out by *Edgar*'s log: 'At two the enemy's fire slackened fast.' Although they were clearly not yet ready to admit defeat, there was opportunity here and Nelson, aware that the British fleet had other

potential enemies further east, seized it. At 14:00 he composed
a letter to be sent ashore under a flag of truce praising the Danes
for their fighting spirit and offering a ceasefire, which if rejected
would see the captured Danish ships burnt with their crews still on
board. This *ruse de guerre* reached the Danish Crown Prince, directing operations from ashore, just as he could clearly see the centre
of the Danish line collapse while bomb-vessels took up position to
bombard the arsenal. By the time the Crown Prince's envoy arrived
on board the *Elephant* the battle had in effect been won, and by
15:15 it was all over.

Nelson wrote to Parker on 3 April declaring that 17 of the
Danish line 'are sunk, burnt, or taken'. In fact of the 11 ships taken
as prizes, ten were too badly damaged or outdated to be of any use
and were burned; only one, the *Holstein*, was counted as a prize. It
was, as Nelson remarked, a hard fight. Total Danish losses were an
estimated 6,000 killed, wounded and captured. Royal Navy losses
were around 1,200 killed and wounded.[32]

While the Danes had been neutralized and were aware that
Tsar Paul had been murdered on 24 March – something that the
British were not aware of – there still appeared to be a threat from
Sweden and Russia. Parker and Nelson therefore sailed further
east into the Baltic headed for Reval and the Russian fleet. At this
point they received news of the murder of Paul and that the new
tsar, Alexander I, had ordered the Russian fleet to avoid hostilities.
Parker was recalled, sailing for England on 5 May 1801, taking with
him five ships of the line and a frigate. Nelson, however, continued east, arriving off Reval on 14 May with the remaining 12 ships
of the line. Nelson found his birds had flown to join the Russian
squadron at Kronstadt and his orders only allowed for action if the
fleets remained separated. Recognizing that the death of Paul and
the collapse of the League had changed the wider strategic and
political context; Nelson assured Alexander that his mission was
of a diplomatic nature. Alexander was unconvinced and three days
later Nelson sailed for England. At this Alexander released all the
captured British merchantmen and ended hostilities, with Sweden
and Denmark following suit. It was the death of Paul I, rather than

the exercise of British seapower at Copenhagen, that was the direct cause of the collapse of the League of Armed Neutrality.[33]

In late July Nelson, flying his flag in the *Medusa* frigate, was appointed to command the British naval defensive flotilla ready to oppose a French invasion from Boulogne. Believing that the best form of defence was attack, a number of raids were mounted against that port. On 4 August a flotilla of gunbrigs and bomb-vessels

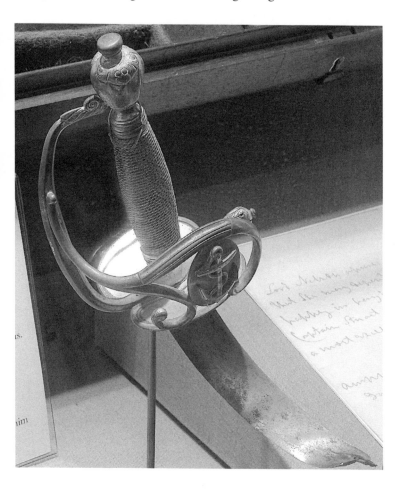

Fig. 1.10. Sword broken in the hand of Captain John Stuart on board HMS *Medusa* on 15 August 1801 during a boat action off Boulogne whilst serving under Nelson.

shelled the harbour but caused little damage. A larger repeat performance with the flotilla organized into four divisions accompanied by boats armed with howitzers on 15 August was again beaten off with 44 men killed and 126 wounded. But by this time the British government was engaging in peace negotiations with France. In order to understand why, it is time to assess the activities of the Royal Navy beyond home waters.

CHAPTER 2

'Nelson's Patent Bridge for Boarding First Rates'

The Mediterranean, 1793–1802

Vice Admiral Samuel 1st Viscount Hood was one of the Royal Navy's most distinguished officers and had seen service in both the Seven Years' War and the American Revolutionary War. In August 1793 Hood, now aged 69, was in command of the 21 ships of the line of the Mediterranean Fleet. The role of the fleet was to negate the French fleet at Toulon, either by blockade or by bringing it to battle, thereby ensuring free passage for British commerce in the Mediterranean. Hood's fleet would also act as a force for power projection throughout the region and was a highly visible British commitment to those countries opposed to Revolutionary France.

During July 1793 counter-revolutionaries in Toulon had removed the radical supporters of the revolution from power. The central government in Paris responded by sending an army to crush the rebellion, *à la guillotine*. With around 50,000 refugees packed into Toulon the situation was reaching crisis point and the authorities turned to their last hope of salvation and opened negotiations with Hood, then blockading Toulon, to enter the port. Hood was not the first or the last Royal Navy officer to find himself faced with a situation that took him beyond his official orders. Communication with London would take weeks; what was required now was for him to exercise his own judgement, not just in naval terms but also with regard to the possible political, diplomatic and strategic repercussions of acting beyond his government's orders and to intervene in an intrastate conflict and humanitarian crisis.[1]

Hood was not found wanting, as detailed in a proclamation he issued to the French people from his flagship, HMS *Victory*, on 23 August. He noted how the leaders of the revolution had preached liberty but had stripped that from the people, they had preached respect but had violated human rights, they had replaced monarchical tyranny with political tyranny. With the country ravaged by famine, the destruction of trade and commerce and the decline of industry, France was in a wretched condition. Britain saw no alternative but the restoration of the French monarchy in order to cease the acts of aggression and violence undertaken by the Republic against its neighbours. It was in this context that Hood masterfully offered the help of his force 'with which I am entrusted by my sovereign [...] to spare the further effusion of human blood, to crush with promptitude the factious, to re-establish regular government in France, and thereby maintain peace and tranquillity in Europe'. 'Trust your hopes,' he continued, 'to the generosity of a *loyal* and *free* nation.'[2]

Of course Hood was not one to miss a glorious opportunity and insisted that he was allowed to occupy the forts defending the town, thereby providing for the security of his fleet and, crucially, to disarm the French fleet which would be held in trust until peace was established in France. This was agreed upon and British forces, now supported by a Spanish fleet of 17 sail of the line, entered Toulon on 28 August 1793. It was a remarkable outcome, for without firing a shot the British had taken control of France's premier Mediterranean naval base and her Mediterranean fleet of 22 sail of the line.

After this initial success things started to unravel. Toulon was difficult to defend, for the town and harbour were dominated by higher ground, Hood would require enough troops to man a 15-mile defensive perimeter, but he did not have sufficient to defend the position: 'Had I five or six thousand good troops I should soon end the war,' he lamented to Henry Dundas. Instead he landed 1,500 marines and sailors from the fleet and two British regiments embarked with his ships under Captain George Elphinstone to occupy key positions. They were soon backed up with a thousand men from the Spanish ships with promises of more. There was also Jacobin discontent in the town and within the French fleet, so Hood sent away four French warships with the most troublesome crews. Apart from taking up defensive positions Elphinstone's force fought a number of skirmishes with Jacobin forces. In the harbour Royal Navy sailors manned gunboats and floating batteries which duelled with shore batteries now assembled by the republican forces. Ashore, sailors and marines fought side by side with British, Spanish and Neapolitan reinforcements which continued to trickle in. Republican batteries were assaulted but the weight of numbers was beginning to tell. At the end of October 1793 the allied forces totalled 16,912 men with only 12,000 fit for duty. The majority were Spaniards and Neapolitans; the British contingent numbered only 2,114. By stripping his fleet of sailors to support operations ashore Hood was forced to turn to the Grand Master of the Knights of Malta to hire 1,500 sailors to help man his fleet.[3] This *ad hoc* force was tasked with holding off around 33,000 French republicans including the inspirational figure of Napoleon Bonaparte.

During November and December 1793 the defence of Toulon started to fall apart and Hood was left with little option but to evacuate. The task now became one of utter destruction – to burn ships, naval stores and damage as much of the dockyard facilities as possible – to prevent Toulon serving as a base for a French fleet. This task fell to, or rather was grasped by, Captain Sir Sidney Smith. On the afternoon of 18 December in the *Swallow*, accompanied by three Spanish and three English gunboats, Smith began his task. He found a confused and dangerous situation ashore. Beating off attacks by republican forces, Smith prepared to burn the dockyard facilities and French warships. At around 20:00 Smith saw Captain Charles Hare's *Vulcan* fireship under tow into the harbour; she would be placed next to the French warships and set on fire. At 22:00 the priming powder on the *Vulcan* was lit and immediately produced a flash explosion which blew Hare 'much scorched' into the water. As the fire spread the *Vulcan*'s double-shotted guns

discharged themselves against the shore. There the general magazine and hemp magazine, storehouses for oil, tar, pitch and tallow
and the mast house were set alight by Smith's men. The French
frigate *Iris* was picked out for special attention and a Spanish team
were tasked with her scuttling, but, unaware there were a thousand barrels of gunpowder on board, they set fire to her. The resul-
tant catastrophic explosion obliterated the *Iris* and the Royal Navy's
Union gunboat, killing her midshipman, Mr Young, and three crew.
The *Terrible* gunboat was also blown out of the water but her crew
survived and were picked up.[4]

The Spaniards failed to complete their task of burning the French
ships in the basin, but even Smith and his men were prevented from
undertaking this by fire from republican positions. He removed
French prisoners from the 74-gun *Héros* and *Thémistocle* before
burning the ships. With their combustible material exhausted and
everything within reach on fire, the explosion of the frigate *Montréal*
left the waters around the *Swallow* foaming with falling timber
and assorted debris. It was clearly time to cut and run and Smith
proceeded to the designated embarkation points for the remaining allied troops, all of whom were safely on board the fleet by the
morning of 19 December. They were joined by 14,877 French loyalists who escaped the slaughter that followed; around 2,000 prisoners and 6,000 men, women and children in Toulon were butchered
or died escaping.

Fifteen French warships were taken by the allies. The British
retained the enormous and unwieldy 120-gun *Commerce de Marseilles*
which was initially converted into a huge store ship and then, due
to her unseaworthiness, a prison hulk. The 74s *Puissant* and *Pompée*
along with three fine frigates, *Perle*, *Arethuse* and *Topaze*, were added
to the Royal Navy. Nine French sail of the line and a host of smaller
vessels were destroyed in Smith's conflagration; in total the French
lost 58 warships of all sizes along with the destruction of the main
stores including valuable shipbuilding timber: 'possibly the single
most crippling blow suffered by the French navy since Quiberon Bay
in 1759'. Although this marked a major blow to French ambitions in
the Mediterranean, left behind were some very good ships includ-

ing the 80-gun *Tonnant* and four 74s with another on the building stocks. Hood's actions highlighted the value of having a naval force on the spot for intervention in an intrastate conflict and, crucially, the immense responsibility that fell on admirals like Hood operating with allies at distance from the Admiralty in London.[5]

Corsica

While assisting the royalists at Toulon, Hood had detached a squadron to support a royalist uprising under General Paoli on the French island of Corsica. Hood thought the harbour at San Fiorenzo would make an excellent rendezvous for his fleet but the French-controlled land defences would have to be seized. On 8 February 1794 the 74-gun *Fortitude*, assisted by the *Juno*, was directed to attack a round tower guarding San Fiorenzo Bay at Mortella Point. Two and a half hours' worth of cannon fire failed to make any impression on the thick walls of the 'Mortello' tower and the *Fortitude* hauled off 'much damaged by red-hot shot' from two 18pdrs on top of the parapet. The tower also resisted two days' close-range fire from land batteries until red-hot shot set fire to the backing of the parapet. The tower then surrendered; out of a 33-man garrison only two had been mortally wounded. With this tower seized sailors hauled a number of 18pdrs up a 700ft cliff to help reduce a redoubt at Fornelli.[6]

With his anchorage safe, Hood moved on to besieging the Corsican capital of Bastia. General David Dundas, in command of 1,400 troops, refused to cooperate with Hood's plans. The siege of Bastia was, therefore, largely a naval affair. Naval guns were landed and sailors and marines provided British support to 1,200 Corsican irregulars. The bombardment commenced on 11 April and the siege lasted until the town's provisions ran out. A flag of truce was run up on 19 May and Bastia formally surrendered on the 21st. *Agamemnon*'s Captain Horatio Nelson wrote, 'I may say truly, that this has been a Naval Expedition: our boats prevented any thing from getting in by sea, and our sailors hauling up great guns, and then fighting them on shore.'[7]

While Hood sailed to look for the French Toulon fleet, supposedly at sea, a British detachment sailed to attack the town of Calvi. With reinforcements from Gibraltar under Lieutenant General Sir Charles Stuart now arrived, Nelson commanded the naval contribution. The 1,450 troops were disembarked on 19 June and joined by sailors who took with them hammocks, sandbags, casks of beef, bags of bread and three pipes of wine. 'Dragging cannon up steep mountains, and carrying shot and shells, has been our constant employment,' Nelson wrote on 27 June. On the same day, Hood in the *Victory* arrived. Several more days were spent in preparing the batteries until, on 4 July, the bombardment of Calvi began. On 12 July Nelson was 'a little hurt' by sand and gravel kicked up by a French shell; he would, in fact, lose the sight in his right eye. Sickness ravaged the besieging forces; of the sailors ashore a third were unfit for duty. The siege continued until Calvi finally fell on 10 August and two French frigates in the bay were seized. Naval dynamism had been contrasted with some less than enthusiastic attitudes amongst army officers, prompting Nelson to declare, 'They hate us sailors; we are too active for them. We accomplish our business sooner than they like.' [8]

Hood's concern over the French Toulon fleet was entirely valid, for seven sail of the line and four or five frigates had put to sea on 5 June. Hood chased them down with 13 sail of the line and four frigates, sighting them on the 10th. The French ran for the safety of Gourjean Bay where Hood left Vice Admiral William Hotham with eight sail of the line to blockade them while he sailed for Corsica. Hotham maintained the blockade until blown off station when the French made a run for it, finally arriving back at Toulon.

In November 1794 Hood sailed for England with effective command of the Mediterranean Fleet now devolving to Hotham. With Hood back in England, having failed to provide Hotham with instructions or knowledge of the intentions of the government, and with a change at the Admiralty, Lord Spencer replacing Chatham as First Lord, guidance on British policy in the Mediterranean was sorely lacking. Hotham, dutiful and eminently capable in subordinate positions, was not up to commanding a theatre like the

Mediterranean and was very much out on a limb.[9]

On 14 March Hotham engaged the French and took two sail of the line, but with four of his own ships damaged he broke off action. His priority was to keep his numerically inferior fleet 'in being' as an effective fighting force. By doing so he provided security to Corsica and Italy, as without his fleet both would fall to the French. What was perhaps frustrating for a younger generation of captains under his command, eager for glory and promotion, was Hotham's apparent lack of aggressive spirit. By the time of his next brush with the French fleet on 13 July Hotham, ill and weighed down with responsibility for the fleet, was displaying signs of mental break-down. Reinforced to 23 sail of the line, in light winds he found it difficult to close with the French fleet and after taking one French ship, which blew up, Hotham called off the action again. Vice Admiral Samuel Goodall, his second in command, was disgusted, 'kicking his hat about the deck in a frenzy of rage'. While the risks of continuing the attack were great, Nelson admitted, 'so was the object'. The French fleet eventually made it back to Toulon.[10]

Nelson vented his frustrations by harrying French positions along the Gulf of Genoa, cutting out French ships and seizing French merchantmen such as the convoy of 12 ships he attacked in the Bay of Alassio on 26 August. He took ten and drove one on shore while the final ship was burned. Nelson was also acting as the front line of British diplomacy, corresponding with Austrian generals and British representatives such as Sir Gilbert Elliot, newly installed viceroy of Corsica.[11]

On 14 September six French sail of the line and three frigates put to sea to reinforce the Brest fleet for the invasion operations planned for late 1795. This detachment was chased by a British force sent by Hotham to cover an important British convoy of 63 merchant ships from the eastern Mediterranean. It was too late. The British 74-gun *Censeur* struggling under a jury rig was captured along with 30 British merchant ships. Unable to make the Channel, the French put into the Spanish port of Cadiz. A second French fleet escaped from Toulon in late September, cruising towards the eastern Mediterranean in expectation of attacking the same British convoy.

They missed it and instead played havoc with British, Russian and Neapolitan shipping off Smyrna before arriving back in Toulon on 5 February 1796.

Hotham had maintained his fleet in being to support British diplomacy, preserve crucial alliances and protect Corsica. But both French cruises illustrated the dangers posed if the enemy could get to sea and of missing opportunities to destroy them. While such cruises could not change the wider strategic situation, they did pose real dangers to British trade. Moreover, for the Royal Navy every French cruise involved detaching forces to hunt them down and remove the danger, leading to a dispersal of effort and increased wear and tear on ships and men. The only way to protect British trade was to lock up enemy fleets in port or decisively defeat them in battle.[12]

Hotham struck his flag on 1 November. Command of the Mediterranean Fleet devolved to Admiral Hyde Parker until Hotham's permanent successor, Admiral Sir John Jervis, arrived. Jervis's thinking was demonstrated by his first actions upon hoisting his flag on HMS *Victory* on 3 December. Discipline and drill were tightened, and ready supplies of fresh victuals were sourced to ensure ships' crews remained fit and healthy. But most importantly, Jervis thought it was his prime objective to negate the Toulon fleet, either by bringing it to battle and destroying it, or keeping it bottled up in Toulon. To that end, he sailed on 13 December to cruise between Toulon and Minorca.

While Jervis intended to keep a very close watch on Toulon, events ashore in early 1796 started to alter the situation in the Mediterranean. In Italy, French success under General Bonaparte culminated in the seizure of Leghorn in late June. This denied the now Commodore Nelson in HMS *Captain* a crucial operating base for his detached squadron in those waters. Without victuals and stores supplied from Leghorn, Nelson seized Porto Ferrajo on the island of Elba on 10 July 1796, relocating some of the repair and victualling support personnel to that port, before heading back to blockade Leghorn.

The Spanish declaration of war, 1796

Spain had been an ally of Britain at Toulon, but 1795 had seen a French invasion of Catalonia and the loss of Bilbao and Vitoria. With Castile and Madrid coming under threat in July 1795 Spain made peace with France; just as in Italy, French success on land far outweighed British influence at sea. War between Britain and Spain became a reality in October 1796. The Royal Navy was now outnumbered in the Mediterranean by 40 sail of the line to 30, denied access to Italian bases and was now faced with the hostile Spanish fleet base at Cadiz posing a threat to British interests and commerce. Spencer realized this would effectively 'drive us from the Mediterranean'. Gibraltar was not a useful base for westward traffic, so Spencer decided to concentrate British naval forces into two commands. One would be the traditional Channel command, the other would be stationed at Lisbon and be responsible for the waters between Gibraltar and Cape Finisterre to preserve the British alliance with Portugal, intercept Spanish trade, protect British trade, and keep Lisbon open as an entrepôt into European markets, while 'taking every opportunity of annoying the enemy'.[13]

Spencer's worst nightmare turned into reality with a cruise by 19 ships of the line under the Spanish Admiral Juan de Lángara, who left Cadiz and combined with the French fleet at Toulon, providing a potentially decisive concentration of force. Separately, the French retook Corsica and, with Nelson having evacuated Leghorn, the British strategic withdrawal from the Mediterranean became a reality when on 2 December Jervis's fleet arrived at Gibraltar to victual and repair. Nelson, still in the Mediterranean with a frigate squadron to evacuate Elba, remarked to Lieutenant General de Burgh at Porto Ferrajo on 29 December 1796, 'The object of our fleet in future is the defence of Portugal, and keeping in the Mediterranean the Combined Fleets.'[14]

Jervis arrived off the Tagus on 22 December 1796, but lost the 74-gun *Bombay Castle* on the dangerous bar of the river, reducing his command to 14 ships of the line. As the new year dawned not a single British ship of the line was in Mediterranean waters.

In January 1797 Nelson, flying his flag in the frigate *La Minerve*, completed the withdrawal and headed for Jervis's fleet now at sea off Cape St Vincent. On the night of 11 February *La Minerve* passed through the Spanish fleet, now at sea to convoy an essential shipment of quicksilver for the South American mines. Nelson joined with Jervis on the 13th with this vital intelligence.[15]

The battle of Cape St Vincent, 14 February 1797

Despite being outnumbered by the 23 Spanish ships of the line, Jervis was not one to miss an opportunity for battle. Aware of the poor state of the Spanish ships and with his force augmented to 15 ships of the line, including six very powerful three-deckers, he knew that, given the naval situation in the Channel and the Mediterranean and with French success on land, 'a victory is very essential to England at this moment'.[16]

As the Spanish ships loomed out of the haze a conversation occurred between Jervis and his flag captain, Robert Calder:

'There are eight sail of the line, Sir John.'
'Very well, sir.'
'There are twenty sail of the line, Sir John.'
'Very well, sir.'
'There are twenty five sail of the line, Sir John.'
'Very well, sir.'
'There are twenty seven sail of the line, Sir John […] near twice our own number.'
'Enough, sir, no more of that; the die is cast, and if there are fifty sail I will go through them.'

The Spanish ships were formed into two loose groups: while five ships of the line escorted the convoy carrying quicksilver, the other group of 18 sail of the line tried to close the gap that had opened up between the two groups. That gap was precisely where Jervis was headed and, with the *Culloden* leading his line, he won the race, passing up the starboard side of the larger Spanish group, cannonading as they went. The *Príncipe de Asturias* with the convoy tried to pass ahead of the *Victory* and join with the main body but was raked ahead and astern causing her to bear up 'in great confusion'. The British ships tacked in succession between the two Spanish groups, the larger of which was now to the north-east of Jervis's fleet. This group now tried to close with the ships of the convoy a second time, and in doing so attacked Jervis's rearward ships.[17]

Jervis signalled his rear under Vice Admiral Sir Charles Thompson to intercept this move but in the confusion of battle Thompson did not see the signal. Jervis was tactically astute and had amended the fighting instructions for the Mediterranean Fleet with a specific instruction for such a case. While his van cut through the enemy line from a leeward position and engaged from the wind-ward side, the British centre and rear would engage their respective opponents to prevent them supporting the now isolated enemy van which would be defeated in detail. Seeing the danger, aware of Jervis's tactical thinking and intentions and interpreting 'take suit-able stations for mutual support' included in Jervis's signal, Nelson in HMS *Captain* wore out of the British formation and recrossed the line ahead of the rearmost British ship, the *Excellent*, before heading for the Spanish van. Following her tack at the head of the British line, *Culloden* was now bearing down on the Spanish van and Jervis ordered Collingwood in the *Excellent* to tack and join *Culloden* and *Captain*. The three British ships were shortly supported by the *Blenheim* and *Prince George*. The Spanish had been prevented from reforming their fleet.[18]

Nelson had headed for the imposing shape of the 136-gun *Santísima Trinidad*, a three-decker recently reconstructed to include a fourth gundeck. *Captain* suffered damage aloft in this uneven duel but her fire was augmented by the *Culloden*. Meanwhile Collingwood was busy battering the 112-gun *Salvador del Mundo* and then the 74-gun *San Isidro*, the latter striking her colours while the former, just as *Victory* was about to rake her, also hauled down her colours. Collingwood moved onto the *San Nicolás*, already damaged by the *Captain*, forcing her into evasive action which led to her running into the *San José*, before *Excellent* went on to tackle the *Santísima Trinidad*. *Captain* had suffered much damage to masts and rigging: 'not a sail,

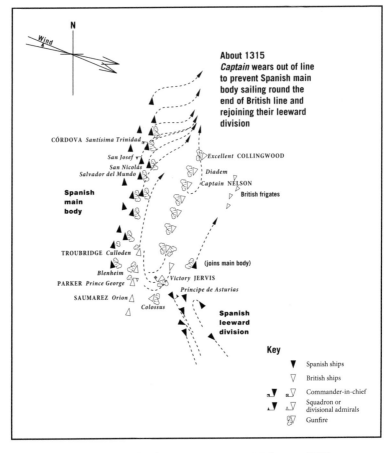

N

Wind

About 1315
Captain wears out of line
to prevent Spanish main
body sailing round the
end of British line and
rejoining their leeward
division

CÓRDOVA *Santísima Trinidad*

San Josef   *Excellent* COLLINGWOOD

San Nicolás   *Diadem*
Salvador del Mundo   *Captain* NELSON

Spanish main body   ▽ British frigates

TROUBRIDGE *Culloden*   (joins main body)

Blenheim
PARKER *Prince George*   *Victory* JERVIS

SAUMAREZ *Orion*   *Príncipe de Asturias*
          Colossus

Spanish leeward division

Key

▼   Spanish ships
▽   British ships
▼ ▽   Commander-in-chief
▼ ▽   Squadron or divisional admirals
    Gunfire

Fig. 2.1. The battle of Cape St Vincent, 14 February 1797.

shroud, or rope standing, the wheel shot away, and incapable of further service in the line or in chase,' Nelson recalled. She could still provide a useful service and Nelson directed Captain Miller to run the ship into the *San Nicolás*.

Lieutenant Pierson of the 69th Regiment of Foot led several soldiers onto the *San Nicolás*. While this was happening one soldier broke open the quarter-galley windows before leaping into the cabin of the *San Nicolás*, followed closely by Nelson and others. They were fired on, but broke open the cabin's locked doors, before pouring out onto the deck. The Spanish commodore fell as Nelson pushed for the quarterdeck where he found Lieutenant Berry in possession of the poop and the Spanish ensign hauled down. At this point fire came from the stern of the *San José* and, directing more men into the *San Nicolás*, Nelson ordered those around him to board the first rate which quickly surrendered. Nelson recalled how 'on the quarterdeck of a Spanish First-rate, extravagant as the story may seem, did I receive the swords of the vanquished Spaniards, which as I received I gave to William Fearney, my bargeman, who placed them, with the greatest sang-froid, under his arm'. Using one Spanish ship as a boarding bridge to capture another was certainly unique and 'Nelson's Patent Bridge for Boarding First Rates' helped to bring his actions at the battle to popular attention.[19]

Fifteen British ships had aggressively attacked 23 Spanish sail of the line, capturing four of them (two of which were three-deckers) in the process. Exact Spanish losses were 261 killed and 342 wounded on the four prizes alone: the *San Nicolás* had 144 men killed and 59 wounded, the *San José* 46 killed and 96 wounded, the crew of the *Santísima Trinidad* suffered over 200 casualties. Jervis's fleet lost 73 killed and 227 seriously wounded, the majority in the *Captain*, 24 killed and 56 wounded, the *Blenheim*, 12 killed and 47 wounded, the *Excellent*, 11 killed and 12 wounded and the *Culloden*, 10 killed and 47 wounded.[20]

To the prizes and the victory can be added another important outcome: the battle provided the nation with a new naval hero. Nelson, using his friendship with Sir Gilbert Elliot and his political connections, made sure that his role was played up to the full. Moreover, his account was carefully edited by Lord Spencer. All this ensured that Nelson's version of the battle would become the accepted version with, of course, him as the hero of the day. By doing so Nelson downplayed the role of others, causing some dissention and jealously in the fleet.

To the public Nelson was the hero of St Vincent and his actions brought him much acclaim. He was made a Knight of the Bath and his promotion, on seniority, to rear admiral followed. Jervis was raised to the peerage as Earl of St Vincent. Nelson was clearly acting upon his admiral's intent, if not specific orders. Sir Robert Calder,

Jervis's flag captain, noted that Nelson's move was unauthorized. 'It certainly was so,' Jervis responded, 'and if you ever commit such a breach of your orders I will forgive you also.' It was also a manoeuvre that was based upon an assessment of Spanish fighting capabilities and seamanship, or, more accurately, a lack of them. Nelson in the *Captain* engaged a much superior part of the enemy fleet, placing his ship in extreme danger, and against better-trained, manned and motivated ships it would have been almost suicidal. Yet he had the confidence of his commander and knew that his brother officers' support for his bold move would be forthcoming.[21]

After repairing his ships Jervis arrived off Cadiz on 2 April to blockade the 26 enemy sail of the line there. The main British fleet would take up position off the entrance to Cadiz harbour, arranged in a crescent shape with Jervis, now flying his flag in the *Ville de Paris*, in the centre of the formation. Inshore of this was an advance or inshore squadron under the command of Rear Admiral Nelson. Jervis hoped to provoke the Spanish fleet to weigh anchor and come out for a decisive showdown, but it remained at anchor. On 3 July an attempt to bombard Cadiz was made by gunboats, ships' boats and the bomb-vessel *Thunder*. This force was attacked by Spanish gunboats leading to vicious hand-to-hand fighting between boat crews, with Nelson, visibly leading from the front, in the thick of it again. It was really no place for an admiral but Jervis and Nelson were both aware that blockade was a hard but monotonous duty which impacted upon the morale and discipline of the men.

The assault on Tenerife

With the blockade of Cadiz continuing into July and St Vincent determined to carry the conflict to the Spaniards, largely to occupy the time and the minds of his crews, news reached him of Spanish treasure galleons sheltering at Santa Cruz de Tenerife. Unfortunately a small British raid in April 1797 had provided the Spanish governor with a warning that his town was of interest to the British and he had been busy improving the defences and raising the number of men available to resist an assault.[22]

Unaware of this, Nelson, sent by Jervis to attack the town in a 'sudden and vigorous assault', set about drawing up a meticulous plan showing considerable attention to detail. It called for a swift and intense night-time attack by sailors and marines to the north of the town, capturing the forts there and then turning the guns on the town. With complete surprise this would outwit the Spaniards who would, of course, inevitably surrender. Nelson, now in the 74-gun *Theseus*, had with him the cream of those captains available at Cadiz. There was Thomas Troubridge in the *Culloden* and Samuel Hood in the *Zealous*, both 74-gun ships. In addition, there were three frigates, Thomas Fremantle in the *Seahorse*, John Waller in the *Emerald* and Richard Bowen in the *Terpsichore*, along with the *Fox* cutter. Nelson communicated the plan personally to his captains, ensuring all were aware of the aim of and their roles in the operation. The plan displayed a keen understanding of the importance of avoiding strong points, but landing to take them from either the flank or rear. What it lacked was anything more than rudimentary knowledge of the Spanish defences.[23]

The British arrived off Santa Cruz on 21 July but bad weather and contrary currents prevented a surprise assault, the key part of the plan. As the assault went in on the 21st the strong currents made it difficult for boats to keep to Nelson's plan, with darkness adding to the confusion. The boats were recalled to the ships. A second landing attempt on the 22nd under Thomas Troubridge did make it ashore but was also called off. Any element of surprise had been completely lost. 'My pride suffered', Nelson later admitted, and when a deserter from the shore brought news that the Spanish defences were lightly manned and morale was low, Nelson decided on another attack, this time a full-frontal assault on Santa Cruz using all the available men of the fleet. The attack on 25 July was a bloody shambles, for the defenders were in fact well prepared and highly motivated. Ships' boats used to transport men from the fleet to the shore were smashed by shot and only five from the first wave made it to their target. Those men who did get ashore were met with heavy small-arms fire. A group of around 350 made it into the town but were forced to surrender. The Spanish governor provided food to his captives and boats to take them back to the British fleet. During the assault Nelson had been hit by a musket ball above his right elbow, severing an artery. He was taken back to the *Theseus* where it was discovered that the wound necessitated the immediate amputation of the arm. Nelson now gave up, and with his men returned to the squadron he headed for Cadiz.

Despite careful planning and verbal and written communication of the plan to his captains, Nelson, in his first independent command, had failed. The ill-judged assaults had been bloody: 153 men were killed or drowned, double the number killed at St Vincent, and 110 wounded, including Fremantle. In comparison the Spaniards lost only 30 dead and 40 wounded. Once surprise had been lost, a more experienced commander would have left well alone; instead Nelson's headstrong actions cost the lives of many of his men. 'I shall,' he wrote after arriving off Cadiz on 16 August, 'no longer be considered as useful.'[24]

The Nile campaign

St Vincent's main priority remained the blockade of Cadiz, a strategic consideration for his fleet and one which comprised 'a considerable portion of the defence of the [British] Empire'. If Cadiz could not be blockaded, the British Isles would be open to invasion and the empire exposed to attack from Spanish and French naval forces. When news of French preparations at Toulon and Genoa for a substantial naval expedition reached London, it confirmed the government view that a British naval force should re-enter the Mediterranean. The reason, as Spencer informed St Vincent, was that 'the appearance of a British squadron in the Mediterranean is a condition on which the fate of Europe may at this moment be stated to depend, you will not be surprised that we are disposed to strain every nerve and incur considerable hazard in effecting it'. This was a strategy not without risk, for re-entering the Mediterranean would leave no strategic reserve in home waters, but the arrival of a British fleet would be an important sign of support to Austria and Russia.[25]

Following a period of convalescence in England, Nelson arrived with the fleet on 29 April, flying his flag in the 74-gun *Vanguard*. St Vincent was delighted: 'the arrival of Admiral Nelson has given me new life'. While perfectly suited to blockading Cadiz, St Vincent's fleet had a critical lack of frigates to scout out enemy intentions. Therefore he dispatched Nelson's *Vanguard*, accompanied by the *Orion*, Captain Sir James Saumarez, and *Alexander*, Captain Alexander Ball, both 74s, along with three frigates, *Emerald* (36), *Terpsichore* (32) and *Bonne Citoyenne* (20), to discover what the French were up to.[26]

On 19 May Nelson was watching Toulon when his ships were hit by a gale blowing them all the way to Sardinia. Nelson arrived back on station on 31 May but the massive French fleet of 72 warships, including 13 sail of the line and 400 transports convoying 36,000 troops, was nowhere to be seen. It had in fact sailed on 20 May, with Vice Admiral François-Paul Brueys entertaining Napoleon aboard his 120-gun *L'Orient*. On 10 June Napoleon attacked Malta, its harbour of Valetta a crucial strategic base for projecting power in the Mediterranean. The city surrendered two days later. Napoleon sailed to the east and on 1 July the great expedition reached Alexandria. By the end of the month Napoleon was master of Egypt.

On 7 June Nelson had been reinforced: he now had 13 74-gun ships, one 50-gun ship and a sixth-rate brig sloop, the *Mutine*, to search for the French. But that search was hampered because British merchantmen, usually a vital source of intelligence, had been driven from the Mediterranean after the Royal Navy had withdrawn in 1797. There were enemy and neutral merchantmen but this raised the issue of obtaining reliable and accurate intelligence. Such ships had to be caught, and here Nelson's lack of frigates was crippling. Acting on information from a Tunisian warship, Nelson headed first to Sicily. After receiving news of the attack on Malta he sailed for Valetta but then learnt of the island's fall. Weighing up the situation, Nelson came to the only conclusion possible: the French expedition was headed for Egypt. He followed suit, covering up to 150 miles a day, unknowingly overtook the French on 24/25 June and when the city of Alexandria was sighted on 28 June there were only merchant vessels and Turkish warships in the bay. On the morning of 30 June Nelson sailed for Turkey. Just over 24 hours later the great French expedition was anchoring in Alexandria harbour.[27]

On 28 July Nelson's luck changed, for he received definite intelligence that the French were in Egypt. With the *Swiftsure* and *Alexander* operating ahead of the fleet, on 1 August the *Zealous* and *Goliath* spotted the French fleet anchored in a defensive position in Aboukir Bay. Nelson had used the time chasing down the French to communicate his intent to those under his command. His plan for battle envisaged finding the French in an irregular order, in which case he would attack in 'separate divisions', each kept 'in the closest order possible' to attack the French with a mass concentration of British gunnery. This would allow him to destroy the enemy fleet. If he caught the French at sea, his fleet would divide into three parts: two to attack the French warships while the third destroyed the transports.[28]

During those weeks a number of his captains were invited to dine aboard the *Vanguard*. There was also at least one full conference on 18 July with all captains called to the *Vanguard*. This allowed Nelson to discuss his tactical methods and how they might be employed in a number of scenarios. By fostering strong bonds between his captains and with himself, Nelson knew his subordinates would act with unity in striving to achieve his intent: 'Each knew his duty, and I was sure each would feel for a French ship,' he later recalled. This spirit is what he referred to in a letter of 8 January 1799: 'I had the happiness to command a Band of Brothers'. Through his tactical orders and his meetings with subordinates, Nelson created a unity of purpose. This included communicating what he intended his fleet to do if he found the French at anchor.[29]

The battle of the Nile, 1 August 1798

Anchored in Aboukir Bay, the northern end of Brueys' fleet was near the shallows of Aboukir Island with his 13 sail of the line stretching to the south-east in a shallow convex line. Brueys had positioned his flagship, *L'Orient*, in the centre with his 80-gun ships towards the rear. His four frigates were stationed closer inshore. Protected by the shallows and with broadsides presented to any attacker, Brueys thought his fleet safe. In order to help each ship manoeuvre individually to obtain the best field of fire, their anchor cables were fitted with springs, ropes run through an aft gunport and attached to the cable allowing sailors to haul and shift the ships' position.

Nelson's fleet lost some cohesion, with *Alexander*, *Swiftsure* and *Culloden* all separated from the main group bunched around *Vanguard*. Faced with the prospect of starting an action that would undoubtedly go on into the night, something usually avoided in battle at sea owing to navigational hazards and the potential for friendly fire, Nelson made the momentous decision to attack forthwith, instructing his fleet to concentrate on the enemy van and centre. But with the fleet lacking the cohesion his pre-battle thinking had sought, the leading ships would bear the brunt of French defensive fire to take up key positions, with those trailing behind having to take their guidance from the first in action. With *Goliath* and *Zealous* racing each other for the honour of leading the British line into the fight, at 17:30, abreast of Aboukir Island, Nelson ordered the fleet 'to form the line as most convenient'. This was, in effect, abandoning all the careful tactical preparation Nelson had put in over the preceding few weeks. But it was a clear sign of the trust and confidence instilled between commander and subordinates. 'I knew what stuff I had under me,' he wrote after battle, 'so I went into the attack with only a few ships, perfectly sure that the others would follow me.' [30]

It was fortunate that Captain Foley in the *Goliath* won the race, for according to an eyewitness, he was in possession of superior French charts of the bay which guided him round Aboukir Island avoiding the shallows and allowing him to take a line inside that of the *Zealous*. Noticing the distance between the head of the French line and the shallows and aware of his commander's intent to concentrate on the van and centre, Foley not only saw a glorious opportunity to round the head of the line and attack from the shore side but possessed the acumen and moral courage to act on his instincts. The discussion between Foley and the *Goliath*'s master is recounted by midshipman George Elliot: both men 'agreed there was room to pass between the ship and her anchor. [...] I heard Foley say, that he should not be surprised to find the Frenchman <u>unprepared</u> for

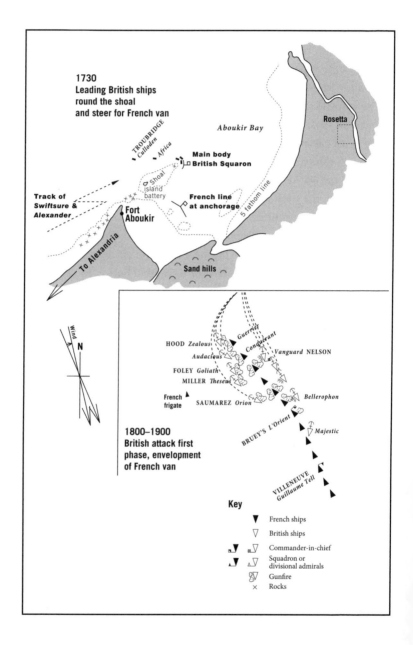

Fig. 2.2. The battle of the Nile, 1 August 1798.

action <u>on the inner side</u>.' Where Foley went others could follow, and with British ships taking up a more conventional station on the outer side of the French fleet, the head would be caught between a deadly crossfire. 'At 15 minutes past 6,' *Goliath*'s log recounts, 'crossed the van of the enemy's line and Commenced the Action.'[31]

Hood in the *Zealous* followed Foley, both pounding the lead French ship, the *Guerrier,* as they rounded her. The next two British ships, *Audacious* and *Orion*, whose captain, Saumarez, passed inshore of the first three British ships, also rounded the head of the French line and engaged ships from the shore side. Captain Miller in the *Theseus* actually passed between *Guerrier* and the second French ship, *Conquérant*. During the final advance Nelson slowed the *Vanguard* to move his ship further down the battle-line, allowing it to exercise control over the middle and rear ships of his fleet. This allowed him to place the *Vanguard* on the seaward side of the French *Spartiate*, third in the enemy line, which was engaged on the inner side by Miller's *Theseus*. *Minotuar* and *Defence* followed suit, the former engaging the *Spartiate* and *Aquilion* and the latter the *Peuple Sovereign*. This concentration of firepower crushed the head of the French line, whose five ships were engaged by eight British. *Conquérant* surrendered after only 12 minutes of British gunnery.

Towards the rear of the British line, *Culloden* passed too close to Aboukir Island and ran aground, preventing her 74 guns getting into action, but her misfortune provided a marker for *Alexander* and *Swiftsure* who both managed to avoid the same fate. Nelson had instructed his captains to anchor by the stern which, with springs attached, would allow a degree of tactical manoeuvre. Something went wrong on the *Majestic*, for in failing to anchor she was hit by fire from the *Tonnant*, then ran onto the *Heureux* and was exposed to her fire without the ability to respond effectively until after an hour she moved further down the French line.

With darkness falling, and with British ships following Nelson's order to carry four lanterns astern for recognition in the gloom, at around 19:00 *Bellerophon* took up a position to engage the massive *L'Orient* not from her bow quarter as intended but on the broadside. Not surprisingly, *Bellerophon* was battered by her far superior opponent before drifting, dismasted, out of the battle. It was now that the *Alexander* and *Swiftsure* helped turn a British victory into a crushing defeat for the French. In textbook fashion *Alexander* passed through the French line and anchored on her springs off *L'Orient*'s stern port quarter while *Swiftsure* took up a position off her bow starboard quarter. The final British ship, the 50-gun *Leander*, anchored between the *Peuple Sovereign* and the *Franklin*, the latter ahead of *L'Orient*.

L'Orient was now caught in a crossfire and, as *Swiftsure*'s log recalls, 'at 3 mins past 9 observed the *L'Orient* on fire'. Admiral Brueys had been wounded in the arm and the head before being virtually truncated. It became obvious to the British ships that the fire was spreading and they took what action they could to prepare for the inevitable outcome. On *Swiftsure* the gun ports were closed and sailors ordered below decks as figures could be seen leaping from the French ship. Given her position, Captain Hallowell kept the *Swiftsure* close, hoping that burning debris would be blown clear over his ship. The French ships *Heureux* and *Mercure* both cut their cables. At 21:37 *L'Orient* was destroyed in a cataclysmic explosion. *Swiftsure*, to the windward, escaped without too much damage; a section of *L'Orient*'s mast hit her, which Hallowell would later turn into a coffin for Nelson. The crew of the *Alexander*, downwind, spent the next two hours putting out fires. All firing stopped for a short time as the shock of the destruction of the French flagship brought a mutual paralysis over the fleets.

Franklin restarted the action but she soon surrendered – the fight had gone from the French fleet. What was left of the rear now tried to escape. Captain Aristide Du Petit Thouars of the 80-gun *Tonnant* had lost both legs and an arm in the action but continued, propped up in a barrel of wheat, to direct the fire of his ship. He had instructed her colours be literally nailed to the mast. Around 03:00 on 2 August, with crews on both sides exhausted, all firing ceased. At that point every French ship ahead of the now obliterated flagship *L'Orient* had surrendered.

Around the time *Spartiate* struck to the *Vanguard*, sometime close to 20:30 on 1 August, Nelson had been wounded on the

Extirpation of the Plagues of Egypt;– Destruction of Revolutionary Crocodiles;– or – The British Hero cleansing y͏e Mouth of y͏e Nile

Fig. 2.3. *Extirpation of the Plagues of Egypt.* Nelson, wielding a club of 'British Oak', sets about the French crocodiles, one of which, representing *L'Orient*, explodes in the background.

Fig. 2.4. Nelson and the 'Victors of the Nile', whom he later called his 'Band of Brothers'.

forehead, leaving him with a deep gash down to the skull and
suffering from concussion, impacting upon his ability to manage the
fleet, if indeed anything much could have been done in the confusion and darkness. But in the early hours of 2 August he ordered
those British ships at the head of the line that could sail to make
their way to the rear of the enemy fleet. *Tonnant* and *Timoléan*
still flew their colours and there was the *Guillaume Tell*, Admiral
Pierre-Charles de Villeneuve, and the *Généreux* to deal with as well
as a couple of French frigates. *Heureux* and *Mercure* had by now run
aground, to be followed by *Timoléan*, whose crew prepared to fight
her to the last. At 11:30 on 2 August Villeneuve made the decision
to escape. The final actions of the battle did not take place until the
morning of 3 August when the *Tonnant* finally surrendered and the
Timoléan was burnt by her crew.[32]

Nelson had destroyed the French Mediterranean fleet and won
the most decisive naval battle of the century; two of Brueys' 13
sail of the line had been burnt and nine taken. Of these only three
were taken into the Royal Navy, the *Spartiate* and *Tonnant* under
their original names and the *Franklin* as the *Canopus*. Nelson's fleet
had lost 218 dead and 677 wounded. Throughout Nelson's fleet,
losses were greater on the ships that engaged to the outer side of
enemy ships and lighter on those on the inside. In contrast, 5,225
Frenchmen were killed, drowned, burned or missing. Such a blow
to French naval power completely changed the strategic situation in
the Mediterranean. Now the French army, and Bonaparte himself,
were trapped in Egypt and his ambitions in the East were dealt a
moral as well as a physical blow. It also exposed French possessions
in the Mediterranean to attack, gave hope to Turkey and Russia
and provided enhanced security to British interests. The battle
also ensured that Britain would never again be forced to abandon
the Mediterranean. For the French navy, the Nile was a shattering
psychological blow from which it never recovered.

Captain Foley certainly acted independently of his orders in
rounding the French line but most certainly in the knowledge of
what Nelson intended by concentrating force against the French van
and centre. Nelson did not single out any of his captains for specific

praise in his official dispatches, insisting, as he told his captains, that 'in the Battle the conduct of every Officer was equal'. In the face of a superior fleet, it was an aggressive Royal Navy ethos, based on superior seamanship, discipline and gunnery, which won through.

Nelson arrived off Naples on 22 September 1798, making repairs to the *Vanguard*, but by mid-October was ready to blockade Malta. He was back at Naples in early November assisting with the evacuation of the court from Naples to Palermo following a disastrous campaign. While a master of fleet command, the intricacies of politicking and diplomacy were sometimes beyond Nelson and for the latter part of 1798 and the early months of 1799 he and his squadron were sucked into a myopic view which ignored the wider strategic situation to the detriment of the naval context. In effect he was guilty of a dereliction of duty.[33]

The siege of Acre

With his army stranded in Egypt, Napoleon resolved to return to Europe by land via Turkey and in January 1799 headed into Syria with around 13,000 men. After a number of successes, on 15 March he had the walled city of Acre in sight, arriving there two days later. Anchored in the bay were Commodore Sir Sidney Smith's 80-gun *Tigre* and 74-gun *Theseus* – yet again British warships were in his way.

Smith had set to work strengthening the city's medieval defences, landing marines and seamen who positioned ships' guns, undertook repairs and generally boosted the morale of the ragtag Ottoman forces defending the city. On 18 March Smith's *Tigre* engaged in perhaps the most decisive action of the campaign, seizing Napoleon's siege train as it was shipped up from Egypt in gunboats. The guns were, of course, added to the defences of the city, while the gunboats were armed with carronades to harass enemy movements along the coastal road to the city. *Tigre* and *Theseus* were each anchored to provide covering fire to the flanks of the city.

Napoleon's batteries, limited to 12pdrs because of the loss of his siege train, still pounded the medieval walls of Acre, creating

Fig. 2.5. Admiral Sir William Sidney Smith, in a typically
dashing pose, defending the ramparts of Acre.

a breach before a major assault went in on 28 March which was beaten back by the defenders. On 7 April a sally by the defenders ended in the deaths of Major Oldfield of the *Theseus* and Lieutenant Wright. A second siege train, shipped from Alexandria, landed at Jaffa and hauled overland, arrived at the French camp on 27 April. Serious inroads were made into the city's defences. For the defenders a relief column was defeated by the French on 16 April, but a second force arrived by sea on 7 May. Napoleon resolved to storm the town before they could land but again the assault was unsuccessful; this time *Tigre*'s two 68pdr carronades had been placed on the mole to cover one of the city's gates. On 10 May Napoleon launched the eleventh and final assault which was again beaten off. His army packed up and marched back to Egypt on 20 May. On 23 August Napoleon fled Egypt, leaving behind his army in order to overthrow the regime in Paris. As for Smith, he had led from the front, often on the ramparts or at the breaches. Napoleon would later claim, 'That man made me miss my destiny.' [34]

The cruise of Bruix

With the French Mediterranean fleet now removed from the equation and his own fleet reinforced, St Vincent could implement operations designed to assist power projection in the Mediterranean. Towards the end of October 1798 he detached a small squadron under Sir John Duckworth with troops drawn from Lisbon to attack Minorca in a combined operation. On 15 November the garrison of the island surrendered and Port Mahon could now be added to the Royal Navy's network of bases. [35]

Despite the success of the previous five years, the Royal Navy did not have absolute 'command of the sea' but rather areas of more localized 'sea control'. Given the vagaries of conditions at sea and the often dispersed nature of naval fleets, even this 'local control' was liable to fail at critical moments. One was in late April 1799 when 24 ships of the line under Admiral Étienne Bruix escaped from Brest, a clear failure of Bridport's distant blockade policy, and arrived in the Mediterranean. This really could change the strategic situation.

With St Vincent ashore ill, command of the Mediterranean Fleet had devolved to Admiral George Elphinstone, Lord Keith. On 3 May Keith found himself trapped between Bruix's ships and the 28 Spanish ships in Cadiz. Keith stood out with his 15 sail of the line ready for battle but Bruix declined and headed into the Mediterranean. With four ships of the line with Duckworth at Minorca, three with Nelson at Malta and another four at Naples, two with Smith in the east, plus the allied warships of Russia, Portugal and Naples, there was a real prospect that Bruix might crush each of these in detail. Keith needed to concentrate his forces, settling on Minorca, as Duckworth's capture of the island proved of immediate benefit as a logistical base. In the end, Bruix headed for Toulon and convoyed supplies to the French army in Italy before heading back to Cadiz, picking up the 28 Spanish warships there and heading back for Brest, where he anchored on 8 August. Placing land-centric objects above defeating British seapower, Bruix had missed a glorious opportunity to defeat the Royal Navy in the Mediterranean and perhaps change the course of the war.

All this dragged Nelson from his involvement in Neapolitan scheming. As he concentrated his forces off western Sicily, he was joined on 5 June by Duckworth from Minorca. Faced with conflicting priorities, Nelson dithered, though he retained some professional focus on the task at hand, on 20 May drawing up a sailing order in case he brought Bruix to battle. Once the scare was over, Nelson headed for Palermo. Distracted by politicking and Emma Hamilton, in July he disobeyed direct orders from his new commanding officer, Lord Keith, who had superseded St Vincent on 10 June.[36]

When Keith pursued Bruix back into the Channel, on 1 September 1799 Nelson assumed temporary command of the Mediterranean Fleet, but spent much of the next few months at Palermo. He finally went to sea again in January 1800, a cruise which resulted in his meeting Keith, now back in the Mediterranean and installed as the new commander in chief. On 19 February there was a glimpse of the old Nelson: his small squadron consisting of the 80-gun *Foudroyant*, with the 74s *Audacious*, *Northumberland* and *Alexander*, fell in with the French *Commerce de Marseilles*, a store ship,

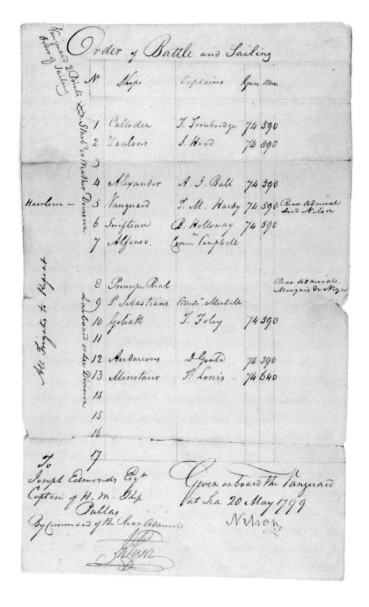

Order of Battle and Sailing

Nº	Ships	Captains	Guns	Men	
1	Culloden	T. Troubridge	74	590	
2	Zealous	S. Hood	74	590	
3					
4	Alexander	A. I. Ball	74	590	
5	Vanguard	T. M. Hardy	74	590	Rear Admiral Lord Nelson
6	Swiftsure	B. Holloway	74	590	
7	Alfonso	Commᵈ Campbell			
8	Principe Real				Rear Admiral Marquis de Niza
9	S. Sebastians	Commᵈ Mitchell			
10	Goliath	T. Foley	74	590	
11					
12	Audacious	D. Gould	74	590	
13	Minotaur	T. Louis	74	640	
14					
15					
16					
17					

Vanguard 2 Points (Order) of Starbᵈ or Weather Division

Haerlem —

Larboard or Lee Division

All Frigates to Repeat

To
Joseph Edmonds Esqᵗ
Captain of H. M. Ship
Pallas
By Command of the Rear Admiral

Given on board the Vanguard
at Sea 20 May 1799
Nelson

Fig. 2.6. Signed by Nelson and dated 1799, this document shows his plans to use two divisions (weather and lee) to attack an enemy fleet. Also note the presence of two Portuguese ships (8 and 9) under Admiral Niza.

escorted by the *Généreux*. After a chase and a brief exchange of shot, one of the two French ships of the line that had escaped his grasp at the Nile had fallen into Nelson's hands. On 30 March the *Foudroyant*, now under Captain Berry, succeeded in taking the last Nile survivor, the *Guillaume Tell*, after a hard fight. Nelson left Naples in the summer of 1800, hauling down his flag and returning to England overland with the Hamiltons, his professional and moral reputation damaged.[37]

On 6 July 1801 Rear Admiral Sir James Saumarez tried to bring his six sail of the line into Algeciras Bay to attack three French warships moored in a defensive position and covered by 14 Spanish gunboats and batteries ashore. The wind dropped, leaving Saumarez exposed. His ships suffered much damage but succeeded in forcing the French to run two of their ships aground, though HMS *Hannibal* also ran aground under fire from the shore and eventually surrendered to the French. Saumarez withdrew, having lost one ship and leaving the two French ships aground. It was a salient example of what can happen to an aggressive attack in coastal waters among shore batteries, shallows and the vagaries of the wind.

Just a few days later, after repairing at Gibraltar, Saumarez with his remaining five sail of the line, the 80-gun *Caesar*, and the 74s *Venerable*, *Superb*, *Spencer* and *Audacious*, fell in with the enemy, who had been reinforced by a Spanish squadron taking them up to nine sail of the line including two 112-gun three-deckers and a 94-gun ship. Saumarez was not only outnumbered, he was outgunned. In a disjointed and confused action, notable for being fought during darkness, the two Spanish three-deckers, *Real Carlos* and *San Hermenegildo*, fired upon each other. The former had already caught fire and eventually exploded, though not before setting fire to the *San Hermenegildo* which also exploded, the loss of life in both ships estimated to be around 1,700 souls. The *Superb* disabled and captured the *St Antoine*. Despite desperate attempts by the French to turn the actions of their *Formidable*, which disabled the *Venerable*, into a glorious episode in French naval history, the outcome was a clear victory for Saumarez who had now obtained revenge for Algeciras Bay and could resume his prime task, the blockade of Cadiz.[38]

Fig. 2.7. Saumarez's action of 12 July 1801 against a combined French
and Spanish fleet was notable for being fought at night.

The Egyptian expedition

After the battle of the Nile and the defence of Acre the French army
trapped in Egypt provided France with a toehold in the region. In
British minds this aroused strong suspicions as to French ambitions
towards India, perhaps acting as a catalyst for a native Indian uprising against British rule. Moreover, by 1801 the war in Europe was
at a stalemate; removing the French from Egypt would prevent them
using it as a bargaining chip to be exchanged for overseas possessions
or even claiming it as permanent conquest at the peace table. The
French army would have to be removed.

The man chosen to command was an amphibious specialist. Sir
Ralph Abercromby had much experience of working with the Royal
Navy in the West Indies during 1795–97 and during the 1799 expedition to Holland. The difficulties of the task now at hand were
considerable; he remarked around this time that 'there are risks in

a British warfare unknown in any other service'. Abercromby had also participated in an unsuccessful raid against Cadiz in 1800: with the first wave ready, Lord Keith's plan for the landing craft went awry; this was compounded by a storm which forced the fleet off station. Keith was now charged with landing the army in Egypt. In fact Keith did learn from his 'bungled' attempts to personally supervise the landing craft at Cadiz and completely handed over that role to the senior captain, Alexander Cochrane. He had been present at Cadiz, but had not been properly briefed by Keith, who instead meddled with the operation before leaving Abercromby to sort out the mess.[39]

Cochrane was now provided with full authority to organize the landing. To represent the army's concerns, Abercromby appointed Colonel Anstruther to work directly with Cochrane. The task facing Cochrance and Anstruther was formidable: to land an assault wave in order of battle under enemy fire, to provide swift reinforcement and build up the forces landed to the full strength of 13,000 men. They were also to ensure continued logistical support from the fleet to the army ashore; this required regular, three-month shipments of victuals, sent out from Britain. The system, using the victualling network at home and in the Mediterranean, primarily the key points of Gibraltar, Minorca and Malta (once it was retaken from the French in September 1800), ensured that Keith's fleet and the British army were sustained in their operations in the eastern Mediterranean.

A planning conference was held on 20 January 1801 while the fleet anchored in Marmaris Bay, Turkey. To get the troops from ship to shore, Cochrane and Anstruther had at their disposal a range of craft. There were 58 flatboats, specialist shallow draft (9in) assault boats. Carried on the decks of troopships and commanded by a naval officer, each could land 50 men. Also available were 37 ships' boats, each carrying 25 men, 84 row boats, carrying ten men each, and 28 artillery-carrying boats. The plan was to land an initial assault wave of ten battalions. To prevent a dangerous gap between assault and reinforcement waves, it was decided to collect the reinforcements inshore, and launch the assault wave from the larger ships farther out, ensuring the sailors would have a shorter row back out to the reinforcements.

On 21 January 1801 assault drills were practised; within five minutes of touching ashore the troops were formed up and ready for action. Not satisfied, Cochrane and Anstruther refined their plans, assembling landing craft in three lines:

Line 1 – flatboats and artillery launches, spaced at 50 yards to
   prevent bunching and allowing room for the landing of Line 3
Line 2 – ships' cutters, their role being to rescue boats in trouble
Line 3 – ships' cutters towing launches with more troops.

To each flank were positioned guide boats to keep the assault wave on target and which were to be used for dressing the advance to ensure the assault would arrive en masse. On their final approach, the flatboats would drop grapnels to allow their sailors to haul off and row for reinforcements. Further practice landings prompted further tweaks to the plan.

Cochrane organized the boats into four divisions. Each division, commanded by a captain, contained boats from a range of ships and, adding further complication, the whole matter of the ships arriving at the transports, the embarkation of troops from the transports into the landing craft and the assembling of the craft into an assault formation would take place during darkness. To obtain order out of a potentially chaotic situation, Cochrane produced embarkation tables showing from which ship each boat was to collect troops and where then to assemble, the tables being distributed to the captains of the four boat divisions.

With a well-practised, coherent plan, the fleet arrived off Alexandria on 2 March 1801. In the shallow waters, the pull inshore would be longer than expected: seven miles from the ships of the line and five miles from the troopships and transports. An in-depth survey of potential landing areas was undertaken by Chief Engineer Major McKerras, but Abercromby was denied his findings, for McKerras's brains were blown out by a French musket ball when his pinnace was attacked by a French gunboat. Abercromby embarked in a pinnace to reconnoitre the potential landing site himself. A heavy swell delayed the landing until 8 March and with the French fully alerted there would be no tactical surprise, but Abercromby had achieved operational surprise due to the French dispersal of their troops across in Egypt. The first assault wave of around 5,000 troops accompanied by 1,000 seamen would face a French force of 2,500 men. Under a heavy fire on the morning of 8 March the assault went in. Fire support came from cutters and gunboats and two bomb-vessels.

The troops had already been in the assault craft for around six hours as they approached the shore, where enemy shot started to land among them. Three boats were hit and as the force closed to 300 yards grape and canister tore through water, wood and flesh; in one boat 22 men were hit. Cochrane's boat was the first ashore, though not by much, as the entire assault happened as if on parade. After a brief period of close-order fighting, the French fled. Meanwhile the flatboats had pushed off and headed for ships containing the reinforcements. The first, crucial assault had cost the Royal Navy seven officers and 90 seamen killed and wounded; army casualties were higher – 625 men. While notably higher than French losses, which were around 200–300 men, the landing was a huge success. All of Abercromby's hopes had been realized thanks to Cochrane's and Anstruther's planning and practice.[40]

The troops had been landed with three days' worth of provisions; once the troops were ashore the fleet landed further provisions using ships' boats: 'without the Ships of War,' one eyewitness wrote, 'it would have been impossible for us to keep up the regular supplies of the Army.' In total there were supplies for 20,000 men for 92 days of bread, 89 days of meat and 83 days of spirits. Additional supplies for 20,000 men were on their way from Malta. The Navy also provided more direct support. On 15 March three gunboats and two bomb-vessels opened fire on Aboukir Castle which surrendered three days later. On 21 March Abercromby defeated a French counterattack, shortly after which the French asked for terms. The objective – removing the French army from Egypt – had been achieved.[41]

LANDING of the BRITISH TROOPS in EGYPT, March 8, 1801.

Fig. 2.8. The successful amphibious assault by British forces on 8 March 1801 was the start of a campaign to remove the French from Egypt.

CHAPTER 3

'The first point to make perfectly certain'

The Global War, 1793–1802

The quotation in the title of this chapter refers to what Henry Dundas thought of the West Indies. For while the war began in Europe, and British war aims concentrated on the European theatre, it was clear from the outset that this would be a global conflict. So while in 1793 Pitt was sending British forces to the Low Countries, Dundas was committed to dealing France a severe blow overseas by expanding the conflict beyond its European dimension. This would, it was initially hoped, be achieved by capturing French West Indian colonies. This strategy was inherently maritime in nature and based upon the operations of the Royal Navy in home and Mediterranean waters to either defeat the French navy in battle or keep it bottled up in port. That would allow for the exercise of British seapower overseas.

During the eighteenth century British trade with Europe had declined. In 1700–01 Europe took 82 per cent of British exports and provided 62 per cent of imports, but by 1797–98 the figures were 21 per cent and 29 per cent respectively. In comparison, British trade with American markets, which included West Indies trade, exploded. In 1700–01 British trade with the Americas (including the West Indies) accounted for 10 per cent of domestic exports and provided 20 per cent of imports (including re-export goods). By 1797–98 trade with America (including the West Indies) had grown to 57 per cent of exports and 31 per cent of imports. British West

Indian exports were worth £7,250,000 in 1788 and the total value
of British investments and their associated services accounted for
somewhere between 7 and 10 per cent of annual income.

There was another element to British concerns: the spread of
republican ideals to the West Indian slave populations who might
wreak havoc on British plantations. In 1791 the French Assembly
had granted citizenship to slaves in the French West Indies, leading
to a state of violent anarchy in many of the islands. It is not hard to
see why 50,000 British colonists were worried by the spread in the
early 1790s of republicanism to the French islands when within the
British islands there were 465,000 slaves.[1]

The West Indies were also crucial for France. West Indian
commerce accounted for around 40 per cent of total French foreign
trade. Exports from French colonies to France averaged around
£8,250,000 in the years before 1793, while the physical aspects of
the trade (including coastal related trade) employed a third of registered French seamen and two-thirds of French mercantile tonnage.[2]

The overwhelming majority of British citizens in the West Indies
were concentrated in islands at either end of the chain of Caribbean
islands, Jamaica and Barbados. So while those two islands could
mount some form of indigenous defence for themselves, the remaining British possessions were seriously exposed to French attack.
Moreover, there was no opportunity for defensive cooperation, and
even Barbados and Jamaica would find it hard to resist a major expedition of around 10,000–15,000 men sent out from France. Jamaica
accounted for half of all British investments in the West Indies and
its loss would, Dundas thought in 1796, 'be complete ruin to our
credit', leaving Britain prostrate at the feet of France.

While local initiatives could be undertaken, the lack of British
resources stationed in the West Indies at the start of the war meant
that any major campaigns would involve major forces sailing from
Britain. There was a clearly understood relationship between
the European and colonial theatres and that any strategy would
be dependent on the Royal Naval defeating French naval power
in Europe, isolating the West Indies from French interference.
Securing British interests would necessitate clearing out French

possessions in the region. This meant that hot-beds of revolutionary fervour and the threat of local attack would be removed, and the use of French islands as launch pads for major expeditions coming in from Europe would be prevented, while commercial and naval resources would be denied to the French war effort. Dundas 'looked to destroy French naval power and France's long-term means of rebuilding it while proportionally expanding British power' by attacking French colonies in the West Indies followed by those in the East Indies. Dundas thought the West Indies to be 'the first point to make perfectly certain' in British grand strategy.[3]

Striking a decisive blow to French naval power in Europe would allow 'the capture of the West Indian islands [which] will prevent their restoring it, and this he states as the principal object proposed by the war in favour of Great Britain in compensation for our charge in it'. Inflicting such blows against French naval power and its means of recovery would provide for long-term maritime security for British interests. Expanding British commerce through colonial conquest would lead to a situation whereby Britain 'would become dominant in both naval power and overseas trade for many years to come'. This would provide the necessary financial underpinning for the British economy and to fund loans and subsidies to the European powers, an essential part of the British strategy of coalition building. Implementing such a global strategy would, however, prove harder in practice.[4]

The local war in the West Indies

Given the distance between Jamaica and Barbados, and the vagaries of wind and weather, the Royal Navy's presence was split into two commands. Vice Admiral Sir John Laforey, flying his flag in the 50-gun *Trusty*, was based at Barbados and accompanied by a small frigate and two or three sloops. To the west, at Jamaica, was Commodore John Ford with his flagship, the 50-gun *Europa*, with a small number of 12pdr frigates and a few smaller ships. Upon the outbreak of war, therefore, the largest Royal Navy ships stationed in the West Indies were the two 50-gun ships flying the flags of the respective commanders. Providing reinforcements took priority over reinforcing the Mediterranean or Channel fleets. Seven ships of the line under Rear Admiral Gardner, and two regiments of foot under Major General Bruce, were sent from Britain to the West Indies on 24 March 1793. In the meantime the war in the West Indies had begun in earnest.[5]

In the Windward Islands Laforey's first target was the island of Tobago, taken by the French during the war of 1775–83 (for more information see *A History of the Royal Navy: The American Revolutionary War* by **Martin Robson**). On 12 April 1793 Major General Cuyler embarked 418 men drawn from the 9th and 60th Regiments, 50 artillerymen and 32 marines onboard the *Trusty*, the sloop *Nautilus*, the armed schooner *Hind* and the merchantman *Hero*. Arriving off Tobago two days later, the troops were landed and in the early hours of the 15th, after the garrison had declined to surrender, the French fort at Scarborough was assaulted and captured, the island capitulating afterwards.

Gardner now arrived at Barbados with his reinforcements, which allowed him to respond to a request for assistance from French royalists on the island of Martinique. The intimation was that the appearance of a British force would inspire the island to declare for the royalist cause. Gardner sailed with the *Queen* and *Duke*, powerful 98-gun three-deckers, and the 74-gun *Hector* and *Monarch*, escorting transports containing 1,100 British troops and 800 French royalists. Landing commenced on 14 April, with assistance coming from French royalist ships. Once the landing was complete, on the 18th two columns attacked the town of Saint Pierre, but the assault turned into a shambles with the royalist troops firing on each other, causing a panic. The British, thinking themselves outnumbered by the garrison, retired. There then followed a hasty evacuation of royalist supporters; those who did not flee were executed by the French.[6]

To the west, Ford at Jamaica had also been receiving calls for help, this time from royalists on the French island of Saint-Domingue. On 9 September Ford set sail with a small force arriving off the island ten days later. He was duly welcomed and the harbour of St Nicholas Mole was delivered to the Royal Navy while other areas of the island followed suit by the end of 1793. While campaigning at a local level was an important aspect of the war in the West Indies, those local campaigns were eclipsed by a number of major expeditions sent from Britain.

The Grey-Jervis expedition

In May 1793 Dundas commenced planning for a major expedition of over 16,356 men under the command of Lieutenant General Sir Charles Grey and Vice Admiral Sir John Jervis, which would sail for the Caribbean in September. It was hoped that the swift attainment of their objectives would allow Grey to send back 10,000 men in the spring of 1794 for European service. Preparations to meet this pressing deadline inevitably fell behind while the problems of balancing overseas and European commitments were thrown into sharp focus in September when the news of Toulon's surrender to Hood arrived. This opportunity might require some of the troops to be diverted; in fact some of Grey's troops were deployed to Flanders. As the timetable continued to slip in October Dundas recommended sending troops to assist the royalist uprising in the Vendée.[7]

The expedition did not finally sail until November 1793 and with the dispersal of forces to a number of other objects, Grey could only muster just over 7,000 men, less than half what was originally intended. On 6 January 1794 Jervis, flying his flag in the 98-gun *Boyne*, arrived off Barbados. Over the next few days his fleet of nearly a hundred warships and transports arrived at Carlisle Bay, Barbados. With an increasing sick list, speed was of absolute necessity before the onset of the sickly season really hit the expedition.

Typical of the type of operation undertaken was the attack on the French island of Martinique in March where the Navy and army combined to good effect. As well as benefiting from good knowledge of the island, Jervis's frigates had been busy attacking French commerce which also denied the enemy intelligence of his arrival. Jervis's ships provided naval gunfire support to the landing of troops to negate enemy batteries. Captain Robert Faulkner of the *Zebra* sloop silenced a French battery at Galion Bay, and at Saint Pierre enemy shipping was seized in the harbour. At the siege of Fort Bourbon in February, 300 seamen were landed from the fleet to haul 70 cannon and their ammunition into position. The fort was bombarded by the *Vesuvius* bomb-vessel during daytime and with fire from gunboats during darkness. Also ashore was Captain Faulkner who commanded a naval battery in the siege which followed naval tradition and fired all of its ammunition in broadsides in just one day, a rate of consumption rather more than the considered fire suited to a land siege.[8]

On 17 March a party of seamen from the *Boyne* rowed to and seized the French frigate *Bienvenue*. Given the ease with which the *Bienvenue* had been attacked – she had been stripped of her crew to man batteries ashore – a combined naval–land assault against Fort Louis and Fort Royal went in on 20 March with the main attack coming from the sea. Special flatboats for landing troops were escorted by gunboats and ships' boats (pinnaces and barges) with more support coming from the 64 guns of the *Asia* and 18 guns of the *Zebra*. In a daring demonstration of seamanship and bravery Faulkner took the *Zebra* under the guns of Fort Louis, grounded her and proceeded to launch an assault from ladders in the rigging and ships' boats used as a bridge to the ramparts, taking the fort in about 30 minutes. Faulkner refloated the *Zebra* and sailed back to the fleet. The loss of Fort Louis directly led to the surrender of the town of Fort Royal and the island, denying France its major naval and commerce-raiding base in the region.[9]

The capture of Martinique was a major strategic success, but it had taken far longer than expected, eating into the campaigning season, and was costly to British manpower in the West Indies. Further success came with the capture of St Lucia and Guadeloupe in April, followed in June by the capture of the capital of Saint-Domingue, Port-au-Prince. This run of success hit the buffers when French reinforcements and an uprising by the French inhabitants of Saint-Domingue took their toll on British forces, who were now suffering heavily from yellow fever as the sickly season effectively ended offensive operations.[10]

Fig. 3.1. Captain Faulkner's HMS *Zebra* assaults and captures
Fort Louis, Martinique, 20 March 1794.

The Abercromby-Christian expedition

Dundas's strategy of preventing French interference in the West
Indies by blockading them in Europe was not infallible. After the
initial success of the Grey-Jervis expedition a French fleet had
arrived off Guadeloupe and the sickly British garrison could not
prevent them gaining a foothold. With Jervis himself ill, the fleet
dispersed and with the hurricane season drawing close, the French
reinforcements from Europe had come like a bolt from the blue.
The French freed slaves and duly called them up for military
service. Grey and Jervis assembled a scratch force which assaulted
French positions but was driven back on 1–2 July 1795. With the
French now ensconced in Guadeloupe, Dundas's strategy for clearing out their West Indies colonies was dealt a further blow by a
wave of republican insurrections that spread across the Caribbean
in 1794–95. They were not confined to French islands; there were
major disturbances, leading to revolts, in British possessions caused
by French revolutionary propaganda from neighbouring islands.

Removing this threat was a recurring consideration.[11]

All this led to a second major expedition to the West Indies in August 1795. The 1795 expedition called for 35,000 men, the single largest British overseas commitment of the wars and an immense logistical challenge. Owing to difficulties in obtaining transport tonnage for the Grey-Jervis expedition, in July 1794 the Admiralty had created the Transport Board, bringing the hiring of vessels under one body. Finding the necessary ships for the force, to be commanded by Major General Sir Ralph Abercromby and Rear Admiral Hugh Christian, took only three months despite gales and foul weather hindering the collection of shipping.[12]

In November 1795 Christian was ready to sail; he did so and straight into a storm which scattered his fleet with substantial losses of men and materiel. This put the expedition back several months and it was not until 20 March 1796 that Christian sailed (for the third time), arriving in Carlisle Bay, Barbados, on 21 April, very late in the campaigning season. Nevertheless, Abercromby's first move was to take possession of the Dutch South American colonies before recapturing most of the islands lost to France. Guadeloupe, however, would continue to be a thorn in the British side, serving as a base for French privateers to prey on British trade and as a launch-pad for potential French expeditions against the British islands.[13]

The Abercromby-Harvey expedition

The nature of the war in the Caribbean was always dependent on the situation in Europe, as Dundas noted – the two were inseparable parts. This was also the belief of William Pitt who told the House of Commons in October 1796:

> While the violence of France has been over-running so great a part of Europe, and everywhere carrying desolation in its progress, your naval exertions have enabled you to counterbalance their successes, by acquisitions in different parts of the globe, and to pave the way for the restoration of peace to your allies, on terms which their own strength might have been unable to procure.[14]

Fig. 3.2. Thomas Byam Martin's soup tureen, presented by a merchant of Antigua, 1797. Naval officers were often the recipients of gifts such as this for their part in protecting British trading and commercial interests.

The need to compensate for lost trade in Europe and the need to keep trade expanding to cover escalating war costs provided an expansionist dynamic to British policy. This was given added impetus as Anglo-Spanish relations deteriorated during 1796 and the colonies of Spain were added to the list of British concerns. When the Spanish declared war on 8 October, Dundas immediately thought of attacking Trinidad and Buenos Aires, but the latter idea was scuppered by a shortage of warships due to the pressing need in the Mediterranean and the threat of invasion at home. Instead Trinidad would be the initial object as it could be taken by more local naval resources. That left the need for land reinforcements, which Dundas cobbled together from British and foreign units as well as drawing on West Indian negro regiments. The convoy from Britain sailed on 15 December 1796 and, like all late sailings to the Caribbean, was hit by gales; it finally set sail again on 4 January

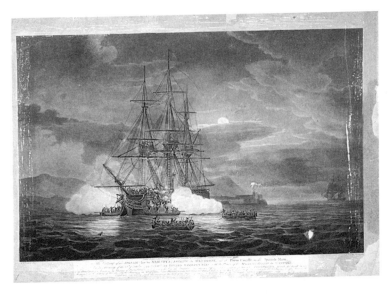

Fig. 3.3. Recapture of the *Hermione*. Following a mutiny in 1797 the Royal
Navy hunted down the ship now in Spanish service. This blight on the reputation of the Navy in the West Indies was removed when she was retaken in
a daring assault by Captain Edward Hamilton's HMS *Surprise* on 25 October
1799. *Hermione* was duly renamed HMS *Retribution* in 1800.

1797. Commanding the land forces was Abercromby, who had
returned to England to consult with Dundas and had sailed ahead of
the convoy, arriving at Martinique and liaising with Admiral Henry
Harvey, now commanding in the West Indies, as to the practicalities
of his plans.

In February 1797 Harvey, flying his flag in the 98-gun *Prince of
Wales*, set a course for Trinidad. He was accompanied by the 74s
Bellona, *Vengeance* and *Invincible* with the 64-gun *Scipio*, the 44-gun
armed transport *Ulysses*, *Arethusa* (38) and *Alarm* (32) frigates and the
16-gun sloops *Favourite*, *Thorn*, *Zebra* and *Victorieuse*, plus the *Terror*
bomb-vessel. Abercromby had managed to muster some 3,743 officers and men to provide the land force. Arriving off the island on
the 16th Harvey found a squadron of Spanish ships, the 80-gun *San
Vicente*, 74s *Gallardo*, *Arrogante* and *San Damaso* and the 34-gun frigate *Santa Cecilia*, and prepared to attack the next day. The Spanish,

Fig. 3.4. Badly wounded in retaking the *Hermione*, Sir Edward Hamilton
was knighted for his bravery and made a Freeman of the City of
London – a clear link between British commercial
interest and the exercise of naval power.

woefully undermanned, set fire to their ships but the *San Damaso*'s
magazines did not explode and the fire went out allowing boats from
Harvey's fleet to tow her away. Abercromby now supervised the
landing of his troops from the *Arethusa*. Once ashore, and with some
of his men starting to lose discipline when they discovered rum,

Abercromby called on the Spanish governor to surrender, which was duly agreed on 18 February, giving the British a commanding presence on the Spanish main.[15]

Once again, initial success was followed by disappointment. In April Harvey and Abercromby moved on to attack Puerto Rico, but the assault was beaten off by strong defences. With the hurricane season approaching, his forces suffering from desertion and generally poor morale and the surf starting to interrupt communications between fleet and shore, Abercromby admitted defeat on 30 April and re-embarked his force. Dundas's strategy to clear out enemy possessions in the West Indies had fallen short. British objectives would now be largely defensive, maintaining British naval superiority in home waters to prevent France and Spain from sending out reinforcements to tip the balance again. After the failure at Puerto Rico the 'heyday of Caribbean warfare was over'.[16]

There were, however, a number issues to tidy up. In October 1797, for a guarantee that republican forces would not attack Jamaica or foster rebellion, Lieutenant Colonel Frederick Maitland agreed to evacuate British forces from Saint-Domingue. 'Thank God,' Maitland wrote with some relief, 'I have at length got Great Britain rid of the whole of the incumbrance of this Island.' Further south in September 1798 a Spanish attack against Belize was beaten off by the 16-gun sloop *Merlin*, ably assisted by a number of armed local vessels.[17]

To such defensive actions were added further captures of enemy colonies, but unlike the great expeditions these were largely locally organized and inexpensive in terms of expenditure and loss of life. In response to an offer from its governor to surrender the Dutch colony of Surinam in the face of a suitably sized force, a thousand troops were transported by a powerful squadron comprising the 98-gun *Prince of Wales*, 74-gun *Invincible*, four frigates, a sloop and a gunbrig which sailed from Martinique arriving off the Dutch colony in August 1799. The governor surrendered to Vice Admiral Lord Hugh Seymour just over a week later. At the Dutch island of Curaçao French privateers were running amok plundering the colony when the British 36-gun frigate *Nereide* under Captain Frederick Watkins happened to be passing. The governor asked Watkins for assistance and offered to surrender the colony in return. Watkins sent word to Seymour asking for reinforcements. In the meantime he landed marines from the *Nereide* to provide some protection to the island's inhabitants and the privateers fled. Watkins accepted the surrender of the island on 13 September.

Once again, events in Europe led to further captures, this time of Danish and Swedish islands and shipping as well as Russian vessels, following the formation of the Baltic League of Armed Neutrality in 1801. Reinforcements were sent out from England but the 5,400 troops sent were small fry compared to the earlier great expeditions. In March 1801 Admiral Sir John Thomas Duckworth implemented a swift and effective campaign taking the Swedish island of St Bartholomew on 20 March 1801; this was followed by the capitulation of the Franco-Dutch garrison on Saint Martin. On 28 March the Danish islands of St Thomas, St Johns and St Croix all surrendered, providing useful bargaining chips which British ministers could use to exert influence over the northern European powers.

Despite the region's economic importance, in human and military terms, the British West Indies campaigns have come in for some vehement criticism. The army lost around half of all troops sent out to the region – 43,750 deaths – and the same number were invalided while campaigning in a region feared for high mortality rates, chiefly due to yellow fever. The naval and transport services also lost heavily – between 19,000 and 24,000 men.[18]

The main argument against Dundas's West Indies strategy was that the troops could have been better used to secure British interests in Europe. Britain always seemed to be able to find troops for overseas operations while acting perfidiously with regard to supporting her European allies, sending 4,000 men to the Low Countries in 1793 yet dispatching 33,000 to the West Indies in 1795. Yet it was actually British reaction to events in Europe that drained resources away from the West Indies campaigns. Importantly British leaders did not expect victories in the West Indies to bring France down; instead they would help pay for the war and make it popular at home while exhausting and demoralizing the French.[19]

While criticism of the butcher's bill can rightly be justified, set against the context of a maritime war the value of the West Indies campaigns was not just what Britain protected and gained. Given their economic importance and as a nursery for seamen, attacking French colonies and therefore their ocean-going trade had a number of wider effects, as Dundas had always recognized. Perhaps the final assessment comes from the raw figures: by 1797 imports from the West Indies totalled over £7 million per year, by far the single largest source of imports into Britain, while re-exports of colonial goods increased by 81 per cent between 1793 and 1797. Put simply overseas trade, and particularly the West Indies trade, provided the necessary financial resources to keep Britain in the fight against France and then Spain.[20]

The East Indies

While in economic terms nowhere was more important for Britain than the Caribbean, British operations against French, then Dutch and Spanish colonial possessions were not confined to the West Indies. As with the campaigns in the West Indies, the war in the East Indies began with a number of local initiatives. In fact as early as November 1791 Commodore William Cornwallis in the 38-gun *Minerva* frigate detached the 36-gun frigates *Phoenix* and *Perseverance* to search for the French 38-gun *Résolue* convoying ships supposedly carrying supplies to the Sultan of Mysore, Tipu Sahib, who was then in conflict with the East India Company. A hot action ensued in which the French ship struck but the convoy was found to be legitimate. When news of the war in Europe did reach Calcutta on 1 June 1793 French commercial possessions were immediately seized without a fight. The French fortress of Pondicherry, however, was a tougher nut to crack. The siege lasted 22 days, with Cornwallis in the *Minerva* and three East Indiamen blockading the fort by sea, preventing the French frigate *Cybèle* from resupplying the garrison.[21]

A far greater problem than French Indian possessions was posed by a couple of specks in the Indian Ocean, the islands of Île de France and Bourbon. The Île de France served as a key base for

French privateers to prey on valuable East Indiamen plying their trade between the subcontinent and England. Combined with the presence of French warships, including the *Cybèle* and the 36-gun *Prudente*, in Indian waters, privateers posed a real danger to merchantmen. On 27 September 1793 the 30-gun merchantman *Princess-Royal* heading for Penang was captured by the three French privateers off the island of Java. The next month, off Île de France, a small British force comprising the 50-gun *Centurion* and the 44-gun *Diomede* engaged the *Cybèle*, *Prudente*, the 20-gun *Jean Bart* and the 14-gun *Courier* in an inconclusive action. *Centurion* and *Cybèle* and *Prudente* were all damaged but the French ships managed to make it back to Île de France.

As in the Caribbean, it was reinforcements from England that allowed major offensives to take place. On 11 September 1794 Commodore Peter Rainier, flying his flag as commander in chief in the East Indies in the 74-gun *Suffolk*, reached Madras in company with the *Swift* sloop after a remarkable voyage in which he had convoyed 12 merchantmen, not losing a single ship or having touched land once since leaving England. Even more remarkable was that out of a ship's company in excess of 600 the number of sick on this long ocean voyage to a notoriously unhealthy location never exceeded the number of sick that had been on board while resting off Spithead, somewhere between 20 and 30 men. In fact it was only once the ship's company came into contact with the Indian shore that the sick rate increased.

Rainier had been here before: as captain of the *Burford* in the American Revolutionary War he had fought against the famous French Admiral Pierre André de Suffren. His past experience of warfare in the Indian Ocean was a key factor in his current appointment, for the geographical extent of Rainier's command was mind boggling. He was responsible for the maritime security of British interests stretching from the Cape of Good Hope in the west to Canton in the east, including the Persian Gulf, the Bay of Bengal, the South China Sea and waters around Indonesia. The tempo of operations in the East was determined by the weather, with merchantmen following the trade winds to the east between January and April;

later in the year the winds blew from the north-east, with homeward vessels leaving the East in December to March. Either way, Île
de France was on the route to and from the East Indies. Moreover,
during the winter Madras was on a lee shore, so the Royal Navy had
opened up Penang to protect the East while the fleet would winter
at Bombay. All this added further complication to Rainier's remit,
as did the dispersed nature of his command which created communication problems with his subordinates stationed from the Red Sea
to the South China Sea as well as communication problems with
London, which took an average of six months.[22]

On his arrival at Madras in September 1794 Rainier found the
only ships to hand were the *Heroine* and *Orpheus*, two 32-gun frigates. At Mauritius, of course, were the *Centurion* and *Diomede*, but
the action described above had driven them off station and Rainier
concluded that an effective blockade of the island was not practi-
cable with his meagre resources. He also had the *Resistance* under his
command but had no idea of her precise location in the South China
Sea. Rainier's initial objective was defensive, to protect the lucrative
British East India trade (the value of East India imports in 1797 was
over £6.5 million, second only to the West Indies islands). In early
1795 therefore he stationed ships to protect the trade at Ceylon and
Malacca. But again European developments, this time the French
occupation of the Netherlands, provided the opportunity for more
active measures.[23]

Now Ceylon might, at least theoretically, fall into French hands
so Rainier, promoted to rear admiral, moved quickly and, largely
on his own initiative, forced the Dutch to capitulate on 31 August
1795. This had the added benefit of granting his ships permanent
access to Trincomalee harbour. Other Dutch colonies were ripe for
the picking, so concurrent with the Ceylon expedition Rainier had
dispatched the *Resistance* and *Orpheus* to seize Malacca. Rainier's next
target was the Dutch island of Amboyna and its surrounding spice
islands. On 15 February Rainier, in the *Suffolk*, arrived off Amboyna
with the *Centurion, Resistance, Orpheus, Swift* and a number of armed
East India ships. This show of force ensured that the Dutch spice
islands fell peacefully into British hands.

Such opportunistic seizures were important for a number of reasons. They removed the islands from the enemy, affecting Dutch and hence French trade while enhancing that of Britain. Taking them also denied enemy naval vessels and privateers the use of their harbours while providing secure bases from which British merchantmen and naval ships could operate. Finally, while the East Indies offered little chance for naval glory, they did offer rewards of a more material nature. At Amboyna and Banda British forces found a bonanza in captured goods and prize money. The five naval captains each received the sum of £15,000 each in prize money, and Rainier's pot, as commander in chief, would have been even higher. Rainier was absent from Indian waters for a total of 16 months, returning to Madras on 13 February 1797. While this might be seen as a dereliction of his prime duty of protecting British trade, he had been acting in the knowledge that events further to the west had, or so it seemed, enhanced the security of the British position in India.[24]

Capture of the Cape

The key strategic position on the sea line of communications to the East Indies and the Far East was the Dutch colony at the Cape of Good Hope. British ministers could simply not tolerate an enemy holding a position which could cut trade and communications with the East while denying vital provisions from the Cape to British ships. Sir Francis Baring, chairman of the East India Company, likened its importance to the exercise of maritime power in the East as Gibraltar was to the Mediterranean. In fact Baring wrote to Dundas on 4 January offering the use of East India Company ships to transport troops, as the capture of the Cape would not only provide an essential logistical node for supplying ships on passage but would allow Britain to control all communication to the East. Here is clear evidence of the links between commercial interest, government and the exercise of maritime power through the Royal Navy. There was also a concern about the Cape falling into French hands: Captain John Blankett remarked to Dundas, 'What was a feather in the hands of Holland will become a sword in the hands of France.'[25]

A combined naval and land force was dispatched from Britain in March 1795 under the command of Rear Admiral Sir George Elphinstone (later Lord Keith) with Major General John Craig commanding a detachment from the 78th Regiment of Foot. The expedition, with Elphinstone flying his flag in the 74-gun *Monarch*, also comprised the 74-gun *Victorious* and *Arrogant*, the 64-gun ships *America* and *Stately*, and two 16-gun sloops, the *Echo* and *Rattlesnake*, all of which arrived off the Dutch colony on 12 July. This show of force failed to persuade the Dutch governor to hand the colony over to British protection, and offensive operations commenced.

As in all overseas expeditions, the sailors of the fleet were expected to fulfil a myriad of tasks. On 14 July 450 soldiers from the 78th Foot and 350 marines from the fleet were landed and took possession of Simonstown, which the Dutch governor had threatened to burn rather than see fall into British hands. The Dutch continued to put up a stiff fight, and with a base from which to conduct land operations, Elphinstone landed a thousand sailors from the fleet organized into two battalions and commanded by Captains Hardy (*Echo*) and Spranger (*Rattlesnake*). Added to the 78th Foot and the marines already ashore, this force of 1,800 men was assisted by a gunboat and launches from the fleet equipped with 24pdr and 18pdr carronades to provide naval gunfire support. On 7 August the infantry, marines and sailors began their advance on Cape Town with the flotilla assisted by the *America* and *Echo* closing to the shore to provide covering fire to the line of march. This drove the Dutch from a number of successive defensive positions including their camp at Muizenberg. The following day the Dutch counterattacked but were beaten off. Craig remarked of the sailors, 'They manoeuvred with a regularity which would not have discredited veteran troops.' Despite these successes, a lack of field guns and transport hampered progress ashore until the arrival of 14 East Indiamen on 3 September brought reinforcements to Elphinstone and Craig which forced the Dutch to abandon a planned counterattack. Elphinstone and Craig now decided to bring matters to a head by assaulting Cape Town and the operation commenced on 14 September. Seeing the game was up, the Dutch governor bowed to the inevitable and next day agreed to capitulate.[26]

Yet that was not the end of the story. As already noted, the Royal Navy's blockade of enemy ports in Europe was not infallible. In February 1796 a small Dutch squadron had escaped from the Texel determined to recover the Cape colony. It arrived in the waters off the Cape on 3 August and Elphinstone sailed to bring it to battle. The Dutch, under-strength and faced with an overwhelmingly superior force, surrendered to Elphinstone on 17 August.

A far greater danger was posed in the Indian Ocean, for while Elphinstone was dealing with the Dutch squadron, a French squadron under Rear Admiral Pierre Sercey had slipped past the Cape and sailed to Île de France. Sercey's four frigates, *Forte*, *Vertu*, *Régénérée* and *Seine*, when added to the *Prudent* and *Cybèle*, provided the French with a powerful raiding force to prey on British shipping. With Rainier absent the only British ship on the Indian station was the 28-gun frigate *Carysfort* under Captain James Alexander. Alexander, benefiting from captured intelligence outlining Sercey's plans for commerce raiding in the Bay of Bengal, responded by bluffing the French into believing there were four sail of the line at Madras. Sercey, suitably discouraged, headed further east.

On 8 September Sercey's squadron fell in with the *Arrogant* and *Victorious* and although both British ships suffered damage in a hot action with their smaller but numerically superior opponents they inflicted sufficient damage on Sercey's ships to bring their commerce-raiding plans to a halt and they headed to Batavia to repair. Sercey then sailed to intercept British trade coming round the eastern part of Java but he remained wary of Rainier's presence owing to his action with the *Arrogant* and *Victorious*. On 28 January 1797 the *Cybèle*, in advance of his squadron, sighted five ships. They were in fact British East Indiamen and aboard the East India Company ship *Woodford* was Captain Charles Lennox, the senior officer. Lennox, knowing that to give the appearance of fleeing would mark his ships as merchantmen, resolved on bluff. He hoisted Rainier's blue rear admiral's flag and, with his ships responding with suitable naval signals, detached two of his Indiamen to chase down the *Cybèle*. Convinced he was facing Rainier's two ships of the line and four frigates, Sercey fell for the ruse and fled back to Île de France, thereby losing the opportunity to capture five valuable Indiamen.

The situation changed in the East again with Spain entering the war. Rainier planned an attack on the Spanish possession of Manila in the Philippines but this was aborted when news reached India of peace between France and Austria, theoretically freeing up French forces for a possible attack on British interests in the East. Some credence for this belief might have been reinforced by further enemy attempts to interdict British trade. A Franco-Spanish squadron did try to capture the lucrative homeward China trade but Rainier had enhanced the escort, originally just the 64-gun *Intrepid*, with the 38-gun frigates *Arrogant* and *Virgine*. They arrived in good time, for on 27 January 1799 the Franco-Spanish squadron of two 74s and four frigates appeared off Macao. Captain Hargood of the *Intrepid* immediately sailed to bring them to combat, closely followed by the *Arrogant* and *Virgine*. As it was late, both squadrons anchored, and at first light the British were surprised to see their superior enemy had fled, 'their running away' being put down to 'their dread of a conflict that would in all probability have terminated in their disgrace'.[27]

The combined squadron split, the French and Spanish ships going their separate ways. Attacks on British commerce in the East wound down during 1799 as losses took their toll on the French force. The *Forte* was captured by the *Sybille*, and the *Preneuse* was run aground by the *Adamant* and burned, while the *Vertu*, *Régénérée* and *Seine* returned to France. Rainier also suffered loss: the *Resistance* was struck by lightning and exploded in July 1798 with only one man surviving to recount the tale.

The Red Sea expedition

On 5 November 1798 a letter dated 18 June reached Rainier appearing to confirm that a French expedition was headed for Egypt and from there to India. A force had been dispatched from England to the Red Sea to attack any French attempt to embark troops for a sea journey to India. In fact Rainier had been forewarned of the French plans and pre-empted Admiralty instructions by dispatching the *Centurion* and the 18-gun *Albatross* to the Red Sea. Commodore Blankett, with the force from England comprising the 50-gun *Leopard*, *Daedalus* frigate and the *Orestes* sloop, found these ships in the Red Sea upon his arrival in April 1799. In August the frigates *Daudalus* and *Fox* bombarded a French position at Kosseir, though to little effect. In September Aden was occupied by British forces but was later evacuated. After a fraught few months during which he was completely in the dark as to events further west, in July 1799 Rainier received a letter from Blankett confirming his arrival in the Red Sea and within a week had received another letter, this time from Sir Sidney Smith, recounting Napoleon's defeat in battle.[28]

With India now safe and Napoleon fleeing back to France, operations in the Red Sea wound down, until the 1801 Keith-Abercromby expedition headed for Egypt. On 22 March 1801 Blankett seized Suez and sent troops overland to join up with Abercromby's force. Blankett, ill and dying, was replaced by Commodore Sir Home Riggs Popham, who liaised with a force of 6,000 troops under General Sir David Baird sent from Bombay to assist with the Egyptian operation and which endured passage by sea, land and then the River Nile to reach Alexandria. Part of Popham's remit was to foster cordial relations with the Arab peoples of the Red Sea hopefully leading to a restoration of commerce with the East India Company. Popham the naval officer was, in effect, representing British commercial interests by engaging in diplomacy with Arab leaders, always a tricky prospect. A number of times he was held at gunpoint, while the natives continually tried to entice seamen from the fleet to desert. If all this was not enough, and ever the scientific officer, during his 18 months Popham surveyed the entire length of the Red Sea, producing the first two English detailed charts of the sea.[29]

The war at sea in the East effectively wound down, with many of the Dutch islands returned at the Peace of Amiens in 1802 including the Cape, Malacca and Amboyna. Given its importance as a naval base, Trincomalee was retained, Rainier using it as a fleet base, and in India the handing over of Pondicherry to France was delayed.

Fig. 3.5. The remarkable and controversial Sir Home Riggs Popham.

The Peace of Amiens

By 1801 Britain had secured its position in the West Indies and the East Indies. The French and Spanish navies had been dealt a number of heavy blows, the League of Armed Neutrality had fallen apart and the French had been removed from Egypt. As a sop to Napoleon, in the Peace of Amiens, the preliminaries of which were signed on 30 September 1801, the majority of colonial captures from France and

Holland were returned. The assumption was that with French naval power in clear decline, if war restarted, as many believed it would, then they could be taken again.

Amiens provides a useful pause at which to take stock of the effect of the wars on Britain and the key advantages that the Royal Navy possessed by 1801. The first was the complex administrative systems of repair, victualling and the issue of lemon juice which now allowed a tight blockade of the major French and Spanish naval bases, thereby allowing the exercise of maritime power globally. This was a zero sum game, for if the enemy was not at sea, his seamanship skills and morale were being undermined. Moreover, the numbers of captured, killed and wounded French sailors had cut their available manpower by around half from the estimate of 85,000 available pre-1793. By 1801 France had lost a total of 371 warships of all sizes, including 55 sail of the line – 67 per cent of her battlefleet strength. Spain had lost 77 warships, of which ten were sail of the line, and the Dutch 95 warships, of which 18 were sail of the line. With Britain in control of Baltic access, the vital stores needed to make good these losses were largely denied to France and her allies.[30]

While enemy naval strength diminished, the Royal Navy grew in size: it had 69,868 sailors on its books in 1793 but that figure had risen to 125,061 in 1801. While it had lost 20 sail of the line, 60 frigates and 120 smaller vessels between 1793 and 1802, captures and ship construction more than made up for those losses: by 1802 there were 27 former French sail of the line, 17 Dutch, five Spanish and one former Danish ship commissioned into the Royal Navy, and its overall strength had increased markedly from 422 warships in 1790 to 768 in 1800.[31]

At the same time, British trade had grown. The merchant fleet had increased from 14,440 vessels in 1793 to 17,207 in 1802, giving some indication of the development of overseas trade that was essential to ship imports and exports. During 1793–1802 British imports increased by 70 per cent, more than half of this due to expanded West Indies trade; exports doubled and re-export of goods grew by 187.2 per cent. Key here was maritime security provided by the

Royal Navy, but increased trade also provided the finance and long-term credit which allowed increased naval expenditure, which in 1793 was £2.4 million but had skyrocketed to £14.7 million in 1801. Total military expenditure had increased from £19.6 million in 1793 to £50.9 million in 1801.[32]

The Peace of Amiens also provided an opportunity for the First Lord of the Admiralty, St Vincent, to take stock of a number of perceived issues in naval administration. He believed that naval administration was not only inefficient but corrupt, 'rotten to the very core' in his own words. Believing that much of the work paid for in the dockyards was not actually carried out and that all contractors were corrupt he approached his task with a reforming zeal. The major problem was that much of his efforts were misdirected and by 1803 he had 'wrecked morale and efficiency, reduced the yards' workforce by a fifth, and badly damaged their capacity to recruit'. His approach to timber and other material contracts left the Navy with a shortage of crucial supplies in 1803–04 just when it was being remobilized for war. Stocks of timber in May 1804 were 36,570 loads, less than the consumption figures for 1801 of 39,700 loads. To put that into perspective, to build a single 74-gun ship consumed 3,212 loads of timber. The debate over St Vincent's tenure turned political through his Commission of Naval Enquiry which rather than dealing with real structural issues made personal attacks on individuals with whom St Vincent disagreed and, in part, played a role in the demise of the Addington ministry.[33]

Yet progress had been made. The Transport Board had been established in 1794 and the victualling system was enabling the Navy to maintain operational effectiveness beyond the capacity of its enemies. With reference to St Vincent's particular *bête noire*, the Royal Dockyards, here dock capacity of Portsmouth and Plymouth had doubled between 1753 and 1801, reflecting the strategic support required to refitting the ships of the Channel Fleet and thereby maintaining an effective blockade of French ports. With the decision to copper the hulls of the entire fleet between 1779 and 1782 to prevent *teredo navalis* (ship worm) from burrowing into the hull, replacing worn and damaged cooper sheathing and thereby allow-

ing for greater speed in chasing down enemy squadrons, was excep-
tionally important. A 74-gun ship of the line required re-coppering
after four to five years of active service and a full refit would take a
ship of the line out of active service for three to four months. The
dockyard workforce only doubled in size between 1755 and 1815,
compared with a tripling of the size of the Navy itself. Given this
disparity, by the time of Amiens the dockyards were struggling to
meet the unprecedented requirements placed upon them over eight
years of global conflict, rather than being the dens of corruption St
Vincent believed they were. St Vincent's tenure came to an end in
May 1804 when he resigned along with the Addington ministry.[34]

While fighting its enemies during 1793–1802 was expensive,
British strategy under Dundas and Pitt, balancing European security with overseas expansion based upon the Royal Navy's ability to
destroy French and Spanish naval power, had kept Britain in the war
and laid solid foundations for any future conflict. Given Napoleon's
growing ambition, future conflict was a real prospect even as the
ink was drying on the Treaty of Amiens.

CHAPTER 4

'I do not say they cannot come, I merely say they cannot come by sea'

The Invasion Threat, 1802–05

On 12 July 1803 Captain George Cockburn was appointed to the 38-gun *Phaeton*, initially for service in the Channel, but in September he was called back to London to be briefed on a new mission, to convey a new British minister to the United States. But there was more to this mission than safely delivering the minister. In November Cockburn was at New York awaiting orders. With his presence drawing the ire of the Americans, who tried to tempt his crew to desert, on 28 December the East Indiaman *Sir Edward Hughes* joined him; this ship Cockburn would escort to India, for she was to carry American specie, compensation to Britain for losses sustained by loyalists during the American Revolutionary War, to India. *Sir Edward Hughes* picked up half the shipment in New York and the remaining part in Norfolk. When both ships sailed on 28 January 1804 they contained $400,000. They safely put into Madras on 26 May 1804. While Cockburn did very well out of his 'freight' commission, the voyage of two ships seems like a small occurrence in a global war. Yet it goes straight to the heart of what the conflict was about for Great Britain, for the British war effort was sustained by the free flow of trade and money.[1]

Moreover, the ability of British insurers to sustain losses when they did occur was remarkable and this was based on London's dominance of the global financial services sector. This market was controlled by three heavyweights for much of the wars: the merchant banker Sir Francis Baring, Director of the East India Company from 1779, Julius Angerstein, known as the 'father of Lloyds', and Richard Thornton, who specialized in Baltic trade. Later on a fourth name, that of Nathan Rothschild, was added. Angerstein made £490,000 during the conflict, set against trifling losses of £1,000. Thornton underwrote one shipment of specie as a subsidy to Russia to the tune of £250,000 on his personal account. When Thornton died in 1865 his estate, valued at £2.8 million, was one of the largest on record. Nathan Rothschild was crucial in raising funds in Europe to pay for the British campaign in Spain and Portugal during 1812–14, but he could only raise those funds because Napoleon could not defeat Britain through direct military action, an invasion or economic warfare.[2]

The French invasion threat

At Amiens Britain had made some vague commitments about handing Malta over to Napoleon, something which the government were unwilling to turn into reality. With Russian interest in the fate of the island, and Napoleon's insistence that it be evacuated, the British government stood firm, insisting on a formal ten-year tenure of the island, crucial for projecting seapower in the Mediterranean. In return Britain demanded that France withdraw troops from the Low Countries. Sensing that further conflict was looming, on 10 March the Admiralty started fitting out ships for sea that had been decommissioned after Amiens and began placing squadrons off the major French naval bases including stationing Admiral William Cornwallis off Brest. Cornwallis was on station on 17 May 1803, the day before Britain declared war on France.

This caught Napoleon by surprise, with his navy unprepared and dispersed in a number of ports. He had, however, been dreaming up invasion plans and assembling a flotilla of invasion craft while concentrating land forces around the invasion ports, a policy given

Fig. 4.1. *The Plum Pudding in Danger*. A manic Napoleon carves for himself continental Europe while the relaxed Pitt, using a trident, is busy helping himself to the rest of the world.

further impetus after the British declaration of war. In June 1803 700 French vessels were laid down in the Channel ports and rivers. In early July construction orders for a total of 2,410 vessels were dispatched. As the building project intensified the costs spiralled beyond all initial calculations: 29,917,500 francs for the hulls and rigging alone.[3]

For while Britain remained sheltered behind her 'Wooden Walls', British diplomacy and money could, as in 1793–1802, build anti-French coalitions. Thus in order to build a continental French empire, Napoleon first needed to solve the problem of England's continued defiance and that involved a cross-Channel invasion.[4]

By May 1804 there were 1,273 vessels ready to ferry French troops, horses, artillery and the necessary equipment across the Channel. On July 20 Napoleon was ready to attempt a practice embarkation and ordered the flotilla to sea, but the weather deteriorated, wrecking 20 vessels and drowning between 200 and 400 men. Even worse for Napoleon, such disastrous exercises could be seen from the opposite shore. Clearly French naval control of the Channel was necessary and that required the defeat of the Royal Navy in battle, and for that Napoleon needed a large battlefleet which started him on a course that would end in the waters off Cape Trafalgar.

In September 1804 Napoleon's plan called for Vice Admiral Pierre Villeneuve to sail with at least ten ships of the line from Toulon, avoid action with Nelson who was watching the port, pick up French ships from Cadiz, sail for the West Indies, join with a French force of six sail of the line that had evaded the British blockade to escape from Rochefort, reinforce Martinique and then retake St Lucia and St Domingo. With a second naval force raising hell along the African coast, British planners would be at a loss to define Napoleon's key object but he believed that drawing naval forces from home waters to meet the colonial threat would leave the British Isles exposed. Villeneuve would return from the West Indies, pick up more ships from Ferrol and Rochefort and head for the invasion port of Boulogne. In the meantime the Brest fleet under Admiral Honoré Ganteaume would land 18,000 French troops in Ireland, distracting any remaining Royal Navy ships left in home waters, before heading back to assist Villeneuve in escorting the invasion flotilla. This ambitious, complicated and detailed plan called for coordination on a global scale and had all the hallmarks of Napoleon's genius for land warfare. The problem was that in terms of understanding seapower he was a rank amateur. Not only did his wild plan rely on the British playing along, it also displayed Napoleon's complete lack of understanding of the problems that weather and the time lag in communications could cause for even simple naval planning in the age of sail.[5]

Nevertheless, given the potential acute nature of the threat and the lack of a continental enemy to distract Napoleon, the strategic essentials for the Royal Navy in 1803 were defeating any French invasion attempt and supporting operations in the Mediterranean. Further complications came in late 1804 with the entry of Spain into the war. Napoleon had forced Madrid into paying him an indemnity to allow Spain to preserve nominal neutrality; in late 1804 it was rumoured that a further payment would be made to France. The British government now decided to act. Having already warned Madrid that the original payment was viewed as a *casus belli*, London was concerned over Spanish naval preparations, particularly a Spanish squadron of four frigates returning from South America, laden with specie.

The British plan was to present an overwhelming force to peacefully seize the vessels. When the Spaniards were intercepted on 5 October 1804, the Royal Navy could only manage to collect four frigates for the attack. The Spanish commander naturally resisted the seizure, but after a short engagement one of his frigates, the 34-gun *Mercedes*, exploded, sending men, women, children and a large amount of cash to the bottom. The three remaining vessels were seized and valued at £1 million. The Spanish government was outraged and declared war on 12 December. This now gave Napoleon access to the Spanish navy, with six battleships at Cartagena, nine at Ferrol and 16 in the main Spanish fleet base at Cadiz. Spain's entry into the war swung the naval situation back towards France. The key question for the British government was how to counter Napoleon's plans.

Defence against invasion

Despite the building of the Royal Military Canal behind Romney Marsh, begun in 1803 but not finished until after Trafalgar, the building of 74 Martello towers along the south coast between Eastbourne and Folkestone, and volunteers flooding to a Home Defence force (a sort of Georgian 'Dad's Army') and the concentration of the militia and the regular army in the south-east, the ultimate security of the British Isles rested on command of the sea. Informed opinion thought invasion was highly unlikely owing to the strategic deployment of the Royal Navy and the inherent difficulties in amphibious warfare, particularly the effect of weather. The necessary wind direction to launch an invasion would bring the French on to a lee shore in heavy surf while anything more than a moderate wind would throw the invasion force into utter confusion. Naval officers knew that the large French invasion force of gunboats, prams and other small vessels would be no match for the Royal Navy squadron stationed in the Downs. Without the protection of a battlefleet the invasion flotilla would be sent to the bottom of the

Fig. 4.2. *Let them boast of invasion*. The French invasion threat is
nothing but 'vapour and smoke', something most
naval officers would have agreed with.

Channel. Napoleon's plans to concentrate the necessary battlefleet
in the Channel would be frustrated by the Royal Navy's blockade.
If the French and Spanish did come out, they would be met by an
overwhelming concentration of British naval force.[6]

The first line of British naval defence was the deployment along
the French and Dutch coastlines of a flotilla consisting of 170
vessels, mainly composed of frigates and gun vessels, but including 21 ships of the line. Their role was to watch the invasion ports
and gather intelligence regarding enemy fleet movements while
preventing any of the smaller enemy ships actually getting out of
their own harbours. The second line was a squadron of ships of the
line and frigates in the Downs now under the direct command of
Lord Keith. With a large part of the squadron often stationed off
the key invasion port of Boulogne, its job was to attack the invasion flotilla at sea. The third and final layer of naval defence was
the Sea Fencibles, a naval volunteer service of 25,000 men and 800

gunboats to protect the various possible landing sites along the south coast from Swansea in the west to Great Yarmouth in the east.[7]

This was the classic way to use seapower to defend against an invasion. As Sir Edward Pellew stated to parliament in March 1804, with 1,000 invasion barges collected in Boulogne:

> they cannot all get out in one day, or in one night either; and when they do come out, I trust *that our 500 cockle-shells alone*, as an Honourable Admiral has called a very manageable and very active part of our force, will be able to give a good account of them [...] I do not really see in the arrangement of our naval defence anything to excite the apprehensions even of the most timid among us.

This mirrors St Vincent's thinking when he was alleged to have remarked to the House of Lords, 'I do not say they cannot come, I merely say they cannot come by sea.' 'They were dull, weary, eventless months,' wrote Mahan, 'those months of watching and waiting of the big ships before the French arsenals. Purposeless they surely seemed to many, but they saved England [...] Those far distant, storm-beaten ships, upon which the Grand Army never looked, stood between it and the domination of the world.' This gives the impression of a passive defence, but as in 1801 the situation required offensive measures.[8]

Among a number of offensive plans was a proposal to sink stone-filled ships in the Channel off Boulogne, to use Robert Fulton's 'catamaran' torpedoes and attacks using rockets. On 1 October 1804 Lord Keith moored his fleet off Boulogne and launched an attack using fireships and clockwork fused explosive 'catamarans' (said to resemble a floating coffin). Anxiously watched by Pitt in Walmer Castle and Dundas, now First Lord of the Admiralty and ennobled as Lord Melville, on board the fleet, it was certainly spectacular as the whole of the coast seemed to erupt in conflagration, and explosions sent columns of flame into the night sky. But like many such attacks it delivered little material success. Keith observed from on board the *Monarch* with the man charged with this unconventional warfare, Sir Home Popham. After the attack Keith informed the

Admiralty that 'no extensive injury seems to have been sustained' to the enemy, though he noted that 'it is evident that there has been very considerable confusion among them'. According to Popham the major success of the operation was to deter the French from stationing ships in the roadstead outside Boulogne harbour, a not inconsiderable effect, as the flotilla would take several days to launch from inside the harbour, leaving those outside extremely exposed to further attack. On 8 December a further attack was unsuccessful. Further to the north Sir Sidney Smith was in command of a flotilla tasked with attacking the invasion craft collecting in the ports of Flushing and Ostend. He tried a number of attacks both on the craft inshore and while they were being transferred to Boulogne, but the inherent problems of working close to a fortified lee shore prevented him achieving much lasting success. Eventually the French managed to slowly move the invasion craft along the coast to Boulogne under the protection of shore-based batteries.[9]

The Trafalgar campaign

When Rear Admiral Édouard Thomas Burgues de Missiessy slipped past the British blockade of Brest on 11 January 1805 there was concern at the Admiralty that he might be heading for the Mediterranean. He was in fact heading for the West Indies. When Villeneuve slipped anchor on 17 January and sailed from Toulon, British frigates reported his sailing to Nelson, who was left with a decision to make: either to follow Villeneuve and bring him to battle or to focus on the defence of Sicily. While Nelson has sometimes been regarded as a classic fighting admiral concerned with decisive battle, his decision making now displayed an enhanced understanding of seapower. Nelson was there to 'command the Mediterranean, and the permanence of that command hung on the integrity of Sicily'. Despite his desire to destroy Villeneuve's fleet, 'Never once did he expose what was his essential function to defend for an uncertain chance contact with the enemy's fleet.' In fact Villeneuve sailed into strong winds and, with a number of ships receiving damage, put back into Toulon.[10]

The state of the opposing forces at the start of March 1805 is detailed in Table 4.1. Villeneuve sailed from Toulon on 30 March with 11 ships of the line and six frigates, picked up one French and six Spanish line of battle from Cadiz, then headed for Martinique, arriving there on 13 May. Nelson was keen for Villeneuve to come out, explaining in August 1804 that 'every opportunity has been offered the enemy to put to sea, for it is there that we hope to realize the hopes and expectations of our country'. But a major problem was his chronic lack of frigates, 'the eyes of a Fleet'. Without sufficient frigates it was difficult to gather intelligence regarding the movements of the enemy. This had hampered his response to Villeneuve's first sortie and now, once again, caused problems. After taking on victuals from Sardinia, on 4 April he learned that Villeneuve was out. Again, his first thought was Sicily, and it was there on 18 April that he received intelligence that Villeneuve had headed into the Atlantic. Unsure of Villeneuve's intent, Nelson followed, arriving off Gibraltar on 6 May. Faced with a superior enemy, detached squadrons under Sir Robert Calder and Sir John Orde had followed orthodox policy and fallen back on the Channel Fleet.[11]

Nelson did not, and took a momentous decision based on intelligence from Rear Admiral Donald Campbell, a British officer serving in the Portuguese navy, that Villeneuve was heading for the West Indies. Nelson, acting on his own initiative without orders from London, set off in pursuit with ten sail of the line on 11 May 1805. He was not taken in by Napoleon's plan; instead his reason for following Villeneuve was clear, for, with the Mediterranean now safe, 'I cannot forgo the desire of getting, if possible, at the Enemy'.[12]

With the importance of the West Indies to the British economy understood by all, even if Villeneuve's passage was a feint, as most believed, along with Collingwood, that the object was 'to draw our force from home', it still had to be dealt with. 'I was in a thousand fears for Jamaica,' wrote Nelson, concerned about the damage Villeneuve might cause. 'I was bred, as you know, in the good old school, and taught to appreciate the value of our West

India possessions.' The fears for Jamaica were well founded – the island accounted for half of all British investments in the region. Again evident is the understanding that naval officers like Nelson had of the true centre of gravity of the British war effort: maritime commerce.[13]

Under orders to wait for 40 days in the West Indies, Villeneuve now dealt with a thorn in the side of French interests in the region. Upon arriving off Martinique his fleet had been fired upon by HM sloop of war *Diamond Rock*, but this was no ordinary Royal Navy warship. In one of the most remarkable events in the history of the Royal Navy a small 600ft high rocky island off the coast of Martinique had been seized by British forces in early 1804 and commissioned into the Royal Navy. The rock was defended by a garrison of 107 men manning two 24pdr guns and two long 18pdrs which had been hauled to the pinnacle of the rock and placed on gun platforms, giving them a range of two miles. Crucially a 3,000-gallon tank had been constructed to provide fresh water. Fort-de-France the capital of Martinique, had remained under a virtual blockade for 18 months. At 08:00 on 31 May Villeneuve attacked. With suitable provisions and ammunition the defenders could have held out for a long time, but an earth tremor had cracked the water tank and in soaring temperatures the garrison was left with no alternative but to surrender. Casualties were two killed and a single man wounded, compared to the 50 killed or wounded amongst the attackers. Villeneuve left the West Indies on 5 June, heading back to Europe and the French invasion flotilla.[14]

Table 4.1. State of the opposing forces at the start of March 1805.

French and Spanish navies	
Texel	9 ships of the line, 80 transports, 25,000 men
Boulogne	Invasion flotilla, 130,000 men
Brest	21 ships of the line
Rochefort	2 ships of the line

Lorient	1 ship of the line
Ferrol	5 ships of the line, 10 Spanish ships of the line
Cadiz	1 ship of the line, 6 Spanish ships of the line ready to sail
Cartagena	6 Spanish ships of the line
Toulon	11 ships of the line
At sea in the West Indies	6 battleships under Missiessy

Royal Navy

The Downs, Lord Keith, watching the Texel and Straits of Dover	11 small ships of the line
Channel Feet, Cornwallis, watching Brest	20–24 ships of the line (the actual number on station at any one time varied due to revictualling, watering and repairing)
Blockading Rochefort	no ships because of the naval force sent after Missiessy
Blockading Ferrol	8 ships of the line
Blockading Cadiz	Orde, 6 ships of the line
Mediterranean Fleet	Nelson, 12 ships of the line
West Indies	4 ships of the line, plus Cochrane's squadron to arrive with 6 more

Nelson arrived off Barbados on 4 June and received news of Villeneuve's presence. Next day he heard that a French fleet was at sea but, acting on incorrect intelligence, headed for Trinidad, thereby missing the chance of bringing Villeneuve to action in the West Indies. Arriving at Trinidad on 7 June he learned of the fall of *Diamond Rock* and, with further intelligence of Villeneuve landing troops at Guadeloupe before heading north, by 12 June Nelson was convinced that Villeneuve was on his way back to Europe. He sent the fast-sailing *Curieux* to warn the Admiralty. *Curieux* sighted Villeneuve's fleet on 19 June but instead of returning to

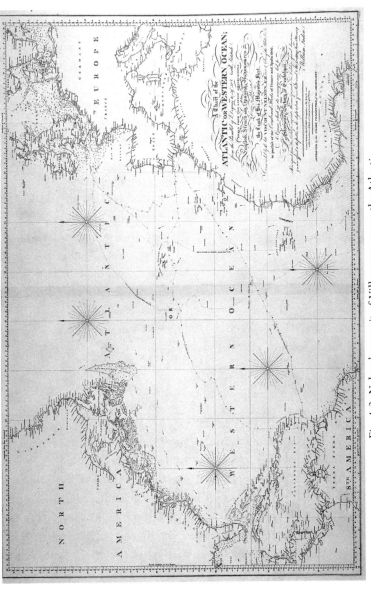

Fig. 4.3. Nelson's pursuit of Villeneuve across the Atlantic.

THE RIGHT HON: LORD BARHAM.
ADMIRAL of the RED SQUADRON.
Engraved by Miss M Dourlier, from an original Drawing by
I. DOWNMAN. A.

Fig. 4.4. Admiral Charles Middleton, Lord Barham, the true mastermind
behind the success of the Trafalgar campaign.

inform Nelson she made all speed for England. Nelson himself
raced back across the Atlantic believing Villeneuve was headed for
the Mediterranean and on 19 June anchored off Gibraltar 'without having obtained the smallest intelligence of the Enemy's fleet'.
Hunting down an enemy fleet at sea was very much like looking for
a needle in a haystack and was reliant on accurate and timely intelligence and a large slice of good fortune.[15]

Calder's action

The Admiralty received *Curieux*'s warning of the likely arrival of Villeneuve's fleet back in European waters just before midnight on 8 July. The First Lord of the Admiralty, Admiral Charles Middleton, Lord Barham, who had replaced Melville on 2 May, had gone to bed and no one was willing to wake him. Next morning the 79-year-old Barham, furious at the precious hours lost and still dressed in his nightgown, organized his fleet dispositions to await the arrival of Villeneuve. Barham was the true architect of the successful outcome of the Trafalgar campaign.

In fact Nelson and Barham both thought that the Mediterranean was Villeneuve's object, but here providence intervened. The *Curieux* had shadowed Villeneuve as he was heading north not south. Recognizing that the most important consideration was the Royal Navy's continued superiority in the Channel to prevent any French invasion attempt, Barham decided to intercept Villeneuve off the north-west coast of Spain. It was a master class in maritime grand strategy. Admiral Cornwallis was stationed to cover the French invasion ports and Barham presumed that Nelson would be able to deal with the Spanish ships at Cadiz. But the crucial element was the placing of Vice Admiral Sir Robert Calder's 15 ships of the line one hundred miles west of Cape Finisterre.

Nelson arrived at Gibraltar on 19 July 1805. The question was where was Villeneuve? The answer hove into Calder's view through the foggy gloom around 11:00 on 22 July off Cape Finisterre. Faced with 20 French and Spanish sail of the line Calder knew he was outnumbered but drew confidence from his superiority in heavy ships – four 98-gun three-deckers, *Glory*, *Barfleur*, *Windsor Castle*, and his flagship the *Prince of Wales* against a single three-decker in the enemy fleet. This levelled the odds as naval opinion thought the heavier guns of a three-decker allowed it to hold its own against two 74s.

Around 12:00 Calder cleared for action and an hour later ordered the fleet into line of battle. Relying on the frigate *Sirius* to keep him informed of enemy manoeuvres, from the quarterdeck of the *Prince of Wales* Calder could see little through the fog. Both fleets manoeuvred for position. Calder tacked to prevent Villeneuve's escape while he tried to ensure his rear was not exposed. *Sirius* actually ran past a number of enemy ships of the line, but they followed the unwritten convention of not firing upon frigates. At 17:15 the 74-gun *Hero* emerged from fog and was fired upon by the *Argonauta*, at which point the *España* opened up against the retreating *Sirius*. *Hero* followed the movements of Villeneuve's fleet by coming onto a starboard tack, a manoeuvre made on Captain Gardner's initiative, and returned fire at 17:20. Calder had already hoisted the signal to engage the enemy as closely as possible and, informed of the change in position of the enemy fleet, at 17:50 signalled the fleet to tack in succession to bring them alongside the enemy. In fact, before the signal was even raised the ships following in *Hero's* wake, *Triumph* (74), *Barfleur*, *Agamemnon* (64), *Windsor-Castle* and the 74-gun *Defiance*, had already followed Gardner's initiative in tacking without orders, thereby bringing on a general action. Calder's ships sought out opponents in the fog, as thick gun smoke added to the poor visibility, and the fight degenerated into a number of confused and insular combats.

After tacking, the *Windsor-Castle* found herself ranged against two French ships of the line, a frigate and a brig, as a Spanish ship of the line also came up to add her weight to the combat. *Windsor-Castle* suffered much damage aloft in this engagement as Calder in the *Prince of Wales* came to her assistance. The *Dragon* was ordered to remain with the disabled *Windsor-Castle*. Yet the British ships inflicted more damage on the enemy fleet, especially to the 74-gun *Firme*, the 80-gun *San Rafael* and the 64-gun *España*, which had dropped to leeward and hence were closer to the British guns. Cosmao-Kerjulien's 74-gun *Pluton* tried bravely to shield the *Firme* from the British fire but the latter struck around 20:00. He did save the *España* with the assistance of *Mont-Blanc* and *Atlas*, but the latter took so much damage that she too needed rescuing. *San Rafael* struck not long after her compatriot.

Calder's fleet had lost cohesion in the fight and with night falling and the enemy still within range he signalled to cease action, although in the poor visibility this was not fully acted upon for over an hour. The *Windsor-Castle* and the *Malta* suffered ten and five killed, 35 and 40 wounded respectively. Total losses in the British fleet amounted to 39 officers and men killed with 159 wounded. Villeneuve lost 476 killed and wounded, with the two captured Spanish ships suffering three-quarters of those: 53 killed and 114 wounded in the *San Rafael* and 41 killed and 97 wounded in the *Firme*.[16]

Calder's *Prince of Wales* spent the night repairing damage as he ascertained the state of his fleet. As the light aided visibility next morning, the British fleet found itself in two groups: the main fleet was about 17 miles from the enemy while *Barfleur*, *Hero*, *Triumph* and *Agamemnon* were lying only six miles away from Villeneuve's fleet. Calder decided to regroup his ships and at 09:00 set a course to the north-east. He later maintained that not one of his ships was 'in a state to carry sufficient sail to take them to windward' and therefore to renew the attack. Villeneuve tried to renew the action but was deterred by Calder's movements from closing for action. On 24 July Calder found himself with the weather gauge but, instead of closing for battle, took his prizes and damaged ships towards Cornwallis. Villeneuve headed to the south and by early evening both fleets were out of touch.[17]

Calder's engagement was seen as very much a lost opportunity. He was criticized for not following up the success of 22 July and making the combat decisive in a Nelsonic style. In his dispatches to the Admiralty Calder stated clearly that the enemy 'had every advantage of wind and weather during the whole day' while the fog prevented him from using signals to coordinate his fleet. Despite this, no one could have disagreed with his comment that 'every ship was conducted in the most masterly style; and I beg leave here publicly to return every captain, officer, and man, whom I had the honour to command on that day, my most grateful thanks, for their conspicuously gallant and very judicious good conduct'.[18]

The problem was very much caused by the Admiralty failing to print the whole of his dispatches. The British press, perhaps expecting another Nile or St Vincent, lambasted Calder for a lack of fighting spirit, though as *The Times* pithily noted, 'We have been so habituated to triumph over the fleets of France and Spain, that our expectations become immoderate, through success.' Nelson, at least initially, thought Calder had been hard done by: 'I should have fought the Enemy, and so did my friend Calder; but who can say that he will be more successful than another?' Calder would face trial in December 1805, after Trafalgar, and although the court martial cleared him of cowardice, the charge of 'not having done his utmost to renew the said engagement, and to take or destroy every ship of the enemy, has been proved'. This 'error in judgement' was the reason the court found him 'severely reprimanded'.[19]

Yet Calder's action was the crucial moment of the entire Trafalgar campaign. Although he faced a numerically superior enemy, he had achieved a tactical success with operational and strategic impact. Barham had placed him there to prevent Villeneuve entering the Channel and joining with the Brest fleet, an object which Calder clearly achieved. Barham's mastery of maritime strategy had put an end to Napoleon's invasion plans. Villeneuve's decision not to bring about further action with Calder and instead to head south was based on the fact that after crossing the Atlantic to the West Indies and back, then fighting a close-range action against the Royal Navy, his fleet was in a terrible state. Here again is clear evidence of the superiority of the British victualling system and the crucial decision to distribute lemon juice to the Royal Navy's Channel Fleet having an operational and strategic effect. In stark contrast, with no such victualling network and no preventative distribution of anti-scorbutic, Villeneuve's fleet had over 1,700 men sick even before the fight with Calder added to his manpower problems. Collecting the sick on board two Spanish ships and one French ship which he sent to Vigo, he was also faced with the prospect of finding somewhere to repair his damaged ships. There was no option but to head for Cadiz where he arrived on 22 August, pushing past the inferior blockading force.[20]

Unfortunately for Villeneuve, and as further evidence of the superiority of the professional bureaucracy of the British Admiralty, Cadiz was the one place where Napoleon had not collected provisions in anticipation of Villeneuve's return. Adding to his woes, disease had ravaged the hinterland, while the city itself, heavily reliant on imported foodstuffs, had been cut off from its coastal supplies by the Royal Navy's blockade. The blockade had also cut off any prospect of receiving much needed naval stores, and with French and Spanish trade almost destroyed by the Royal Navy there was little chance of receiving fresh seamen desperately needed to replace the sick. All this added to ill will between the French and Spaniards as morale plummeted.

With Calder's action preventing Villeneuve from covering an invasion attempt on 26 August, a full two months before the battle of Trafalgar, Napoleon decided to deal with Britain's new ally, Austria, before returning to his invasion plan. Villeneuve would play a part here, for on 28 September he received orders to convoy French troops to Naples. Faced with contrary winds and dissent in his fleet, it was not until mid-October, when he received news that Admiral François Étienne de Rosily was on his way to relieve him of command, that Villeneuve resolved to sail.

Nelson had sailed for the Channel Fleet, then spent 25 days ashore. On 2 September he received news that Villeneuve had been found in Cadiz. On 4 September Nelson received his orders to take command of the fleet off Cadiz. Before heading back to the *Victory*, Nelson picked up 50 copies of a revised version of Sir Home Popham's telegraphic code, an extremely useful tool for fleet signalling. Nelson, on board the *Victory*, weighed anchor at Portsmouth on 15 September.

Given the role that Nelson's ship would play in the campaign and battle, it is interesting to assess the make-up of her crew. Of the 821 men on board *Victory*, 514 were English, 89 Irish, 66 Scottish, 30 Welsh, one from the Isle of Man and one soul listed as 'British'. Drawn from British overseas possessions were six men from Malta, two Canadians, two from India and a single Jamaican. There were four listed as West Indian and one as African. From other overseas nations, by far the largest number were the 22 Americans, followed by nine Italians, seven Dutchmen, four Frenchmen, four Swedes, two Germans, two Swiss, two Danes, two Norwegians, a Brazilian and a Portuguese. The remaining 48 were 'unknown'. When divided into the relevant rates, 42 of the crew were boys between 12 and 18, 86 were landsmen, 194 were rated as ordinary seamen and the highly skilled able seamen numbered 211. Of the remaining crew, 146 were Royal Marines, 77 were non-commissioned warrant and petty officers (comprising 60 petty officers and 16 warrant officers: the master and his six mates, a surgeon, purser, boatswain, carpenter and two carpenter's mates, a gunner, an armourer and a cook). There were 46 supernumeraries such as assistant surgeons, clerks, a victualling agent and supply men. There were 21 midshipmen aged between 16 and 29 years. There were nine commissioned officers, all lieutenants, and the ship's captain, in this case Thomas Hardy. Admirals took with them a number of officers as their flag staff; on board *Victory* Nelson had with him a flag lieutenant, chaplain, secretary and a steward.[21]

Nelson and his crew arrived off Cadiz on the evening of 28 September. Keen to tempt Villeneuve out, Nelson moved the fleet around 50 miles to the west over the horizon. Left to watch over Cadiz was a force of frigates under Sir Henry Blackwood. Midway between the two was a squadron under Captain Duff of the *Mars*, with *Defence* and *Colossus*, to pass signals. Nelson had two worries: the first was the perennial lack of frigates which might lead to Villeneuve shaking off any pursuit, as he had done when crossing the Atlantic. The second was the constant drain on his resources. He had dispatched six sail of the line to draw victuals for the fleet from the stores at Gibraltar. On 14 October he allowed Calder to return for his court martial in his flagship *Prince of Wales* and two days later the *Donegal* was sent to Gibraltar. He now faced 33 enemy sail of the line with 27 of his own. If action were to commence, the crucial factor would be Nelson's plans for defeating a superior force.

CHAPTER 5

'Engage the Enemy more closely'

The Battle of Trafalgar, 1805

Building on the tactical influence of Rodney at the Saints in 1782, where the British fleet broke the enemy line (for more information see *A History of the Royal Navy: The American Revolutionary War* by **Martin Robson**), of Howe's plan for the Glorious First of June and of Jervis's plan for a two-column attack during his Mediterranean command, by the time of Trafalgar Nelson was ready to add his own experiences of fleet tactics in order not just to beat but to annihilate the enemy. His plans were not clear 'tactical doctrines' as we would understand them today, but more a collection of ideas that he instilled into those under his command through their trust and faith in him. Battle was a confused affair, so keeping station and fleet manoeuvres were less important than individual seamanship, ethos and *élan*, and close-range gunnery, especially when faced with an enemy like the French and the Spanish who Nelson believed would be unable to put up much of a fight.

During the chase to the West Indies he circulated a plan to his captains. The intent was clear from the outset:

> The business of an English commander-in-chief being first to bring the Enemy's fleet to battle on the most advantageous terms to himself (I mean that of laying his ships close on board the enemy as expeditiously as possible and secondly to continue them there without separating until the business is decided).

121

With all manoeuvring done prior to the combat, Nelson would cut the enemy line and engage from the leeward to crush their van, just as at the Nile. Once the enemy fleet was engaged, 'The great object is for us to support each other', as the ships' captains would be in the best position to know how to use their ship, either to 'lay themselves alongside' an enemy or to help comrades already in action. In September he outlined a refined version of the close-quarter 'pell-mell' battle to Sir Richard Keats of HMS *Superb*. A force of fast two-decked ships would be placed to windward, seizing the initiative and pinning the enemy. The rest of the attack would be 'in two lines, led by myself and Collingwood, and I am confident I shall capture either their Van and Centre, or their Centre and Rear'.[1]

Crucial to Nelson's plan would be individual captains acting on their initiative to mutually support each other. Of his 27 captains, only eight had previously served under him and just one, Thomas Hardy, had been present at all of Nelson's previous battles. In order to build up the 'Band of Brothers' concept which was so crucial at the Nile, he again used informal dinners in *Victory*'s great cabin during the voyage back from the West Indies and while off Cadiz. On 28 September he held a dinner for the senior officers to celebrate his 46th birthday, with another for the junior captains on 30 September.

It was during these meetings that he explained the 'Nelson touch': 'it was like an electric shock. Some shed tears, all approved – It was new – it was singular – it was simple!'; and, from admirals downwards, it was repeated: 'It must succeed, if ever they will allow us to get at them!' On 3 October he wrote:

> The Officers who came on board to welcome my return, forgot my rank as Commander-in-Chief in the enthusiasm with which they greeted me. As soon as these emotions were past, I laid before them the Plan I had previously arranged for attacking the Enemy; and it was not only my pleasure to find it generally approved, but clearly perceived and understood.

Creating a feeling of confidence and mutual support among the fleet was not limited to culinary occasions. On 9 October Captain Robert

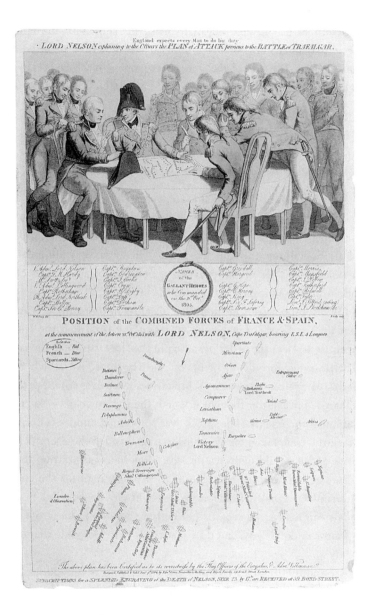

Fig. 5.1. Nelson explaining his plan of attack to his officers.

Moorsom of the *Revenge* began to paint his ship with the famous 'Nelson chequer': two or three broad bands of yellow paint around the hull with the lids of the gun ports painted black to create the chequerboard pattern. On 10 October Captain George Duff wrote:

> I am sorry the rain has begun to night, as it will spoil my fine work, having been employed for this week past to paint the ship *à la Nelson*, which most of the Fleet are doing. He is so good and pleasant a man, that we all wish to do what he likes, without any kind of orders.

Nelson's radical consensual leadership style was his mark of true genius; his intent was not to control and direct his captains but to bring them into his way of thinking, to get them to buy into his vision, by talking through his ideas. This was very different to the autocratic style of the previous generation of admirals such as Rodney and St Vincent.[2]

On 9 October Nelson simplified his ideas into one mission statement for the fleet. In order not to waste any time that the enemy might use to flee, the order of sailing in the fleet was to be the order of battle which would form up on the flagships. An attack from windward against the enemy's broadsides was dangerous, perhaps foolhardy, but Nelson thought it worth the risk to achieve the annihilation of the enemy. The attack was to be made under full sail to reduce the time taken for the ships to pass through the enemy's field of fire and it would deliver a decisive blow by concentrating three-deckers at the head of the columns to drive straight for the enemy commanders. Finally, if anyone was left in any doubt: 'But in case Signals can neither be seen or perfectly understood,' he wrote, 'no Captain can do very wrong if he places his Ship alongside that of an Enemy'.[3]

Around 07:00 on 19 October 1805 Captain Prowse's *Sirius*, part of the inshore squadron watching over Cadiz harbour, hoisted 'The enemy is coming out or under sail'. In the advance squadron Captain Duff's *Mars* relayed the signal to the *Victory* stationed 50 miles out to sea. Nelson, excited at the prospect of action, hoisted the signals 'General chase' and then 'Prepare for battle' and headed for the Straits of Gibraltar. He was to be disappointed, for on the morning of 20 October, in heavy rain, fog and squalls, there was no sign of Villeneuve.

In fact the combined Franco-Spanish fleet had difficulty getting out of port and was still sailing sluggishly south until around 23:00 on the 20th when Villeneuve spotted the British fleet and ordered his ships into line of battle, but poor ship handling led to gaps opening up in his already confused line. Realizing he could not reach the Mediterranean with Nelson bearing down, around 08:00 on 21 October Villeneuve's flagship, the *Bucentaure*, ran up the signal for the entire fleet to reverse course and to head for Cadiz. It took two hours to complete the manoeuvre, by which time his fleet was disordered, formed up in an irregular crescent shape, with some ships bunched together and gaps in other places in the line.

Shortly after daylight Nelson appeared on the *Victory*'s deck wearing his usual blue admiral's frockcoat with his four orders of knighthood embroidered on the left breast. At 06:40 on 21 October Nelson hoisted signal 72 to 'Form order of sailing in two columns' and then number 13, 'Prepare for battle'. On the *Royal Sovereign* Cuthbert Collingwood was also excited at the prospect of battle but remained remarkably calm in front of his servant:

> I entered the Admiral's cabin about daylight, and found him already up and dressing. He asked if I had seen the French fleet; and on my replying that I had not, he told me to look out at them, adding that, in a very short time, we should see a great deal more of them. I then observed a crowd of ships to leeward; but I could not help looking with still greater interest at the Admiral, who, during all this time, was shaving himself with a composure that astonished me.

Collingwood gave some sound advice to a lieutenant: 'You had better put on silk stockings, as I have done: for if one should get a shot in the leg, they would be so much more manageable for the surgeon.' He then went up on deck to encourage the men before addressing the officers: 'Now, gentlemen, let us do something to-day which the world may talk of hereafter.'[4]

Nelson's attack in two divisions was now well under way, Collingwood aiming to cut off the enemy van while Nelson destroyed the rear. But then Villeneuve began his about turn. Nelson, astounded and unsure as to Villeneuve's intent and keen to ensure he did not escape, signalled to 'make more sail' and ordered faster sailing vessels to pass slower comrades. In the light winds the attack was delivered at walking pace, but there was plenty to do. Ships' surgeons laid out their bandages and gruesome operating tools, officers' cabins were broken down and stowed and sails were prepared to serve as stretchers. Lieutenant William Pryce Cumby on the *Bellerophon*, where some of the crew had written 'Victory or Death' on her guns, recalled the men were piped to dinner at 11:00, as 'Englishmen would fight all the better for having a comfortable meal'. On *Victory*, after beating to quarters at 11:00 to make final preparations, the crew were served a dinner of pork and wine.[5]

'In such a bustling, and it may be said, trying as well as serious time,' William Robinson of the *Revenge* later wrote:

> it is curious to note the different dispositions of the British sailor. Some would be offering a guinea for a glass of grog, whilst others were making a sort of mutual verbal will, such as, if one of Johnny Crapeau's shots (a term given to the French), knocks my head off, you will take all my effects; and if you are killed, and I am not, why, I will have yours, and this is generally agreed to.

At around 11:25 Nelson decided to 'amuse the fleet' with a signal, and following a brief conversation with the *Victory*'s signal lieutenant, John Pascoe, the most famous signal ever given at sea was hoisted using Sir Home Popham's code: 'England expects that every man will do his duty.' A second message followed, this time for Collingwood: 'I intend to pass through the enemy's line to prevent them getting into Cadiz.' There then followed the signal to anchor at the close of the action. Nearing the enemy line, *Victory* hoisted a last instruction to the fleet: 'Engage the Enemy more closely.'[6]

Collingwood's battle

With bands playing 'Hearts of Oak', 'Britons Strike Home' and 'Rule Britannia' Nelson's and Collingwood's ships neared the

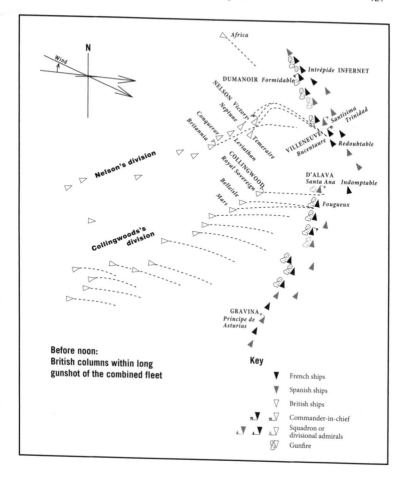

Fig. 5.2. The battle of Trafalgar, 21 October 1805.

enemy line. Collingwood's division was ahead and around midday the first shots were fired at his flagship from the French *Fougueux*. The British ships responded by hoisting union flags, the white ensign and battle flags. Around this time Henry Blackwood left the *Victory*, Nelson remarking, 'God bless you Blackwood. I shall never speak to you again.'[7]

The powerful three-decked 100-gun *Royal Sovereign* had a reputation as a slow vessel, but her copper sheeting had been recently repaired and she now began to pull ahead of her compatriots. This exacerbated the variable sailing qualities in Collingwood's lee column which delivered its attack in a slanted line *en echelon* rather than a concentrated blow. The violence of his attack was therefore dissipated along the rear of the enemy fleet. Nelson, perhaps concerned that with *Victory* and *Royal Sovereign* leading the attacks both commanders might be incapacitated, had been adamant that the *Belleisle* should lead Collingwood's attack. But Nelson was unwilling to let the *Temeraire* pass him at the head of the weather column, so it is not surprising that Collingwood ignored Nelson and spearheaded the advance.

Coming under fire at around 12:00, *Royal Sovereign* sailed through about 20 minutes of desultory enemy fire until at around 400 yards they opened up with their broadsides. Covering this final distance would take five to six minutes, during which the *Royal Sovereign* would endure two to three broadsides from each enemy ship while she kept her first, crucial broadside ready for the right moment. It was up to Collingwood's flag captain, Edward Rotherham, to sail the ship, so there was little for Collingwood to do other than to choose which enemy ships to engage. 'What would Nelson give to be here!' he exclaimed as his ship was the first to break the enemy line. Watching from *Victory* Nelson declared, 'See how that noble fellow, Collingwood, takes his ship into action. How I envy him!'[8]

At 12:20 the *Royal Sovereign* burst through the enemy line, raking the stern of the 112-gun *Santa Ana* with a devastating double-shotted broadside and raking the bow of the 74-gun *Fougueux* before tangling with the *Santa Ana*. The first Spanish close-range broadside heeled *Royal Sovereign* over a couple of feet while Collingwood nonchalantly munched on an apple. Completely dismasted and with her sides 'almost entirely beat in' *Santa Ana* surrendered around 14:20 having sustained 97 killed and 141 wounded compared to the 47 killed and 94 wounded on board *Royal Sovereign*. One midshipman recalled, 'It is shocking to see many brave seamen mangled so, some with their heads half shot away, others with their entrails mashed lying panting on the deck, the greatest slaughter was on the quarterdeck and Poop.' Severely damaged, *Royal Sovereign* was taken in tow by Blackwood's *Euryalus*. In assisting *Royal Sovereign*, Captain William

Hargood had directed his *Belleisle* astern of *Santa Ana* and ahead of *Fougueux*, engaging in a desperate struggle with the latter. With the French *Achille* firing off Hargood's quarter, by 14:00 *Belleisle*'s mainmast was shot away and with the French *Neptune* joining in the assault, *Belleisle* was reduced to a floating wreck, her colours nailed to the stump of the mizzen-mast. Despite being engaged by a total of nine ships of the Combined Fleet and sustaining 25 per cent casualties, *Belleisle* continued to deliver broadside after broadside until the *Swiftsure*, *Polyphemus* and *Defiance* came to her aid. Hargood even managed to capture the Spanish *Argonauta*, which had been battered by and then nominally surrendered to the *Achille*. When an officer from *Argonauta* was rowed over to present his sword to Hargood, he arrived just in time to take afternoon tea with *Belleisle*'s officers.[9]

Belleisle had been followed into action by Captain George Duff's *Mars*, but some manoeuvring by the French *Pluton* to close a gap forced *Mars* into a collision with the *Santa Ana*, leaving her vulnerable to raking fire from the *Algeciras* and *Monarca*. *Leviathan* now came up to help Duff but could not prevent *Mars*'s crew suffering 29 men killed and 69 wounded as she was crippled by enemy fire, taking her out of the battle. Duff himself was decapitated by a roundshot. The 80-gun *Tonnant*, captained by Charles Tyler, had by now ploughed into the increasingly confused mêlée ahead of the *Monarca* and astern of the *Pluton*, before locking with the *Algeciras*. So hot was the close-range action that *Tonnant*'s crew directed their fire-fighting pump onto the ships' sides to prevent the muzzle flashes setting fire to both ships. In a pattern to be repeated that day, *Tonnant*'s upper decks were swept by French musketry and several attempts at boarding were beaten off before superior gunnery discipline, heavier broadsides and a more rapid rate of British fire told. *Algeciras* struck around 14:30.

With gun smoke affecting visibility, the *Bellerophon* now joined the fray, becoming sandwiched between the French *Aigle* and the *Monarca* and *Montañés*. Small-arms fire also swept her quarterdeck, only four men escaping unharmed from the 58 stationed there. The captain of marines was hit by eight musket balls and Captain John Cooke mortally wounded. Lieutenant Cumby now found himself with the unenviable task of commanding a ship engaged by five enemy vessels. He himself threw an enemy hand grenade overboard while another, he later recalled:

> thrown in at a lower deck port, and in its explosion has blown off the scuttle of the Gunners Store Room, setting fire to the store room and forcing open the door into the magazine passage, <u>most providentially</u> this door was so placed with respect to that opening from the passage into the magazine that the same blast which <u>blew open </u>the storeroom door <u>shut to</u> the door of the magazine otherwise we must all in both shops inevitably have been blown up together.

Bellerophon's superior gunnery told as *Aigle* dropped out of the action and was raked by *Bellerophon* and *Revenge* while *Monarca* surrendered to the *Bellerophon*. *Bellerophon* had suffered 27 killed and 123 wounded but had inflicted 250 dead and wounded on *Monarca*.[10]

Of all the Royal Navy ships in action that day the *Colossus* incurred the highest casualties of 40 killed and 160 wounded, the latter including her captain. Suffering heavy fire during her final advance, she engaged the French *Swiftsure* (the ship taken from Captain Hallowell in 1801) and *Argonaute*. After ten minutes' fire the latter dropped out of the action but *Colossus*'s respite was short-lived as the Spanish *Bahama* joined the attack. *Swiftsure* was temporarily forced out of the action but when she re-joined was raked by *Colossus*. At 15:30 the *Orion* delivered the final blow to *Swiftsure*, bringing down her mainmast and the gallant Frenchman struck to the *Colossus* who was later towed clear by the *Agamemnon*. The experience of the *Colossus* was directly related to two factors. First, as noted, the shock of Collingwood's attack was dissipated owing to his advance *en echelon*. Second, poor fleet management in the rear of the Combined Fleet had created an accidental and unorthodox battle formation with ships drawn up two or three deep. This not only absorbed further the shock of Collingwood's attack but also prevented his ships from attacking the enemy rear from leeward. Collingwood now had six ships in action and the seventh, the *Achille*, engaged first the *Montañés*, then the *Argonauta* for an hour, before taking on her French namesake, the *Achille*, as well as the

Berwick (captured from the British in 1795), battering the latter into submission. It was now that gunnery really began to tell, for fresh British ships were engaging multiple enemy ships, which had already sustained damage, with deadly effect to take them completely out of the action. This was the case with the *Defence*, which between 14:20 and 15:20 engaged the French ship *Berwick*, inflicting so much damage aloft that it dropped out of the battle to eventually strike to the *Achille*. *Defence* was then attacked by the Spanish 74-gun *San Idelfonso* which would haul down its colours when the *Polyphemus* arrived on the scene. The disparity in casualties was again noticeable: 36 on the *Defence* compared to 160 on *San Idelfonso*.

With Captain Moorsom of the *Revenge* declaring 'We shall want all of our shot when we get close in: never mind their firing: when I fire a carronade from the quarterdeck, that will be a signal for you to begin, and I know you will do your duty as Englishmen', his ship scraped the bow of the *Aigle* before emptying two broadsides into her. Moorsom now took on the 112-gun *Príncipe de Asturias* and at one point was engaged by four enemy ships. The mighty Spaniard had tried to use her superior crew numbers to attempt a boarding but as William Robinson recalled, 'our marines with their small arms, and the carronades on the poop, loaded with canister shot, swept them off so fast'. Relief came from the *Dreadnought* and, at around 15:00, the *Thunderer* under the command of Lieutenant John Stockham who, seeing a number of enemy ships had struck, joined the action at a crucial junction and placed his ship across the bow of the *Príncipe de Asturias*, driving her off. *Thunderer* now prepared to answer Collingwood's signal to sail northwards to meet the threat posed by Admiral Pierre Dumanoir's squadron.[11]

One of three three-deckers in Collingwood's division, the notoriously slow-sailing *Dreadnought*, rounded the rear of the enemy fleet around 14:00 and crashed into the already damaged *San Juan Nepomuceno*, forcing her to strike after just 15 minutes of close action. Leaving the Spaniard to be taken by Captain Philip Charles Durham's *Defiance*, *Dreadnought* moved on to the *Príncipe de Asturias*, delivering broadsides into her as she started to flee towards Cadiz carrying the mortally wounded Admiral Federico Carlos Gravina with her. After passing between *San Idelfonso* and the French *Achille*, Durham fired into the *Príncipe de Asturias* but *Defiance* sustained much damage aloft before taking on and capturing *Aigle*, after which her crew occupied the already stricken *San Juan Nepomuceno*.

Bringing up the rear of Collingwood's division was his final three-decker, *Prince*. Once again, fresh British gunnery wreaked havoc on already damaged enemy ships, this time the French *Achille*, which she engaged at around 16:30, bringing down masts and starting a fire which once it caught hold could not be extinguished. Sometime between 17:30 and 17:45 *Achille*'s magazines detonated:

> It was a sight the most awful and grand that can be conceived. In a moment the hull burst into a cloud of smoke and fire. A column of vivid flame shot up to an enormous height in the atmosphere and terminated by expanding into an immense globe, representing for a few seconds, a prodigious tree in flames, speckled with many dark spots, which the pieces of timber and bodies of men occasioned while they were suspended in the clouds.

This macabre spectacle brought an end to the fighting at the rear of the Combined Fleet. Out of 19 enemy ships only five escaped and made it to Cadiz. Villeneuve's rear had been destroyed. But what of Nelson? [12]

Nelson and *Victory*

Nelson's approach had been much more cohesive and compact than Collingwood's; the only question remaining was where he should deliver his knockout blow. He was searching out the flag of Villeneuve and headed towards the van of the enemy line but once they unfurled their colours he turned to starboard a little and headed for the 11th ship in the line, the *Bucentaure*, which he could now see carried Villeneuve's flag. Again, light winds slowed the advance, and as *Victory* closed with the enemy line she was exposed to the combined fire of seven or eight ships. The fire was hot, and 500 yards out *Victory*'s wheel was destroyed and she was steered using a tiller in the gunroom. While talking with

Captain Hardy, John Scott, Nelson's private secretary, was almost cut in two by a roundshot and his body thrown overboard by a sailor and Captain Charles Adair of the Royal Marines. Shortly afterwards a shot passed between Hardy and Nelson, while a splinter tore the buckle off Hardy's shoe. Both men stopped, 'to survey each other with inquiring looks, each supposing the other to be wounded. His Lordship then smiled, and said: "This is too warm work, Hardy, to last long" and declared that through all the battles he had been in, he had never witnessed more cool courage than was displayed by the *Victory*'s crew on this occasion.' A bar shot ploughed into a file of Adair's Royal Marines standing to attention on the poop deck, killing eight.[13]

Nelson's fight would be very different to Collingwood's. With damage aloft slowing her down, *Victory* was closely seconded by *Temeraire*. Moreover, Nelson had four three-deckers near the head of his attack to drive through the Combined Fleet and isolate it from Collingwood's destruction of its rear. Yet, while gaps had opened up at the rear of the Combined Fleet, protecting Villeneuve's *Bucentaure* were the *Redoubtable* and *Neptune*. Hardy recognized that heading directly for Villeneuve would probably entail running *Victory* into an opponent, so at around 13:00 he directed *Victory* through the enemy line astern of the *Bucentaure* and ahead of the *Redoutable*. As *Victory* passed *Bucentaure* her boatswain, William Wilmet, fired the port 68pdr carronade, loaded with 500 musket balls and a roundshot, into the stern of Villeneuve's flagship before a rolling broadside from double- and even triple-shotted guns caused horrific damage and casualties and took *Bucentaure* out of the action. Meanwhile *Victory*'s starboard guns were firing into the *Redoubtable*.

Redoubtable was one of the smallest French 74s, and her captain, Jean Lucas, of similar stature at just under five feet tall. But both men and ship fought like giants, for she was perhaps the best-officered and manned ship in Villeneuve's fleet. Moreover, Lucas eschewed gunnery and instead had spent much time training his men in hand-to-hand combat and boarding actions. Significantly his crew were supplemented by soldiers embarked at Cadiz and stationed aloft to sweep the enemy decks with musket fire. Musket balls

Fig. 5.3. Captain Charles Adair was one of the many casualties on *Victory*'s quarterdeck as French snipers targeted senior British officers.

peppered *Victory*'s woodwork and crew; in a short space of time her upper deck was a scene of carnage. Captain Adair called for marines to be moved from working guns below to provide small-arms fire from the decks but to no avail, for they were working their guns in a frenzy. As Marine Second Lieutenant Lewis Rotely recalled:

Plate 1. Model of HMS *Kent*. The 74-gun, two-decked sailing
warship was the backbone of the Royal Navy.

Plate 2. Boat actions such as this involving Nelson off Cadiz in 1797 (before the loss of his right arm at Tenerife) were an important part of the Royal Navy's aggressive blockades of key ports. Not only did they keep the enemy on their toes and sometimes lead to the capture of enemy warships, but they allowed the gathering of intelligence and provided the prospect of promotion for junior officers.

Plate 3. *The Destruction of 'L'Orient' at the Battle of the Nile, 1 August 1798* by George Arnald. Nelson was later presented with a macabre gift by Captain Benjamin Hallowell, a coffin carved from from *L'Orient*'s mainmast.

Plate 4. *The Battle of Trafalgar, 21 October 1805* by Nicholas Pocock. The beginning of the action. In the foreground is the van of the combined Franco-Spanish fleet. In the centre, Nelson's division is in action, as is

Plate 5. *The Battle of Trafalgar, 2.30pm* by W.L. Wyllie. *Victory* forms the focus of this painting, at centre left; next to her (left to right) are *Fougueux*, *Temeraire* and *Redoubtable*. In the far right foreground is the shattered *Santísima Trinidad*.

Plate 6. HMS *Victory*, sailors' messing facilities and hammocks slung between guns.

Plate 7. HMS *Victory*'s dining cabin was used by Nelson to entertain senior officers and discuss his pre-battle plans in October 1805.

Plate 8. The world's most famous warship and a living museum of the Georgian navy, HMS *Victory* is pictured in 2011 before her major restoration work commenced.

Fig. 5.4. HMS *Victory*'s gundeck. Marine Second Lieutenant Lewis
Rotely compared the middle gundeck to the 'infernal regions,
where every man appeared a devil'.

We were engaging on both sides; every gun was going off. A man
should witness a battle in a three-decker from the middle deck, for
it beggars all description: it bewilders the senses of sight and hearing.
There was the fire from above, the fire from below, besides the fire
from the deck I was upon, the guns recoiling with violence, reports
louder than thunder, the decks heaving and the sides straining. I
fancied myself in the infernal regions, where every man appeared a
devil. Lips might move, but orders and hearing were out of the question; everything was done by signs.

By this time Adair had only ten marines with him and he inevitably fell, killed by a musket ball. At around 13:15 Nelson was also
struck by a musket ball, fell to the deck and was taken below to the
cockpit. He was one of 57 men killed on board *Victory* either in the
engagement or within a few days of the battle; a further 102 were
wounded.[14]

The majority of *Victory*'s upper-deck guns were now silent and the deck almost deserted, but below the seamen kept sending double- and triple-shotted fire into *Redoubtable*'s hull. Sensing the importance of immediate action, Lucas gathered his crew for a do-or-die mass boarding. Just as the main yard was being placed to create a bridge to *Victory*'s decks, *Redoubtable* and *Victory* crashed into *Temeraire*, herself rendered almost unmanageable by a raking broadside from *Neptune*, sandwiching Lucas between two British three-deckers. A 68pdr carronade from *Victory* now slaughtered many of those preparing to board, while *Redoubtable*'s hull was rocked by a broadside from *Temeraire*. Lucas later claimed this alone inflicted more than 200 casualties on his crew.

Temeraire now faced a new threat as the *Fougueux*, already engaged by the *Belleisle* and *Mars*, was coming up to assist her flagship. *Fougueux* delivered a broadside into the *Temeraire* and her crew prepared to board the apparently helpless ship. But *Temeraire*'s starboard gun crews held their fire until *Fougueux* was within 100 yards, at which point they unleashed two quick broadsides, taking the French ship by surprise, turning her into a floating wreck and mortally wounding her captain. *Fougueux* crashed into, was boarded from and struck to the *Temeraire*.

Victory finally broke free from the *Redoubtable*'s embrace around 14:00 while the tangled hulks of *Temeraire*, *Redoubtable* and *Fougueux* drifted, locked together until *Redoubtable* was finally taken by *Temeraire*'s crew. Lucas gave a frank assessment of the condition of his ship:

> Everywhere the decks were strewn with dead men, lying beneath the debris. Out of a crew of 634 men we had 522 hors de combat; of whom 300 were killed and 222 wounded – nearly all the officers among them [...] The batteries and upper decks were practically abandoned – bare of men, and we were unable longer to offer any resistance. No one who had not seen the state of the *Redoutable* could ever form an idea of her awful condition. Really I know of nothing on board that had not been hit by shot.

Redoubtable was taken in tow to prevent her sinking.[15]

Bucentaure had already taken a terrible pounding before Captain Thomas Fremantle's 98-gun *Neptune* emptied a raking broadside into the stern before he moved to tackle the massive four-decked 136-gun *Santísima Trinidad*, bringing down her masts in the process. *Conqueror* and *Africa* added their firepower and the huge Spanish ship, now a floating wreck, surrendered and was formally taken by the *Prince*. *Leviathan* followed the *Neptune* into action, firing into *Bucentaure*, then assisting Fremantle's fight with the *Santísima Trinidad*. Seeing that *Neptune*'s broadsides were causing so much damage, Captain Henry Bayntum's *Leviathan* headed for the French *Neptune* which fled to windward.

At this point a new threat to Nelson's plan materialized, as several ships from the van of the Combined Fleet were coming round to help their beleaguered centre and rear. Realizing the danger posed by these fresh ships, Bayntum intercepted the Spanish *San Agustín*, deftly turned to port to rake her with a triple-shotted broadside, bringing down her mizzen mast, and then crashed *Leviathan* into her to prevent the Spaniard escaping. *Leviathan*, who had already engaged a number of enemy ships, suffered 26 casualties. There is no greater testament to the superiority of British gunnery than the fact that when *San Agustín* struck to the *Leviathan* her casualties numbered 380, over half her crew. *Leviathan* now came under raking fire from Captain Infernet's *Intrépide* before she in turn was attacked by Captain Henry Digby's 64-gun *Africa*. Digby's sacrifice saved *Leviathan* but his crew suffered 62 casualties in 45 minutes before assistance came from Edward Codrington's *Orion*.

At around 13:35 *Conqueror* became the latest British ship to rake *Bucentaure*'s stern from close range. With Villeneuve's ship now a floating wreck, at 14:00 he struck to the *Conqueror*. The prize party, led by Captain of Marines James Atcherley, found a scene of utter horror:

> The dead, thrown back as they fell, lay along the middle of the decks in heaps, and the shot passing through had frightfully mangled the bodies [...] An extraordinary proportion had lost their heads. A raking shot, which entered the lower deck, had glanced along the beams and

Fig. 5.5. *The Battle of Trafalgar* by Thomas Luny portrays the action around 14:30 and the type of 'pell-mell' battle that Nelson so desired.

through the thickest of the people, and a French officer declared that this shot alone had killed or disabled nearly forty men.

Villeneuve at least was satisfied to have surrendered to Captain Edward Pellew, or so he thought, for when informed that *Conqueror* was in fact commanded by Pellew's brother, Israel, Villeneuve was taken aback: 'His Brother. What, are there two of them? Hélas!' [16]

Rear Admiral the Earl of Northesk in the slow-sailing 100-gun *Britannia* was third in command and now in a position to increase the battering handed out to the Combined Fleet, but he failed to act. *Britannia* therefore played an 'obscure' part in the action and did not pass through the enemy line until around 15:00 after several ships had overtaken him to join in the action. Edward Rotherham, Collingwood's flag captain on *Royal Sovereign*, bluntly stated that Northesk 'behaved notoriously ill'. In contrast, Codrington grasped the opportunity to maximize the impact of his fresh *Orion*, raking the French *Swiftsure* from the stern, bringing down all her masts in one single broadside before providing assistance to *Leviathan* and *Africa* by displaying some superb seamanship. *Intrépide* was determined to fight until wrecked. Codrington laconically noted to his wife, 'this we did [...] in so handsome a way that he had no time to do us much injury', a point reflected in *Orion*'s casualties of one dead and 23 wounded.[17]

Nelson's plan for a pellmell battle had certainly been achieved with the centre and rear of the Combined Fleet largely destroyed, but many of his ships had suffered much damage. In fact the Spanish and French crews certainly put up more of a fight than he was expecting. A number of British ships were now vulnerable to the developing counterattack from the enemy van, though that attack was delayed by the light airs until around 15:00 when Admiral Dumanoir in the 80-gun *Formidable*, along with the *Duguay-Trouin*, *Scipion* and *Mont-Blanc*, took up a position to windward while the Spanish 100-gun *Rayo*, 74-gun *San Francisco de Asís* and the French 74-gun *Héros* fled to the north.

The 74-gun *Ajax* and Captain Edward Berry's 64-gun *Agamemnon* took up a position between the *Intrépide* and Dumanoir's squadron to windward, firing on the latter's ships as they passed. The last two ships of Nelson's division, *Spartiate* and *Minotaur*, had laboured to get into action in the light airs. Now they placed themselves across the head of Dumanoir's ships, raking the *Formidable* from a distance of 25 yards before positioning themselves to protect the vulnerable *Victory*, and in so doing closed with the Spanish 80-gun *Neptuno*, now isolated, and forced her to strike. Drifting, the *Neptuno* now became the third enemy ship to crash into the *Temeraire*. Seeing the *Bucentaure* captured, Dumanoir restricted his role to firing into the mass of ships from long range.

Aware of Nelson's mortal wound, Collingwood had moved his flag to the frigate *Euryalus*, allowing him to exercise command of the fleet. He now ordered six ships to form a line to windward to deter Dumanoir from closing; it worked, as Dumanoir led his ships to the south. With the *Príncipe de Asturias* heading for the safety of Cadiz, any chance of a counterattack by the Combined Fleet had gone and the explosion of the *Achille* marked an end to the action. *Spartiate*'s log noted, 'observed fourteen ships of the Enemy in our possession, including the *Santísima Trinidad*, and the *Santa Ana*, three deckers, two Admiral's ships, and the *Bucentaure*, Admiral Villeneuve'. The

Combined Fleet had been destroyed as Nelson intended.[18]

British success was down to superior gunnery, discipline, seamanship and the aggressive leadership of ships' captains whose willingness to act on their own initiative had been fostered by Nelson's desire for them to mutually support each other and instilled during those dinner meetings. The cost was high, but so were the stakes. Nelson was declared dead by Surgeon William Beatty at 16:30, just as a new danger arose: a storm was clearly brewing to windward. Chaplain Alexander Scott recorded that this was one of Nelson's final concerns, the dying admiral exclaiming to Hardy, 'If I live I'll bring the Fleet to an anchor; if I live I'll anchor.' Yet with many ships suffering damage aloft and to anchors and cable, the fleet was in no state to anchor immediately; instead Collingwood's object was to get the fleet and its prizes into the safety of Gibraltar. On board the *Revenge* William Robinson noted that there was 'a good night's work before us; all our yards, masts, and sails were sadly cut, indeed the whole of the sails were obliged to be unbent, being rendered completely useless, and by the next morning we were partly jury-rigged'. Nelson's desire to anchor was now overruled by Collingwood and it was not until 21:00 that Collingwood gave the order for the fleet to anchor:

> The whole fleet were now in a very perilous situation, many dismasted, all shattered, in thirteen fathom water, off the Shoals of Trafalgar, and when I made the signal to prepare to anchor, few of the ships had an anchor to let go, their cables being shot; but the same good Providence which aided us through such a day, preserved us in the night, by the wind shifting a few points, and drifting the ships off the land.[19]

On the evening of the 22nd the storm was raging and it continued as British ships started to arrive in Gibraltar on the 28th. In the meantime some of the prizes had been scuttled, some were cast adrift with their prize crew still on board to be driven ashore while some made the safety of Cadiz. Matters were complicated by a sortie of enemy ships from Cadiz on 23 October. 'It was a mortifying sight,' Robinson lamented, 'to witness the ships we had fought so hard for,

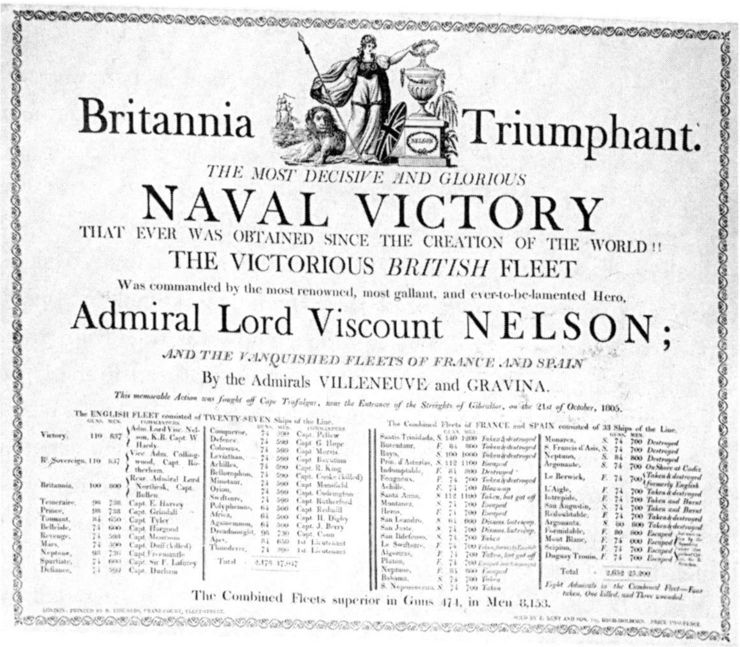

Britannia Triumphant.

THE MOST DECISIVE AND GLORIOUS

NAVAL VICTORY

THAT EVER WAS OBTAINED SINCE THE CREATION OF THE WORLD!!

THE VICTORIOUS *BRITISH* FLEET

Was commanded by the most renowned, most gallant, and ever-to-be-lamented Hero,

Admiral Lord Viscount NELSON;

AND THE VANQUISHED FLEETS OF FRANCE AND SPAIN

By the Admirals VILLENEUVE and GRAVINA.

This memorable Action was fought off Cape Trafalgar, near the Entrance of the Streights of Gibraltar, on the 21st of October, 1805.

The ENGLISH FLEET consisted of TWENTY-SEVEN Ships of the Line.

	Guns.	Men.	Commanders.
Victory,	110	837	Adm. Lord Visc. Nelson, K.B. Capt. W. Hardy.
R^{l} Sovereign,	110	837	Vice Adm. Collingwood, Capt. Rotherham.
Britannia,	100	800	Rear Admiral Lord Northesk, Capt. Bullen.
Temeraire,	98	738	Capt. E. Harvey
Prince,	98	738	Capt. Grindall
Tonnant,	84	650	Capt. Tyler
Belleisle,	74	600	Capt. Hargood
Revenge,	74	598	Capt. Moorsom
Mars,	74	590	Capt. Duff (killed)
Neptune,	98	738	Capt. Freemantle
Spartiate,	74	600	Capt. Sir F. Laforey
Defiance,	74	590	Capt. Durham
Conqueror,	74	590	Capt. Pellew
Defence,	74	590	Capt. G. Hope
Colossus,	74	590	Capt. Morris
Leviathan,	74	590	Capt. Bayntun
Achilles,	74	590	Capt. R. King
Bellerophon,	74	590	Capt. Cooke (killed)
Minotaur,	74	590	Capt. Mansfield
Orion,	74	590	Capt. Codrington
Swiftsure,	74	590	Capt. Rutherford
Polyphemus,	64	500	Capt. Redmill
Africa,	64	500	Capt. H. Digby
Agamemnon,	64	500	Capt. J. Berry
Dreadnought,	98	730	Capt. Conn
Ajax,	84	650	1st Lieutenant
Thunderer,	74	590	1st Lieutenant
Total	2,178	17,947	

The Combined Fleets of FRANCE and SPAIN consisted of 33 Ships of the Line.

		Guns.	Men.	
Santis Trinidada,	S.	140	1200	*Taken & destroyed*
Bucentaur,	F.	84	800	*Taken & destroyed*
Rayo,	S.	100	1000	*Taken & destroyed*
Prin. d'Asturias,	S.	112	1100	*Escaped*
Indomptable,	F.	84	800	*Destroyed*
Fougueux,	F.	74	700	*Taken & destroyed*
Achille,	F.	74	700	*Blown up*
Santa Anna,	S.	112	1100	*Taken, but got off*
Montanez,	S.	74	700	*Escaped*
Heros,	F.	74	700	*Escaped*
San Leandro,	S.	64	600	*Dismas. but escap.*
San Juste,	S.	74	700	*Dismas. but escap.*
San Ildefonso,	S.	74	700	*Taken*
Le Swiftsure,	F.	74	700	*Taken, formerly English*
Algeziras,	F.	74	700	*Taken, but got off*
Pluton,	F.	74	700	*Escaped much damaged*
Neptune,	F.	84	800	*Escaped*
Bahama,	S.	74	700	*Taken*
S. Nepomucena,	S.	74	700	*Taken*
Monarca,	S.	74	700	*Destroyed*
S. Francis d'Asis,	S.	74	700	*Destroyed*
Neptuno,	S.	84	800	*Destroyed*
Argonaute,	S.	74	700	*On Shore at Cadiz*
Le Berwick,	F.	74	700	*Taken & destroyed formerly English*
L'Aigle,	F.	74	700	*Taken & destroyed*
Intrepide,	F.	74	700	*Taken and Burnt*
San Augustin,	S.	74	700	*Taken and Burnt*
Redoubtable,	F.	74	700	*Taken & destroyed*
Argonauta,	S.	80	800	*Taken & destroyed*
Formidable,	F.	80	900	*Escaped*
Mont Blanc,	F.	74	000	*Escaped*
Scipion,	F.	74	700	*Escaped*
Duguay Trouin,	F.	74	700	*Escaped*
Total		2,652	25,200	

Eight Admirals in the Combined Fleet—Four taken, One killed, and Three wounded.

The Combined Fleets superior in Guns 474, in Men 8,153.

LONDON: PRINTED BY R. EDWARDS, CRANE-COURT, FLEET-STREET.

SOLD BY E. KENT AND SON, HIGH-HOLBORN. PRICE TWO-PENCE.

Fig. 5.6. *Britannia Triumphant*: the most decisive victory ever obtained but at a high price, the life of Admiral Nelson.

and had taken as prizes, driven by the elements from our possession, with some of our own men on board as prize masters, and it was a great blight to our victorious success.'[20] Midshipman Henry Walker of the *Bellerophon* was part of the prize crew on the *Monarca* and while not fearing death in the battle, during the storm he 'saw the fear of death so strongly depicted on the countenances of all around me, I wrapped myself up in a Union Jack and lay down upon the deck' until the prize and Walker were saved by the *Orion* and *Donegal*.[21]

Of the ships taken on 21 October only four were saved. Collingwood handed over 1,087 wounded Spaniards, 253 wounded Frenchmen, plus 210 Spanish officers and 4,589 Spanish seamen prisoners to the Spanish authorities in Cadiz, while nearly 3,000 French prisoners, including Villeneuve and Lucas, were sent for internment in England.

Aftermath

The *Victory*, containing Nelson's body, *Tonnant*, *Revenge*, *Colossus*, *Thunderer* and *Bellerophon* all arrived at Gibraltar on 28 October having ridden out the storm. On 2 November *Royal Sovereign*, *Temeraire*, under tow from *Defiance*, and *Orion* arrived, with the four prizes following shortly after. The facilities and shelter of Gibraltar allowed temporary repairs to the most damaged ships before Collingwood could send them home for complete repair. On 4 November one of Trafalgar's loose ends was tidied up when a small squadron under Sir Richard Strachan captured four of the enemy's van ships that had escaped the carnage of 21 October. All of Strachan's prizes were brought home, with each seamen earning £10 13s, or around half a year's pay. By 22 November Collingwood had sent home all the ships that required extensive repairs and was flying his flag in the 98-gun *Queen* with a squadron consisting just of *Prince*, *Dreadnought*, *Orion*, *Swiftsure* and *Thunderer* as he sailed to blockade Cartagena.

Trafalgar crushed the Combined Fleet, with 18 out of 33 ships of the line captured, destroyed or wrecked, thereby putting an end to French and Spanish operational involvement in the Mediterranean. But it did not signal an end to French naval ambitions. There was always the remaining danger that French ships would escape from port, so Trafalgar did not bring an end to the war at sea. It was, however, a crushing psychological blow for the French navy and even more so for the Spanish, spreading loathing for the French amongst the Spanish population and government well before that country erupted in anti-French rebellion in 1808. Importantly, such was the blow to Spanish naval power that it forever cut the link between Spain and her colonies.

Could the French have invaded? Almost certainly not. The Royal Navy was not distracted by French attempts to gain temporary superiority in the Channel by striking at British interests overseas and the chances of a decisive victory for the French at sea were 'almost inconceivable'. What was important in this was Calder's action of 22 July which prevented Villeneuve from entering the Channel and covering the invasion flotilla, forcing the French to call off the invasion and deal with the Austrians. Trafalgar did not prevent the war on land going very badly for Britain, as the continental powers were steamrollered by Napoleon's war machine. Napoleon's inability to invade Britain led to his attempt to undermine the British economy by controlling European trade with Britain through a continental blockade.[22]

Overall, Trafalgar can be seen very much as a turning point for Britain and the final realization of Dundas's strategy of dealing such a blow to French naval power that Britain would have a free hand overseas. After Trafalgar, it was unlikely that Britain would be defeated by France militarily, so it marks the end of the danger that Britain might lose the war: 'Britain had an unchallenged command of the sea, in quantity and quality, materially and psychologically, over all her actual or potential enemies.' Of course there remained a key question after 1805: what type of peace could Britain enforce upon France? It would take another ten years of maritime warfare to preserve British economic prosperity and provide the money to keep fighting and subsidize allies. So while Trafalgar was the last major fleet battle fought by the Royal Navy during the Napoleonic Wars, the Navy did not remain idle after 1805.[23]

CHAPTER 6

'I cannot too much lament not to have arrived a few days sooner'

Home Waters and the Baltic, 1805–15

Three months after Trafalgar William Pitt muttered, 'Oh, my country! How I leave my country!' before dying on 23 January 1806. The optimism of 21 October 1805 had long gone, for in the intervening months France had knocked Austria out of the war, Prussia had remained neutral, and Russia was active but isolated and unable to influence events in Central Europe. Three months after Trafalgar Napoleon had achieved French hegemony in Western and Central Europe, and, despite British supremacy at sea, the naval war was far from over.[1]

There remained the need, stretching back to Dundas's desire expressed in 1793, to remove the French navy as an effective force and to deal with neutral warships which might fall into enemy hands. After the naval losses of 1793–1805 Napoleon was determined to reconstruct his naval forces. This took two forms: an ambitious rebuilding programme and an attempt to seize the navies of the European neutral powers. In the years immediately after Trafalgar Britain possessed 136 ships of the line and 160 frigates while France and her allies could only muster 96 ships of the line and 71 frigates. French rebuilding plans began to bear fruit during 1806–08 when 24 ships of the line were launched or acquired. France continued to

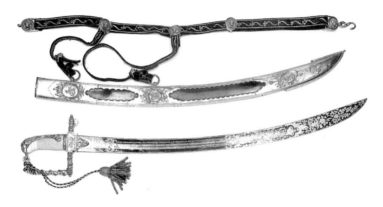

Fig. 6.1. Lloyd's Patriotic Fund £50 sword presented to Lieutenant John
Haswell of HMS *Pallas* for boarding and seizing the French corvette
La Tapageuse in the River Garonne, 6 April 1806.

lay down new ships at an alarming rate: in 1806 eight for every five
laid down by Britain; in 1807 the figures were 12 and 11 respectively. It was only in 1808 that French shipbuilding slackened, with
only three new battleships compared to the 17 laid down for the
Royal Navy. Overall in the years 1804 to 1808 Britain laid down 50
battleships to the 45 laid down in French and Dutch ports. By 1807
Napoleon could theoretically call on 62 French and allied ships of
the line for action against British interests. Of course there were
immense difficulties in turning that into practical effect at sea, and,
apart from the escape of raiding squadrons, the French fleet was
mainly held in port and gained little sea experience after 1805. But
French rebuilding served to preserve the fleet 'in being', as there
were no serious losses unlike in 1794–1805.[2]

The British response

It was not inconceivable that a French, Dutch, Swedish, Danish and
Russian fleet of at least 60 sail of the line might operate in northern waters to close the Baltic to British trade, while only half
this number were needed to convoy a further French attempt to
invade Ireland. French naval construction was concentrated around

Antwerp, a strategic position which would pose a constant threat to British maritime security. The French navy, along with those of her allies, still posed a long-term threat, not just in the war but possibly in a post-war situation. This threat had to be countered by the Royal Navy to preserve and guarantee the future of British maritime supremacy. Some doubt has been cast as to the potential effectiveness of these ships, noting the green timber used in their construction and the difficulties of getting them to sea, to which could be added the dearth of experienced seamen with which to man them. But at the time British ministers just could not run the risk. Thus a prime object for the Royal Navy after Trafalgar was to remove warships from the clutches of Napoleon. In the years 1806–10 Britain would add 101 captured warships to the Royal Navy.[3]

Table 6.1. The European navies, 1805–10. Source: J. Glete, *Navies and Nations: Warships, Navies and State Building in Europe and America, 1500–1860*, vol. 2, pp. 396–400.

	1805		1810	
	Battleships	Cruisers	Battleships	Cruisers
French	41	46	46	38
Spanish	40	50	28	27
Russian	47	16	35	14
Danish	20	16	2	-
Swedish	12	11	13	8
Dutch	15	13	13	9
Portuguese	12	18	11	14
Total	187	170	148	110
Royal Navy	135	192	152	245

The Royal Navy changed post-Trafalgar to reflect the change in emphasis. Looking at the figures in Table 6.1, the most remarkable fact is the increase in cruiser types after 1805. The battlefleet served to protect home security, but it was the smaller ships that exploited British maritime supremacy by promoting and protecting British influence and trade on a global scale crucial to British economic wellbeing. Exercising global power was facilitated by a chain of key strategic naval bases, some in British hands, such as Gibraltar, Malta, Bermuda, English Harbour in Antigua, Trincomalee, Madras, Calcutta and the Cape, but others not under British control, such as Port Mahon, Palermo, Leghorn and Lisbon. The operations of British maritime commerce and the Royal Navy were dependent on such bases and that often involved careful diplomacy combined with naval pressure.

The Baltic

Reacting to rumours that Denmark, under pressure from France, would shut the Baltic to British shipping and hand over her own naval forces to France, the British Foreign Minister George Canning also saw the hand of Russia operating in the background, apparently confirmed when Russia and France became allies at Tilsit on 7 June 1807. In July, with Denmark apparently ready to hand over its fleet to France, the Cabinet decided to attempt a diplomatic solution but also planned for a pre-emptive strike on Danish naval power. A British fleet under Admiral James Gambier, comprising 22 sail of the line with 19,000 troops, was dispatched to Copenhagen. The speed and organization of the expedition was remarkable – having decided on the operation in mid-July, the flotilla was in Baltic waters by mid-August. An attempt to resolve the crisis through diplomatic channels failed and on 16 August British troops were landed on Zeeland. With the Royal Navy using Koge Bay to land more troops, supplies and artillery, a Danish force positioned to block the road to Copenhagen was brushed aside and the city invested.

On 2 September Copenhagen was subjected to a ferocious bombardment from land and sea and by the night of the 5th, with parts of the city on fire, the Danes asked for a truce. This was refused and a British counter offer demanding the surrender of the Danish fleet was made. On 7 September Copenhagen capitulated, giving up the whole of the Danish navy of 18 ships of the line and 52 smaller vessels along with at least 20,000 tons of valuable naval stores. Despite the fact that only four Danish ships of the line and

Fig. 6.2. British tars towing the Danish fleet into harbour, a controversial action which removed the Danish warships from the clutches of Napoleon (top centre). The 'Billy Pitt' boat is rowed by Castlereagh and Liverpool, with Canning towing the Danes. John Bull sings 'Rule Britannia' while the opposition Whigs, including St Vincent, can only offer insults.

some of the smaller craft were incorporated into the Royal Navy, in maritime and military terms the expedition had been a great success, as the objective had been to prevent the Danes handing over their ships to France. Such a move could have led to a large hostile fleet operating in an area of immense strategic and commercial importance to Britain. Politically the operation shocked many contemporary commentators, provided fuel for French propaganda regarding British intentions and pushed the Danes into the arms of France.[4]

The British expedition to Copenhagen presaged a sustained naval commitment to the Baltic between 1808 and 1812. There was no major fleet engagement in this theatre, yet naval forces sparred and influenced the actions of each other. An assessment of these years and of the man in command highlights much about the relationship between naval and political concerns and how that contributed to the overall British war effort. The importance of the Baltic to Britain has already been stated (see Introduction) and it is difficult to disagree with James Davey's assessment that 'Great Britain's importation of Baltic goods was essential to the British way of life, industry and economy'.[5]

On 20 February 1808 Admiral Sir James Saumarez was appointed commander in chief of the Royal Navy's Baltic Fleet. He was to sail with a squadron consisting of his flagship HMS *Victory*, the 74-gun *Centaur*, *Superb*, *Implacable*, *Brunswick*, *Mars*, *Orion*, *Goliath*, *Vanguard*, the 64-gun *Dictator* and *Africa* and five frigates. Following the bombardment of Copenhagen the situation in the Baltic was vexed indeed. Denmark was understandably outraged and now vehemently anti-British, posing a threat to British trade to and from the region, for merchants would now have to pass through 300 miles of hostile Danish waters to enter or exit the Baltic. Then there was the unstable and unpredictable Gustavus IV, King of Sweden, a key British ally when Saumarez took up his command given the general hostility to Britain in northern waters. Russia was, of course, allied to the French after Tilsit and the maintenance of her Baltic fleet at Kronstadt posed a constant danger to British freedom of action in the Baltic. There was also regional power politics, with Russia invading Swedish-held Finland in February 1808 and Denmark declaring war on Sweden the following month. Finally, there was always the danger of a French force crossing from northern Germany and invading Sweden.[6]

Into this complex situation Saumarez now sailed. Things did not get off to an auspicious start. In April the British government had decided to send a force of 10,000 British troops under Sir John Moore to add military assistance to the subsidy of £100,000 a month provided to Sweden for military expenses if Russia did attack her. Moore's mission was a disaster, with disagreements over how British forces should assist the Swedes, culminating in a blazing row between British general and Swedish king in June 1808, which led to Gustavus IV effectively putting Moore under arrest. Moore fled Gothenburg to the safety of the *Victory* and discussed the situation with Saumarez (who had still not passed the Belt into the

Fig. 6.3. Admiral Sir James Saumarez, commander in chief of the
Royal Navy in the Baltic between 1808 and 1812 and at
the forefront of British diplomacy and influence.

Baltic proper) while the government ordered the British troops back to England. When Moore left it was up to Saumarez to display his considerable diplomatic talents to restore some cordiality to Anglo-Swedish relations. This was his main remit for the next five years.

In April 1808 Saumarez was sent further instructions to investigate destroying the Russian Baltic fleet, but his squadron was outnumbered by enemy warships. Instead he used his naval force as a 'fleet in being', to promote British influence through diplomacy and the highly visible symbolism of British maritime power. His prime object, as the Admiralty instructions on 27 June 1808 made patently clear, was to ensure the free flow of British trade and thereby break Napoleon's continental blockade. With Denmark now hostile, Danish gunboats had wreaked havoc on a British convoy on 9 June 1808, destroying or capturing 13 merchantmen and two Royal Navy escorts. This was the Danish interpretation of the *guerre de course*, called the 'Gunboat War' or 'Mosquito War', where flotillas of small but heavily armed and manned and highly manoeuvrable gunboats attacked British trade and could run rings around much larger British warships. Their earlier success was repeated in July 1810 when an entire convoy of 47 ships was taken. Danish gunboats were a constant thorn in the side of British trade and meeting their challenge was a constant drain on Saumarez's fleet, but overall, despite the odd success, the Danes could not challenge British control of the Baltic and the majority of British ships sailing under convoy got through: 2,210 merchant ships transited Danish waters in the last six months of 1809 without loss.[7]

With the British government still not sure of how to manage the fall-out from Copenhagen and with their attention shifting to the developing situation in Iberia (see Chapter 7) and given the distances involved in communicating between the Baltic and London, for much of his command Saumarez was effectively left to run the show, which involved decision making at the political, diplomatic, strategic, operational and tactical levels. One of his first decisions was perhaps his most important. Having left Admiral Samuel Hood in the Gulf of Finland to work with Swedish naval forces, Saumarez was in the Belt picking up a Spanish force which had rebelled against its French masters. On 24 August, Hood spotted the Russian fleet at sea, consisting of 20 ships, bearing down on his four ships of the line and the unready Swedish ships at Örö. Next day Hood sailed with an Anglo-Swedish fleet of 13 sail of the line to engage the Russians. They ran for it, and were chased down by Hood's flagship, the *Centaur*, and the *Implacable* which, thanks to superior seamanship and copper bottoms, caught the *Sevelod*. With *Centaur* trailing behind, it was Thomas Byam Martin in the *Implacable* who battered the Russian ship into submission. With the Russian fleet bearing down on the isolated British ship, Byam Martin was ordered by Hood to abandon his prize and the *Sevelod* was taken in tow towards Rogervik, where the Russian fleet had now sought safety. Hood saw his chance and although both *Centaur* and *Sevelod* ran aground, the latter was burnt and the *Implacable* helped to free the *Centaur*. Heavily outnumbered, the superior speed, seamanship and gunnery coupled with the aggressive ethos of Hood and Byam Martin had chased the Russians into port, destroying one of their ships in the process.[8]

Had Saumarez not been in the Belt and instead had, with his ships added to the force in the Gulf of Finland, caught the Russian fleet, there is little doubt what the outcome would have been. 'I cannot too much lament not to have arrived a few days sooner,' Saumarez wrote. He did arrive off Rogervik on 30 August but in those crucial days between Hood's action and his arrival the Russians had strengthened their position. Saumarez considered the prospect of a second 'Aboukir', destroying Russian naval power in the Baltic at one stroke, and perhaps causing a change in Russian policy. The dangers of making an attack were, however, great and on balance unwise, set against his other tasks. The danger of becoming becalmed in a *fortified* enemy harbour without sufficient troops to seize the enemy batteries weighed against a Nelsonic *coup de main*. As Byam Martin wrote, an attack could not be staged 'with any reasonable hope of success, or without the risk of losing some of his Majesty's ships'. It would be hazardous for a 'powerful squadron of British ships' never mind an Anglo-Swedish force. 'I am confident,' he summed up, 'it would end in disappointment, – if not in disgrace.' The loss of ships and prestige might tip the balance against

Britain in the entire Baltic, with no guarantee of destroying the Russian ships. That would have been a disaster. Instead Saumarez blockaded the port and offered surrender terms to the Russians, which although not surprisingly rejected, was seen favourably at least by them, if not the Admiralty. Saumarez's policy of conciliation and the maintenance of his 'fleet in being' would give him ever growing diplomatic leverage with the Russians over the next few years and help smooth over some of the friction between Britain and Sweden caused by the spat between Gustavus IV and Sir John Moore.[9]

One of the benefits of the Baltic freeze was a decline in naval operations and convoys, allowing Saumarez to return home during this period and leave command of the fleet with Admiral Richard Keats. After wintering in England Saumarez was back in the Baltic in May 1809. In his absence the situation had become more confused, with a coup removing Gustavus from his throne in March 1809. While this complicated his mission, it did not alter the fundamentals of protecting British trade and neutral ships with British licences, keeping an eye on the Russian fleet and attacking them if the opportunity was presented, while keeping his own fleet ready in case Sweden closed her ports. While sorting out their domestic arrangements, the Swedes attacked Russian positions in Finland, with Saumarez providing naval support with ten ships of the line. It was a disaster: Sweden made peace with Russia, giving up the whole of Finland and, of more concern, joining Napoleon's continental blockade. Yet the latter policy was, in effect a *façade*, for Sweden wanted to steer a neutral course and would try to continue an amicable policy towards Britain.

One minor but important success for Saumarez came in May 1809 with the capture of the Danish island of Anholt, in the Kattegat, and the relighting of a lighthouse in those dangerous waters to act as a navigation aid for British merchantmen. Like *Diamond Rock*, HMS *Anholt* was commissioned into the Navy and, in a strange twist of fate, placed under the command of Captain James Maurice who had defended *Diamond Rock* against Villeneuve in 1805. Maurice drove off several Danish attempts to retake the island. Prior to the taking of Anholt, the Danish island of Heligoland had been captured by the

Royal Navy in September 1807, serving as a hub for British smuggling into continental Europe, a centre for collecting intelligence on French movements and the base for British sloops blockading the Elbe, Jade, Weser and Ems rivers, implementing the British Orders in Council (see Chapter 8).[10]

In the spring of 1810 France pressured Sweden to fully enforce the blockade, and while appearances seemed to suggest that might happen, the reality was again a little different. Following his winter break, Saumarez again set out for the Baltic in May 1810; his fleet would consist of 19 ships of the line. His naval duties were much the same as before, with the added task of watching over the now supposedly hostile Swedish fleet. His diplomatic orders from the Foreign Office showed how much he was trusted by the government and how maritime power and British policy were to be enacted through him as a naval officer. He was given the authority to take Britain to war with Sweden if he judged it a necessary last resort.

French pressure on Sweden was seen to have even greater weight following the election of the French Marshal Jean Bernadotte as Crown Prince, Saumarez granting free passage to his barge on 14 October. Surrounded by 19 British warships and up to a thousand merchantmen awaiting convoy, 'there could have been no better way of impressing on Bernadotte both Britain's maritime power and the importance to Sweden and all the Baltic states of the trade that the ships carried'. Under Bernadotte Sweden actually declared war on Britain on 17 November 1810, but Saumarez correctly judged that this would not fundamentally alter relations between Britain and Sweden and so, while fully entitled to take retaliatory measures, he trusted in Swedish assurances that this would be a 'phoney war' to placate Napoleon. Saumarez acted on his own judgement, without reference to London, surmising that the continuance of British trade in the region and the supply of naval stores was of paramount importance. He therefore did not seize Swedish merchantmen, and this policy of understanding, though not without its problems, would shape the next two years of his command. This was crucial, for Bernadotte knew that Sweden could only survive as an independent country through its sea trade and that required the acquiescence of the Royal Navy. By the 1812 campaigning season the Baltic Fleet had been reduced to ten ships of the line. One of the reasons for the reduction had been the catastrophic loss of three such ships in late 1811.[11]

Statistically, during the age of sail sailors were more at risk from disease, accidents and the general dangers of the sea than from battle. The main cause of death was disease, which killed 70,000–80,000 sailors during the French Revolutionary and Napoleonic Wars. This was followed by shipwreck and fire, accounting for 13,000 men, with combat claiming only 6,500 lives. Accidental loss accounted for 101 Royal Navy warships during the wars, and the most catastrophic incident came on 23 December 1811. On that day the 98-gun three-decked *St George*, a veteran of the battle of Copenhagen, was hit by a gale. *St George* was already jury rigged owing to earlier damage and now hit by this new tempest was wrecked on a shoal off the Jutland coast. Only seven from her crew of 738 were saved; those lost included Admiral Robert Reynolds. In company was the 74-gun *Defence*, whose battle honours included the Glorious First of June, the Nile and Trafalgar, and whose captain refused to leave the *St George* without Reynolds's permission. *Defence* suffered the same fate, wrecked on the coast with all but 14 of her crew of 597 perishing. In the same storm the 74-gun *Hero* was lost off the Texel with only 12 of her crew surviving. The total loss of British sailors in this one stormy 24 hours was over 2,000 men, the largest loss of life in a single incident at sea throughout the course of the wars. The contrast with Trafalgar, where the Royal Navy suffered 1,690 casualties of which 430 were killed outright, is stark. It was a sobering reminder of the dangers of seafaring. Battles and their inherent dangers were actually quite rare, but sailors lived a precarious existence just doing their day-to-day jobs.

Despite the losses Saumarez's policy of conciliation reaped rewards in the winter of 1811–12 when Franco-Russian relations, strained ever since the Treaty of Erfurt in 1808, started to break down, leading to Napoleon's invasion of Russia in June 1812. Sweden and Russia, gauging the way the wind was blowing, had already entered into an alliance, and peace between Britain, Sweden and Russia was signed on 17 July. Immediate help to the Russians came in the form of now Rear Admiral Byam Martin who appeared off Riga on 16 July 1812. In fact Saumarez had already positioned British frigates off the north German coastline to intercept French supplies moving by sea.

British and Russian seapower was to prove effective in the wider 1812 campaign, while once again Napoleon displayed his utter ignorance of seapower. In order to ease French logistical problems it was assumed that supplies could be moved up the Baltic by a flotilla of gunboats. This would entail gaining a degree of local sea control, either by defeating the Russian and British navies, by providing suitable escorts for the gunboats, or by seizing a chain of bases along the coastline. This latter scheme would also deny shore facilities and safe harbours to the Russian and British forces. To try to achieve this Napoleon detached 40,000 men to proceed along the Baltic coastline and head for St Petersburg. This force would secure the flank of Marshal MacDonald's corps of 32,500 who were to seize Riga. Not only was Riga an important base for naval operations but was a vital entrepôt into Europe for British goods. MacDonald's force was mainly composed of Prussians and in turn was designed to secure the left flank of Napoleon's central thrust into Russia. Admiral Byam Martin assisted the Russian forces defending Riga as the French laid siege to the city. The Royal Navy's assistance also conveyed a much more important message, as noted by Saumarez, who told Byam Martin on 15 July 1812 that his 'zealous exertions' in defence of the city 'must make upon His Imperial Majesty and the whole of the Russian army, who must derive fresh spirits in seeing a nation, with whom they were so recently in hostility, exerting themselves in giving every support to their cause'.[12]

In September Russian transports, under escort from Byam Martin, deposited a Russo-Swedish force into the rear of the French at Danzig, posing a threat to French communications. Further south a Royal Navy squadron under Admiral George Tate was operating out of Gothenburg where he was joined by elements of the Russian fleet. The routine of naval operations in the Baltic continued, albeit with a new twist. On 28 August Admiral Morris wrote to

Saumarez informing him that while three Royal Navy ships, *Cressy*, *Rose* and *Woodlark*, had sailed convoying 118 merchantmen, three American vessels had been detained. With Tsar Alexander I sending the Russian Baltic fleet to winter in Britain, the priority for the Royal Navy in the final two years of conflict in the Baltic was ensuring that British trade continued to flow, and this was achieved by Saumarez's policy of collecting merchantmen into large, heavily protected convoys, to deter the Danish gunboats.[13]

Aix Roads

In February 1809 Admiral James Gambier's fleet blockading the French at Brest had withdrawn in the face of westerly gales. Admiral Jean-Baptiste Philibert Willaumez had taken advantage, escaping from Brest. His object was to reinforce Martinique before attacking British trade in the West Indies. Sailing with eight sail of the line, including his 120-gun flagship *Océan*, he was observed leaving port by the 74-gun *Revenge* left behind by Gambier. Willaumez headed to a rendezvous inshore of Belle Isle to await reinforcements. One of these forces, of three 40-gun frigates, was driven inshore on 23 February by Sir Robert Stopford who reduced them to absolute wrecks. Trapped in Basque Roads, Willaumez lost the *Jean Bart* but made some progress in getting a boom across the entrance to protect against boats and fireships.

While Willaumez could not achieve anything while he was bottled up, there was the requirement to keep a blockading force off his position and the constant danger that it would be blown off, allowing Willaumez to escape. It was decided that the best way to proceed was to destroy Willaumez; the problem was how? At this point Lord Mulgrave, First Lord of the Admiralty, turned to the ever inventive mind of Captain Thomas Cochrane. It was never likely that the dour and evangelical Gambier and the radical Cochrane would have a good working relationship, nor would Gambier, nor many in his fleet, accept the imposition forced upon them by the Admiralty. While Cochrane considered himself to be under the direct orders of the Admiralty rather than Gambier, Gambier himself never considered Cochrane to be under his command. It was a recipe for disaster; there was no coordinated plan and both went into the subsequent operation with very different interpretations of what their roles were to be.

On the evening of 11 April 1809 Cochrane launched an attack with fireships and boats packed with explosives. Colonel William Congreve had also arrived, bringing some of his rockets to add a new dimension to the action. Thing started well, two explosion ships removing the boom laid by Willaumez, while the fireships equipped with their hellish rockets bore down on the French fleet, causing panic in the dark. Many French ships cut their cables and ran onto mud flats, leaving only two of Willaumez's fleet afloat and able to defend themselves. At first light it was obvious that Cochrane had done his part. Now it was up to Gambier, or so Cochrane believed, to sail in with his fleet and complete the destruction of the enemy. Instead Gambier had intended to use his smaller ships to destroy the stricken enemy ships, keeping the line of battle as a reserve, though it took him half a day to get the former into action. With the tide rising and the French ships now refloating, Cochrane was aghast and tried to place his ship, the *Imperieuse*, in action to force Gambier to act.

Finally, at around 15:00, Gambier's frigates, brigs and bomb-vessels were in place and the action began in earnest. By the time night fell, five enemy sail of the line were destroyed, but next day, assessing that no more could be done, Gambier signalled Cochrane to withdraw. Cochrane ignored this order until Gambier effectively relieved him of his command by sending him with dispatches to the Admiralty. While Cochrane had a right to be annoyed at Gambier's lack of fighting spirit, what he did next was abhorrent to all observers. All in all, it was a successful action, with five sail of the line destroyed, the rest of Willaumez's fleet out of action and, crucially, the danger to the British West Indies dealt with; Gambier was likely to be given a vote of thanks in parliament. But Cochrane made it patently clear to Mulgrave that he would take the unprecedented stance of opposing it. Gambier demanded a court martial for himself and, unsurprisingly, as it was composed of his friends

Fig. 6.4. Destruction of the French fleet in Basque Roads, 12 April 1809,
which left Captain Thomas Cochrane fuming at the perceived inaction
of his superior, Admiral James Gambier.

and those who disliked Cochrane, was acquitted. Cochrane was
outraged and opposed the vote of thanks to Gambier in January
1810. Even though he was offered commands, he became distracted
by politics and never served at sea again for the Royal Navy until in
1814 he was found guilty of defrauding the Stock Exchange, imprisoned and dismissed from the service.[14]

Walcheren

On the evening of 28 July 1809 Captain Sir Home Popham's 74-gun
Venerable dropped anchor off the island of Walcheren to survey and
then mark with boats a landing channel and thereby commence
another British amphibious operation in this strategically vital area.
With a major commitment already made to the Peninsular War,
some commentators have been astounded that 40,000 men could
have been sent on a half-baked attempt to divert French forces from
heading east to fight the Austrians on the Danube. But the expedition was not a diversion to benefit Austria's campaign in the east

— that would be one of the side effects of the operation. Instead it was an opportunist strike at French naval power in the Scheldt estuary and was only undertaken because the forces committed could, it was hoped, be easily evacuated. By 1809 there were six 80-gun ships under construction at Flushing, four 74s at Antwerp, and based out of the Scheldt were ten newly built 74-gun ships under Rear Admiral Missiessy.[15]

While France would have had much difficulty manning these ships, which were built of green timber, and a fair number of those laid down were never completed, it is no surprise that British ministers were extremely worried by such developments in an area of prime strategic importance. The Scheldt estuary was a loaded gun pointing straight up the River Thames to London and was the only large, relatively secure waterway in which a major amphibious force could be assembled and then launched against Britain. Unlike French ports such as Boulogne, which faced the chalk cliffs of southeast England, the Scheldt is directly opposite the open clear and flat terrain of Essex, a far better target for landing an invasion.[16]

By June 1809 the majority of the 400 transport vessels necessary to carry the 29,715 infantry, 8,219 cavalry and 5,434 artillerymen, ammunition, siege train and stores to attack Walcheren had been collected. To provide escort a massive fleet was assembled under the command of Rear Admiral Sir Richard Strachan: 37 ships of the line, five small two-deckers, 24 frigates, 31 sloops, five bomb-vessels, 23 gunbrigs and 120 smaller craft. Strachan arrived off the Scheldt on 29 July, but with English newspapers carrying reports of the preparations, the French had been given ample warning. As often was the case, inclement weather prevented an immediate landing, so the gunboats and bomb-vessels bombarded the town of Veere Gat. On 31 July the weather cleared and a landing was attempted. Two lines of gunboats, 20 and 40 strong, were to lead the assault, row to within grapeshot range of the beach, fire and then draw off to the flanks to allow the troop-carrying flatboats to close to the shore and commence the landing. Everything went according to plan and the landing was a success. Once ashore the troops forced the surrender of Veere Gat on 1 August. Attention then switched to

Flushing: ships' guns were landed and the town was besieged. The entrance to the Scheldt was forced on 11 August and two days later a furious bombardment was opened up on Flushing which lasted for 31 hours until the town surrendered on the 15th.

This was the highlight of the operation. Things now started to get bogged down, a situation compounded by the notorious indecisiveness of the army commander, Lieutenant General the Earl of Chatham. The lack of dynamic leadership was compounded by an outbreak of malaria, 'Walcheren Fever'. On 14 September, with little opportunity of securing any of the major objectives, Chatham left the army to return to England to try and save his own skin in the political fallout. He left behind 9,851 men on the army's sick list. As the land operation wound down during November, defences and docks at Flushing were wrecked and the yard looted of naval supplies – captured timber frames were used in the 74-gun *Chatham* built at Woolwich. A Dutch frigate and a brig were also seized. The last batch of troops were embarked on 23 December. For the loss of 4,000 men, only 106 of whom had died in combat, and the wrecking of the lives of many more who would suffer from the recurring effects of the fever and at a total cost of £835,000, very little lasting damage had been achieved and Missiessy's squadron remained intact.[17]

It would not be the last British commitment in this region. Following Napoleon's defeat at Leipzig in October 1813, to all appearances he was finished and the landing on 13 December 1813 of 8,000 men to operate with the Prussians against Antwerp was designed to secure the key British war aim of a secure Low Countries, though Antwerp itself was not taken. An attack on 8 March 1814 on Bergen-op-Zoom failed. Given the importance of the area to critical British war aims it is not surprising that during 1814–15 the British government was more than prepared to trade most of its colonial conquests in order to free Antwerp from French control. It took the fall of Napoleon in 1814 to achieve that. Finally, during Napoleon's brief 100 days, on 18 June 1815 the Duke of Wellington fought the battle of Waterloo on the road to Antwerp.[18]

CHAPTER 7

'Our maritime superiority'
The Mediterranean and the
Peninsular War, 1805–15

Following Nelson's death, command of the Royal Navy's Mediterranean Fleet was entrusted to Admiral Cuthbert Collingwood
whose mission was to support British diplomatic efforts and prevent
the spread of French influence. This was hampered by a lack of strategic coherence in London and Napoleon's continued success on
land. After crushing Austria in 1805, Napoleon cut Prussia to the
size of a third-rate power in 1806. French success in southern Italy
led to the evacuation of British and Russian forces from the mainland while King Ferdinand I of Naples was evacuated on the 74-gun
HMS *Excellent*. Commanding the Royal Navy force was Sir Sidney
Smith who, along with *Excellent*, had the 64s *Athenien* and *Intrepid*,
the frigate *Juno* and a number of gunboats. He provided ammunition
and guns from *Excellent* to the defenders of the fortress of Gaeta. Off
the River Tiber on 17 April the frigate *Sirius* had attacked a French
flotilla on its way to attack Gaeta, taking a corvette and running
the rest of the flotilla ashore. Smith then assaulted a French position on Capri, before, like Nelson, falling in with the designs of the
Neapolitan court, though this eventually led to the British army's
tactical success at the battle of Maida on 6 July 1806.

Napoleon's success had also brought the war to Russia's doorstep,
as he had started to meddle in Poland and the Ottoman Porte, leading to a Turkish declaration of war against Russia on 30 September
1806. With the Dardanelles closed to Russia her Black Sea fleet was
isolated in the Mediterranean. Britain was keen for the Turkish fleet

to be kept out of French hands, while aggressive naval action would provide a spectacular demonstration of British power to browbeat the Turks into a more conciliatory line. Collingwood had already sent Rear Admiral Thomas Louis in the 80-gun *Canopus*, along with the 74-gun *Thunderer*, 64-gun *Standard*, the frigate *Active* and a sloop, into the eastern Mediterranean where they evacuated the British ambassador to Turkey in late 1806. With Collingwood off Cadiz in January 1807, he received orders to send Sir John Duckworth to demand the complete surrender of the Turkish fleet and naval stores. If the Turks refused Duckworth was to 'cannonade the town, or attack the fleet'. The Turks had anchored a small fleet of one 64-gun, four frigates, four corvettes, two brigs and a small number of gunboats near the mouth of the strait at Abydos. Duckworth's plan was to attack the Turkish squadron and then sail into the Sea of Marmora, anchor and demand the surrender of the rest of the Turkish fleet, composed of 12 ships of the line (two of which were three-deckers) and nine frigates.

Things went badly from the start. Duckworth's fleet of eight ships of the line, two frigates and two bomb-vessels was weakened when on 14 February the 74-gun *Ajax* caught fire and blew up, taking half her crew to the bottom. Five days later Duckworth entered the straits, which were protected by a series of land batteries and fortifications. The Turks opened fire and Duckworth's fleet responded. The efforts of the mercurial Smith forced the Turkish squadron at Abydos ashore where it was destroyed. Duckworth then anchored in the Sea of Marmora before opening diplomatic negotiations. It quickly became clear that the Turks were not willing to play ball, effectively ignoring Duckworth. A midshipman and his boat crew were captured by the Turks while the 13-inch mortar on the *Meteor* bomb-vessel burst. After spending a week and a half posturing, Duckworth withdrew back down the straits. On 3 March, while passing the narrows, the Turkish guns responded to Duckworth's polite and formal 13-gun salute with a furious barrage. Fortunately casualties were relatively light though several ships were damaged by the Turkish fire, including from medieval bombards: HMS *Active* was hit by a huge marble shot and the

Fig. 7.1. Vice Admiral Cuthbert Collingwood, Nelson's great friend and commander in chief of the Mediterranean from Trafalgar until his death on board the *Ville de Paris* on 7 March 1810. Fittingly he rests beside Nelson in St Paul's Cathedral.

Windsor-Castle by one weighing over 800lbs.[1]

While the object had been sound, the implementation of the Dardanelles operation had been a complete shambles. Duckworth lacked the resolve to force the issue and the necessary land forces to take and dismantle the batteries to ensure a safe passage for his ships.

For the loss of 138 men killed and 253 wounded, all that had been achieved was to anger the Turks and drive them further towards the French. It was left to the Russians to defeat the Turkish fleet off Lemnos on 19 June 1807. A British attack on Egypt in March utilizing 5,000 troops from the garrison of Sicily, convoyed in 33 transports and escorted by a ship of the line, a frigate and a sloop, quickly occupied Alexandria. But the position was unsustainable, and with the British forces beset by Albanian troops a convention was agreed with British forces evacuated in September 1807.

The Portuguese fleet

Another crisis over neutral naval power was brewing in Portugal. While trade with Portugal was important, and Portuguese security rested upon the nature of Lisbon's relationship with Madrid, what was really crucial was British commercial access to the Portuguese colony of Brazil. Portugal bought manufactured woollen goods from Britain for export to Brazil, with the imbalance made up by specie shipments, direct from Brazil to England by the Royal Navy and the Falmouth packet service. By the middle of the eighteenth century over £1,000,000 a year was estimated to enter Falmouth alone. Royal Navy captains convoying specie were entitled to about 1 per cent 'freight' commission. In fact it could be argued that as the wellbeing of the British economy was based on trade, insurance and financial services, the requirements to subsidize allies with hard cash and the need to supply British expeditions with cash to pay their way, the Royal Navy's role in guaranteeing an uninterrupted supply of specie was one of the most important tasks it fulfilled. The flow of specie from Brazil to Britain ensured that 'if it appeared [...] that Portugal was seriously threatened by either Spain or France' Britain would intervene.[2]

France demanded Portugal close its ports to British shipping and backed this up with military preparations. Britain responded by signing a secret convention with the Portuguese court guaranteeing that the Portuguese royal family and navy would flee to Brazil if the French invaded. Foreign Secretary George Canning summed up the

British attitude arguing that a Royal Navy squadron would help to 'assist — *i-e in a certain sense to compel* the embarkation'. While this would remove the Portuguese navy from danger, it would also plant a friendly court in South America.[3]

On 16 November the ubiquitous Sir Sidney Smith arrived off the Tagus, his fleet comprising the powerful three-decked 120-gun *Hibernia*, 98-gun *London*, 80-gun *Foudroyant*, six 74s and a frigate. Smith found he was unable to attack the Portuguese fleet with naval force alone and urged the government to send troops to complete the task. In the meantime he offered bluster, warning the Portuguese that Lisbon would suffer 'scenes of horror' as had recently befallen Copenhagen. Without troops there was little Smith could do and it was a combination of British diplomacy, the visible threat posed by the Royal Navy squadron playing on Portuguese minds and, ultimately, the advance of French troops that forced the Portuguese court into evacuating Lisbon. On the morning of 29 November eight Portuguese ships of the line accompanied by four frigates, four smaller vessels and 20 large armed merchantmen carried the royal family out of the Tagus to commence their voyage to Brazil.[4]

The French entered the city unopposed on 30 November. Canning was certainly overjoyed: 'Huzza! Huzza! Huzza! We have saved the Portuguese Royal Family and the Portuguese navy [...] Denmark was saucy and we were obliged to *take her* fleet. Portugal had confidence, and we rescued hers, and will protect her.' He was also relieved that the Russian Mediterranean fleet, which had put into Lisbon while trying to reach the Baltic, were 'quiet spectators'. It is worth considering that by using naval diplomacy to prevent the Portuguese fleet falling into French hands, combined with the expeditionary force to seize the Danish fleet, the British had prevented over 30 ships being added to the French navy, more than Nelson had destroyed at Trafalgar. There was more to seapower than 'decisive' battles.[5]

On 5 December Smith directed Captain Graham Moore of the *Marlborough*, with the ships *Bedford*, *London* and *Monarch*, to escort the Portuguese to Brazil. Moore was to protect Portuguese territory and provide visible support to the Portuguese government. Smith would then send frigates and smaller vessels to enable Moore to protect British trade while attacking any French vessels that might appear. On the afternoon of 22 January, after a voyage of eight weeks, the Portuguese Prince Regent reached All Saints Bay on the coast of the Brazilian province of Bahia. He expressed great thanks for the service provided by *Bedford*, which had assisted the Portuguese ships during the storms. The other British ships *Marlborough*, *London* and *Monarch* had arrived at Rio on 17 January. *Bedford* escorted the Portuguese ships down to Rio, arriving there on 7 March, and finally joined with the rest of the British squadron and the Portuguese convoy. In a classic example of the global nature of the Royal Navy's operations, her crew, formerly of the *Bellerophon* and only six months ago on blockade duty in the Channel, now found themselves promoting British influence and protecting British trade at Rio de Janeiro.[6]

Success at Lisbon was followed up in late December 1807 when a British maritime expedition arrived off the strategically important Portuguese island of Madeira. On 23 December the British commander, William Beresford, learned that the inhabitants had spent the previous two months preparing for a British attack; 'very considerable' works had been constructed to defend Funchal, the regular garrison had been increased and the militia called out. By 13:00 on 24 December the naval force under Rear Admiral Sir Samuel Hood, consisting of the 74-gun *Centaur*, *York* and *Captain*, and the 64-gun *Intrepid*, with the *Africaine*, *Alceste*, *Shannon* and *Success* frigates, was in position to mount an attack on Funchal. News of the evacuation of Lisbon had arrived on the island a few days before, causing all defensive activities to stop. Beresford's intelligence now reported that the people were not 'disinclined to receive the English'. He called upon the Portuguese governor to surrender and this was agreed to on 26 December 1807.[7]

Events in early 1808 once again displayed the importance of blockading enemy ports and proactively denying France naval resources when the Rochefort squadron under Admiral Zacharie Allemand put to sea with five ships of the line, evaded the blockading force and entered the Mediterranean. He anchored in Toulon on 6 February after capturing six British merchant ships. On 7 February ten ships of the line, three frigates, two corvettes and seven armed transports carrying munitions, provisions and French troops, now under overall command of Admiral Honoré Ganteaume, set sail. Arriving off the new French possession of Corfu (handed over by the Russians) on 23 February Ganteaume landed the troops and stores before arriving back in Toulon on 10 April. Collingwood had given chase but for a number of reasons, including poor weather and the failure of his frigates to pass timely intelligence, missed the opportunity to catch him. At least he could be satisfied that the French had achieved little of importance.[8]

Ganteaume's cruise again highlighted the necessity of blockading hostile naval forces and denying the French access to strategic bases. He had sailed past Sicily, whose security was a constant worry for Collingwood and British ministers. Garrisoning the island with 16,000 British troops and providing naval protection to deter a French invasion was a necessary burden for Britain, as Sicily and indeed Malta were essential to projecting maritime power in the western and eastern Mediterranean. Further to the west a French squadron of five sail of the line, a frigate and a brig corvette were still blockaded in Cadiz by Rear Admiral Purvis. While Cadiz was uppermost in ministers' minds, Spanish naval forces at Ferrol, Vigo and Cartagena were also kept under blockade. Then there were the Russian ships and the Portuguese vessels left behind in the Tagus after the evacuation. Admiral Sir Charles Cotton arrived there on 14 January to take over the blockade from Smith, his force comprising ten sail of the line and three smaller vessels.[9]

But this was not a passive blockade. On 13 February two ships' boats from the *Confiance* under the command of the master's mate, Robert Trist, 'in a most gallant manner' captured a French gunboat. A further attack in April by boats from *Nymphe* and the *Blossom* against a brig corvette was less successful: rowing against the tide and with the target defended by a floating battery, the officer leading the assault, Captain Conway Shipley of the *Nymphe*, was killed and the attackers retreated. Cotton's blockade would continue as news began to arrive of a British expedition to Iberia.[10]

The Peninsular War

As so often when momentous events occur, the man on the spot when insurrection against French occupation began to spread through Spain and Portugal in May 1808 was a naval officer. After spending the first half of 1808 blockading the River Tagus, Admiral Cotton started to assist Portuguese forces which had captured a French-held fort at the mouth of the Mondego river, approximately half way between Lisbon and Porto, sending Captain John Bligh of the *Alfred* with 200 Royal Marines and 20 officers to strengthen the position. After receiving information from London that a British military force under Sir Arthur Wellesley was heading for Iberia, Cotton added another hundred marines to the garrison. There had been some uncertainty in the British response to the insurrection in Spain. With enemy warships still sheltering in the harbour at Cadiz, securing them was the main British priority, but the Spaniards were unwilling to let British troops into the city. Instead the British government had settled on committing forces to Portugal.[11]

Such was the situation on 29 July when Wellesley made preparations for landing his 10,000 men at Mondego Bay. The Atlantic coast of Portugal provided many small bays in which a limited force could be put ashore; however, the heavy surf on the lee shore constrained the choices available to land a major force. In fact the conditions at Mondego Bay were far from ideal but it was the only realistic option, a point which Cotton impressed upon Wellesley. Wellesley also pointed to the fact that the 300 marines landed by Cotton and occupying the fort of Figieira provided a degree of security for the landing. Here was one of the key roles that sailors and marines drawn from the fleet could perform time and again, seizing and holding tactical positions for operational and strategic effect, this time in advance of a landing by the army.

Anxious to get the troops ashore, the disembarkation of Wellesley's force started on 1 August in a heavy surf. According to his plan, the infantry would be transferred from their transport ships into smaller boats to be rowed up the Mondego river by seamen from the fleet and deposited on its south bank. The troops were to have supplies for two to three days with bread for a further five days available on the transports. Over 60 men were lost as several boats, crammed with soldiers weighed down with heavy packs, overturned. Landing the troops was a slow process and was not completed until 5 August. No sooner had this been achieved than next day 5,000 reinforcements arrived and took two days to disembark, completing the landing on 8 August. Just over a week later, on the 17th, another 2,700 troops arrived, with a further 2,300 three days later. This rather piecemeal landing was brought to a close on the 24th when a more substantial reinforcement of 11,000 men arrived.[12]

With the French in possession of the city of Lisbon, maritime mobility had allowed Wellesley and Cotton to land the army in a location where the French could not interfere. But the French did eventually come, and Wellesley's victory over them at Vimiero on 21 August occurred as British troops were still landing, thus ensuring that this process could continue undisturbed. By the end of August there were 30,000 British troops in Portugal, the largest single continental commitment up to that date. Of course, Wellesley was still dependent on the fleet for his logistic support, a point he himself recognized:

> I kept the sea always on my flank; the Transports attended the movements of the army as a magazine; and I had at all times, & every day, a short, and easy, communication with them. The Army therefore could never be distressed for provisions or stores, however limited its means of Land Transport, and in case of necessity it might have embarked at any point of the Coast.

French defeat led to a convention between Cotton and the Russians in the Tagus which would see the Russian fleet held by Britain until six months after a general peace. Seven of these ships were sent to England, arriving at Spithead on 6 October, while two were unfit for sea and were repaired in the Tagus. Two ships were returned to Russia in 1813 but the others, in a very poor state, had been sold, with the Russians reimbursed at their original value.[13]

While Wellesley had been busy in the west, on the Catalonian coastline Lord Thomas Cochrane had carried out a remarkable series of operations against the French invading forces with his frigates *Impérieuse* and *Cambrian*. For the French the coast was the one area where they could hope to impose their rule, yet it was also the one area where the Royal Navy could have maximum impact. From late June onwards, Cochrane, utilizing the harbour at Rosas as a base, attacked shore installations and signal towers, blocked the coast road, bombarded French columns and assisted Spanish guerrillas. In July the French tried to take the town of Rosas but were prevented by the actions of the Spanish guerrillas and two Royal Navy ships. By November the French decided the only way to stop Cochrane's activities was to make another attempt to seize and then occupy Rosas. Sensing what was coming, Admiral Collingwood dispatched Captain John West in the *Excellent* and the bomb-vessel *Meteor* to assist in the defence of the town. West landed his seamen and marines, and although an outerwork fell, they put up a determined resistance. When part of the garrison became cut off after a sortie, West led a rescue party, in the process becoming one of the few naval officers to have a horse shot from under him. The arrival of a French siege train to facilitate a regular investment of the town was counterbalanced by the arrival of Cochrane in the *Impérieuse*, the bomb-vessel *Lucifer* and HMS *Fane* to relieve West and the *Excellent*. After further heroics, Cochrane evacuated the last of the marines on 5 December and the town eventually fell to the French.[14]

As well as harrying the French, one of the duties of the Royal Navy was to rescue the British army from sticky situations. Given the manpower available to Britain, this was perhaps even more important than landing the army in the first place. The ability to sweep the army out of the clutches of danger so that it could fight again was absolutely essential. This is the true value of the rescue of Sir John Moore's army from Corunna in 1809. After marching to the interior of Spain to distract the French from completing the destruction of Spanish forces, Moore was forced to flee across northern Spain in a breakneck race against time to find a safe harbour to embark the army before the French could catch up. A fleet of transports awaited Moore at Vigo, but he headed for the town of Corunna, informing the government of his change of plan. Arriving at Corunna on 11 January, Moore found 140 ships in the harbour, but they were store and hospital ships so he commenced the evacuation of his numerous sick and wounded. On 13 January French forces began to press the rearguard. The next day, much to Moore's relief, a flotilla of 110 transports arrived under escort from the mighty *Victory*, *Ville de Paris* and *Barfleur*, accompanied by seven further ships of the line and two frigates. They had been at Vigo, where Moore had originally intended to retreat, but had been delayed by contrary winds from sailing to Corunna. In their command structure was a commissioner from the Royal Navy's Transport Board, Captain James Bowen.

On 16 January Moore's army fought the French to a standstill, providing the necessary breathing space for Bowen to oversee the evacuation of 28,000 men, thereby saving Britain's only deployable army. The loss of this force at a precarious time for Britain could have had a widespread political impact; it is certainly possible that the government could not have survived such a disaster, leading to the Whigs regaining power and perhaps peace talks with Napoleon. Instead the Navy had saved the army and averted a political and strategic crisis. But Moore had paid the ultimate price; mortally wounded by a roundshot, he was buried alone with his glory.[15]

Wellesley's 1809 offensive and victory at Talavera were followed by withdrawal back to Portugal. When the French invaded in 1810 the Royal Navy played a crucial role in supporting Wellesley's operations based around his defensive fortifications of the Lines of Torres Vedras. In January 1809 Admiral Sir George Berkeley had succeeded Cotton on the Lisbon station and after a meeting with Wellesley in June 1809 returned to his fleet by the Tagus, which convinced him that he could utilize the river to supply the army. He established a flotilla of flatboats on the Tagus which could transfer supplies and troops upriver to Abrantes in ten hours rather than the three days it would take by land. Abrantes was a major strategic position; not only did it command the road down the Tagus and into Lisbon but it was also the site of the last bridge over the Tagus which an invading army from the east could use to cross the river and head to Lisbon.[16]

By the time the French arrived in front of the fortifications at

Torres Vedras the Royal Navy was using its signalling expertise to man five signal stations to transmit information along the lines, all using Popham's naval signals. By October 1810 Berkeley had 600 marines and seamen manning 20 gunboats on the Tagus, protecting Wellesley's right flank, while another force of gunboats protected the left, sea flank. That same month 360 naval personnel were sent ashore to take up guard duties while 450 more were organized into a battalion and drilled for shore service. In November, after the French had withdrawn from the immediate vicinity of the lines, Wellesley asked for two battalions to be drawn from the fleet to garrison the forts around Lisbon, thereby freeing up army units for active service. The Admiralty had sent out a trained marine battalion from Chatham to take the place of Berkeley's men ashore; in fact the admiral kept his own men ashore after sending this unit to serve with the army.[17]

If Wellesley's plan to stop the French had failed, the Royal Navy served as the ultimate safeguard by providing the facility to evacuate the army if necessary – the recent example of Corunna proving the value of this capability. Wellesley even created a safe embarkation point at St Julien, only a few miles away from Lisbon if the evacuation were to take place. He was confident that with a large fleet of warships and 45,000 tons of transports he could evacuate the entire army. In February 1810 there were 23,440 tons of transports in the Tagus with 7,000 more tons expected from London and a further 19,000 from Cadiz, Gibraltar and Malta. Once assembled these ships would provide Wellesley with all the tonnage he needed for an evacuation. By May 1810 each vessel had been assigned a specific number, berth and a unit from the army for embarkation. Despite some concerns of Wellesley's regarding possible difficulties if the French seized the south bank of the Tagus, Berkeley was convinced that an evacuation could be still implemented. By March 1811 the Admiralty had collected 256 transport vessels totalling more than 75,000 tons in the Tagus protected by 20 ships of the line, three frigates and eight sloops and brigs, a considerable manpower pool of 13,000 men. One of those ships of the line was HMS *Victory*, arriving on 4 March 1811, the night the French withdrew from the Lines of Torres Vedras; 'fittingly, Nelson's flagship was present at the scene of a victory as decisive as that of Trafalgar'.[18]

Wellesley had implemented a scorched-earth policy in his retreat to the fortified line at Torres Vedras to deny supplies to the invading French, yet his own supply line stretched from Lisbon back to Britain and beyond, and it required the protection of the Royal Navy. As the Anglo-Portuguese army eventually grew to number 60,000–70,000 men, it needed an immense amount of logistical support which was provided by an almost constant stream of convoys into Lisbon that carried victuals, reinforcements, supplies, horses and took away wounded, sick and prisoners, all convoyed by the Royal Navy.

With regard to food for the army, it was the job of the Victualling Board to supply overseas expeditions, and this was achieved from the start of 1809 until the end of 1810. In total 404 victualling convoys sailed from Britain to Iberia between the landings in 1808 and 1814. British exports were halted in 1811 following poor harvests, and alternative supplies were obtained from the Mediterranean and the United States, organized through a Lisbon merchant experienced in the American–Portugal trade. By 1811, 60 per cent of American grain exports went to Iberia. In 1812 this was a million bushels of American flour, and between 1811 and 1812 nearly half of the bread issued to Wellesley's army was made from transatlantic flour. When Britain and America went to war in 1812 (see Chapter 9) neutral and American ships carrying American flour and cereals were even granted exemption from the Royal Navy's blockade by the granting of licences through a British Order in Council. The trade continued until 1813 when alternative sources were found, including Russian wheat from the Mediterranean and Brazilian wheat.[19]

To manage this supply hub, a naval officer had been appointed to Lisbon in 1808 and a store depot was established which eventually employed five clerks, ten coopers with apprentice and foreman, 13 labourers, a porter and five carpenters. By 1811 the depot at Lisbon was so full that Wellesley requested no more supplies should be sent until he required them. The fleet also provided food relief to the population of Lisbon, swollen by great numbers of refugees who had

Fig. 7.2. *A large First Rate, said to be HMS 'Victory', lying off the mouth of the Tagus* (T. Buttersworth), supporting the operations of the British army under Wellesley.

been removed from the region before the Lines of Torres Vedras as part of the scorched-earth policy.

Just as important was a constant supply of specie, gold and silver, for although the 1809 campaign had cost £3 million, that figure doubled the following year and rose to £11 million in 1811. Between 19 November 1812 and 15 July 1813 over £900,000 in specie was shipped to Lisbon in 27 separate deliveries; moreover, the supply line for this stretched right across the Atlantic to South America, a situation only possible through the supremacy of the Royal Navy. Specie was vital for Wellesley, for in order to sustain the support of the Portuguese and Spanish people his army had to 'pay its way' rather than resort to forcible requisitioning like the French.[20]

In 1812, when Wellesley resolved to undertake offensive action, the Navy was a key element in distracting the enemy and preventing the French from concentrating their forces. In 1812 Admiral Edward Pellew, now commanding the Mediterranean Fleet, and Captain Edward Codrington, in command of a squadron off the coast, concluded that 5,000 British troops off the

Catalan coast would assist the Catalan guerrillas to renew their efforts. Wellesley was a keen supporter of this plan, and eventually troops were drawn from the garrison on Sicily to provide for this diversionary force to operate along the coast. Though the forces did not arrive off the coast until after Wellesley had crushed the French at Salamanca on 22 July, during 1812 no French troops were dispatched from eastern Spain to reinforce those trying to stem Wellesley's advance. During this time arms and ammunition continued to be landed for the Spanish guerrillas. As the war shifted to the interior in 1813 and with problems caused by American commerce raiders, the number of ships of the line at Lisbon was reduced to two, with four frigates, with the numbers of cruiser vessels increased to 14 sloops and brigs.[21]

Also in 1812 the ubiquitous Sir Home Popham was wreaking havoc with a detached squadron along the northern coast of Spain. Again, the object was to prevent the French sending troops to help the main French field army. This time the operations did coincide with Wellesley's advance to Salamanca and the French could not spare a single soldier to assist. As well as landing supplies and arms to the Spanish guerrillas, Popham captured the port of Santander on 2 August 1812. He then landed two 24pdrs which sailors began to haul overland towards Burgos where Wellesley was conducting a siege without specialist besieging guns. Popham's crews got within 50 miles of Burgos before Wellesley called off the siege. Popham's command then passed to George Collier who assisted the guerrillas in the capture of Tafalla and then San Sebastian in 1813. The true value of Santander became apparent that year when Wellesley could shift his entire logistical base from Lisbon to Santander, a crucial factor in facilitating the advance to and victory at Vittoria and his campaigns across the Pyrenees and into France in 1814. Also crucial was the continued supply of specie to pay his army during the invasion of France. The last thing he wanted was an interruption to the supply of cash: 'without pay and food,' he stated 'they must plunder; and if they plunder they will ruin us all'. To prevent this, Nathan Rothschild was busy sourcing specie on the continent. That this was possible at all was due to the creditworthiness of London's financial services sector, which in turn was based on trade and the Royal Navy. Specie was then shipped from the Low Countries to the Biscay coastline, again only possible because of the Navy's supremacy at sea.[22]

In June 1813, when he believed American privateers threatened his maritime supply lines, Wellesley criticized the Admiralty, declaring, 'For the first time I believe that it has happened to any British Army [...] its communication by sea is insecure.' Not for the first or last time, Wellesley was exaggerating, and while the Royal Navy's use of the convoy system was never one hundred per cent infallible, the loss of a few ships here and there would not undermine his supply lines. Moreover, given the fact that shipwreck was probably a more pressing danger for ships operating in the often treacherous Bay of Biscay, Wellesley's fears were overblown. In fact it was British maritime power that provided the finance to keep his armies paid and supplied on their campaigns in Portugal, Spain and into France, as recognized by Wellesley himself when he remarked of the Peninsular War:

> If anyone wishes to know the history of this war, I will tell them that it is our maritime superiority [that] gives me the power of maintaining my army while the enemy are unable to do so.[23]

Lissa

As with French naval forces stationed in the ports of the Low Countries and the Atlantic coast, one of Collingwood's key tasks in the Mediterranean was to blockade Toulon, home, by 1809, to 15 French ships of the line and six Russian warships. As before, the blockade was never easy, and on 27 February 1809 a French raid by two frigates and a couple of line of battle attacked the Royal Navy frigate watching the port, the *Proserpine*, forcing her to strike. With seapower playing an integral role in the Peninsular War it was crucial that French naval forces were prevented from intervening. The blockade of Toulon, like that of Brest, could not be absolute, and a number of French ships escaped during the course of the remainder of the war. In the spring of 1809 a French squadron managed to break out and resupply Barcelona, a feat that was again attempted in October of the year. This time part of Collingwood's force hunted them down, two French ships being driven ashore and later burnt. The rest of the convoy of seven storeships, protected by an armed storeship, a xebec and two armed bombards, had sheltered at Rosas, with additional protection coming from shore batteries. Collingwood sent Hallowell's 74-gun *Tigre*, the *Cumberland* (74) and the frigates *Apollo*, *Topaze* and *Volontaire* with three sloops which mounted a boat attack, seizing or destroying the entire French force. Such was the pattern for the rest of the war, with attempts by the French to capture becalmed British ships (the *Temeraire* beat off such an attack on 13 August 1811) or trying to resupply their armies by sea. In return the British aggressively hunted down any ships that escaped.

By that date Collingwood had worn himself to death. He had pleaded for permission to go home, not having seen his family for seven years, and his request was finally granted. He was succeeded by Rear Admiral Martin in March 1810 but died on his flagship, the *Ville de Paris*, on 7 March after 44 years of naval service. He is buried in St Paul's Cathedral next to his great friend Nelson.

By late 1813 Napoleon could in theory call on 21 ships of the line and ten frigates in the Mediterranean ports of Toulon, La Spezia, Genoa, Naples and Venice. But, as at Antwerp, he lacked seamen to man them – crews had been taken for land service in the invasion of Russia in 1812. Then there was the fundamental French problem of assembling disparate ships into a cohesive force. This was something that had affected all French maritime thinking given their need to maintain a presence in both the Atlantic and Mediterranean theatres, leading to the development of Brest and Toulon as the main fleet bases. Events in 1805 had shown that Napoleon's attempts to achieve strategic effect were not only beyond his capabilities but also would have necessitated taking on and defeating the Royal Navy in battle, an unlikely outcome given that the physical and psychological state of his naval force was only growing worse despite the numbers on paper. The blockade of the Mediterranean ports ensured that the

Royal Navy could continue to raid and harass French naval rebuilding efforts and positions along the Italian coastline, especially around Naples as forward protection to the island of Sicily. Farther east, Cephalonia, Ithaca and Santa Maura in the Ionian Islands were taken.[24]

With Pellew commanding the Mediterranean Fleet in 1813 and desperate for a fleet battle to add to his reputation as an outstanding frigate captain, he tried to tempt the French out to play. On 5 November 1813 in a brisk action the wind changed and the French ran back to Toulon. In February 1814 while trying to cover the arrival into Toulon of a 74-gun ship built at Genoa, Pellew again engaged the French but they ran back to Toulon, having successfully added the incoming ship to their strength. Pellew found these months incredibly frustrating and would end the war still frustrated at having missed a major fleet battle. The strategic effect was that the Toulon fleet remained bottled up in port.

One Royal Navy officer who did manage to find a French squadron willing to fight was Captain William Hoste. He was in command of a squadron consisting of his 32-gun ships *Amphion* and *Cerberus* and the 38-gun *Active* operating in the Adriatic. By September 1810 the French had collected a force, to which several Venetian vessels could be added, to free the sea from British control. By March 1811 the Franco-Venetian squadron, comprising three French frigates, three Venetian frigates, two brigs and several smaller vessels, was determined to attack Hoste's base of Lissa, where the British force consisted of the three frigates and the 22-gun sloop *Volage*. On 13 March, with a clear superiority in numbers, the French commander, displaying a suitable aggressive spirit, bore down on Hoste's line. With the signal 'Remember Nelson' flying Hoste prepared to fend off the allied attack, which was, inspired by Nelson's tactics at Trafalgar, a headlong attack in two distinct columns to bring on a pellmell battle. Time and time again, the Royal Navy had placed its faith in superior seamanship, ethos and gunnery. This time, taking up a defensive posture, the same factors were decisive. Hoste's line was compact and the French attack was initially blunted on British gunnery. The French commander, Bernard Dubourdieu, was one of the first to fall and his ship ran aground, at which point two frigates positioned themselves to attack Hoste's *Amphion*.

Here the superior seamanship and comradeship amongst Hoste's squadron played a key role, as *Active*, *Cerberus* and *Volage* beat off the French assault. Hoste manoeuvred *Amphion* to rake one of his opponents, the *Flore*, who struck. *Amphion* was raked in turn by the *Bellona*, but Hoste's superior broadsides defeated her. At this point the British commander signalled a general chase, with *Active* hunting down the Venetian *Corona*. In the heat of the action with *Bellona*, Hoste had been unable to send men across to take *Flore*, which raised her flag again and fled, much to Hoste's chagrin. It had been a brutal encounter, with Royal Navy casualties of 45 killed and 145 wounded, but of the six enemy frigates, only two had escaped, three had been taken and one burnt. The scene of destruction on *Bellona*, testimony to British gunnery, was recorded by Lieutenant O'Brien of the prize crew who thought the 'carnage was dreadful – the dead and the dying lying about in every direction'. He continued:

> every man stationed at one of the guns had been killed, and it was supposed by the same shots (our guns being doubleshotted) which passed through both sides of the ship into the sea. At another gun, the skull of one poor creature was actually lodged in the beam above where he stood, the shot having taken an oblique direction; in short, the scene was heart-rendering and sickening.

Hoste retired to Malta for repair. The British victory at Lissa did not guarantee absolute command of the Adriatic, for the French tried to resupply their garrison on Corfu, as well as other positions, but it did give Hoste local freedom of action.[25]

As along the Italian coast, on the Spanish and even their own coasts the French failure to successfully challenge British seapower allowed the Royal Navy to continue to wage a harrying war along the Adriatic coastline, intercepting French convoys and wiping out enemy merchant traffic, attacking gunboats and flotilla craft and dealing with heavier ships when they appeared. In July 1811 a French grain convoy heading for Ragusa was destroyed and in November a sharp action resulted in the capture of a French frigate

Fig. 7.3. Naval General Service Medals awarded in 1847 to men who participated in Captain Hoste's commendable action at Lissa, 13 March 1811.

and a brig. Next year, when the newly launched 74-gun *Rivoli* sailed
from Venice on her maiden voyage, in company with three brigs and
a couple of gunboats, she was promptly attacked and captured by
the 74-gun *Victorious* and the sloop *Weazel*.

At Cattaro in late 1813 Hoste's sailors hauled two 18pdrs and two
11-inch mortars up Mount Theodore using a system of pulleys and
a kedge anchor. Down in the town the French commander, faced
with the prospect of being bombarded from such a position, surrendered on 6 January 1814. The entire operation, from the initial
landing to complete re-embarkation, had taken only five weeks. It
was certainly no fluke, for shortly afterwards Hoste's crews placed
two 18pdrs on the 1,200ft high Mount Sergius. Further north, in
late October 1813, the Royal Navy commander in the Adriatic, Rear
Admiral Thomas Fremantle, had bombarded the town of Trieste
from his flagship, the 74-gun *Milford*, before landing marines,
seamen and guns to assist the Austrian forces besieging the town,
which fell on 29 October 1813. By February 1814 all French garri-
sons in the Adriatic had been captured.[26]

CHAPTER 8

'The carrier of the commerce of the continent of Europe'

Economic Warfare, 1805–15

With Britain supreme at sea following Trafalgar and France supreme on land, each was the dominant power in its respective 'natural' environment. British maritime supremacy was, at least partially, based on the great fleet battles, but Trafalgar had been fought and won in 1805, yet a definitive peace was not agreed upon until 1814–15. So how could naval battle be seen as a decisive factor? How could navies contribute towards winning the war? With the Royal Navy supreme at sea, a situation which shaped the rest of the war, what did it contribute to British war making between 1805 and 1815?

After Trafalgar Napoleon attempted to rebuild his naval forces through construction and seizing neutral navies; in this strategy he had some material success but could not fundamentally challenge the Royal Navy's control of the sea and so had sought alternative ways to attack Britain. Economic warfare was always integral to British strategy but from 1805 it played an enhanced role in French strategy. By May 1806 Britain had declared a blockade of France which stretched from Brest to the River Elbe. This offered a pretext for Napoleon to implement a long-held plan which was encapsulated in his Berlin Decree of 21 November 1806 and followed by two Milan Decrees in late 1807. They declared the British Isles under blockade and prohibited all commerce between the continent and Britain and her colonies. Napoleon's economic warfare strategy reached its

Fig. 8.1. *The Continental Dockyard*. Napoleon's storehouse contains only minor navies while John Bull's is stuffed with captures from a number of naval engagements with the prospect of more if Napoleon tries to cross the Channel.

zenith during late 1807 and early 1808. The signing of the Treaties of Tilsit in July 1807, between France and Russia, confirmed Napoleon's dominance of continental Europe and left Britain strategically isolated with no major allies in Europe. Napoleon's object was to create an imbalance in British trade, reducing revenue and the inflow of specie; this would also undermine British credit, thereby limiting Britain's ability to pay subsidies to allies and fund military expeditions, all of which were vital for continuing the war against France.[1]

Britain responded with a number of Orders in Council which imposed political and economic terms on neutral trade; there would be long-term repercussions with the United States from this. By 1808 the British government realized the war had become a global contest for economic superiority and that at the end of conflict the accounts would have to be balanced. If Britain ended the wars as the carrier of global trade it would compensate her for the sacrifices made, in the same way that European powers would want territorial compensation for their war efforts. The aim, in Canning's view, was for Britain to become:

> the carrier of the commerce of the continent of Europe, as, no other could, under the above circumstances, trade to the W. Indies and Spanish America but herself; this would annihilate the marine of all the powers in Europe, as, in a few years for want of employment, it would sink into insignificance.

In this case 'England would, by adopting these measures with promptitude and vigour, become mistress of the seas'. British strategy was now focused on dominating global maritime commerce, facilitated by the world's largest merchant marine and protected by the world's largest naval force. This would provide the finance necessary to continue to fight Napoleonic France. The competing military and economic policies of Britain and France left no room for neutrals.[2]

Retaking the Cape

The Cape of Good Hope had been returned to the Dutch at the Peace of Amiens but, given its location on the route to the East, it is not surprising that in July 1805 an expedition was assembling at Cork to retake it. Under the command of Commodore Sir Home Popham and Sir David Baird, it comprised three sail of the line, including Popham's flagship, the 64-gun *Diadem*, two frigates, a couple of gunbrigs, 12 Indiamen and 64 transports containing 5,000 troops, of which 900 men of the 38th Foot were housed on *Diadem*. Popham would also convoy a number of ships heading on to India and all in all there were 120 ships under his command. After the convoy split, Popham's warships, 16 Indiamen and 34 transports, headed for the Cape, arriving there on 3 January 1806. The operation was similar to that of 1795, with the fleet landing the troops in a heavy surf in which 35 Highlanders of the 93rd Foot were drowned when their boat overturned. Seamen and marines landed the heavy artillery. At this point Popham received information of a French fleet at large in the South Atlantic, but retained his focus on the task at hand. On 8 January Dutch forces were defeated, on the 10th they surrendered and by the 12th Baird was in possession of Cape Town. On 4 March the French frigate *Volontaire* arrived off the bay, was lured in by Popham flying Dutch colours and promptly ordered to surrender, which her captain, realizing he had been hoodwinked, assented to.[3]

While the attack on the Cape had gone according to plan, the ever creative Popham now caused something of a stink. On 12 September 1806 dispatches from him arrived at Portsmouth detailing the capture of Buenos Aires. The news was conveyed to London in a carnival procession: eight wagons containing around a million dollars in hard cash (liberated from the Spanish viceroy) were escorted by 30 sailors from HMS *Narcissus*, a Royal Marine band provided suitable martial music and, so no one could miss the spectacle, a salute was fired at every major town on the route. Popham had provided an inkling of what he planned in his dispatches from the Cape which had arrived at the Admiralty on the morning of 24 June. When Popham had originally sailed from Cork, William Pitt was still alive, and, trusting his benevolence and with plans to conquer Spanish America and open it up to British trade circulating in government, Popham thought he had unofficial government authority to attack Spanish America. His dispatches found a new ministry, who had no idea what he was up to, and responded in an *ad hoc* fashion, leading to the dispatch of a number of reinforcements with diverse objects. By the time British reinforcements arrived in South America, the initial expedition had been forced to surrender on 14 August. British policy now resulted in a second disastrous attack against Buenos Aires on 5 July 1807, leading to another humiliating surrender to the Spaniards and the evacuation of the River Plate. Unsurprisingly Popham was recalled to explain himself but escaped censure. Upon taking office the Portland government discussed plans for maritime expeditions in the region, including consulting with Sir Arthur Wellesley about an expedition to attack Mexico.[4]

Such plans took on increased significance as Napoleon exercised his control of Western Europe. This national strategy has often been ridiculed by military historians who insist that British success in the wars was down to the battles won by the Duke of Wellington. This simplistic assessment misses the point. French strength lay in her territory and population, providing a large army, which was used to devastating effect during the Revolution and Empire. The British Army could not decisively defeat the French in battle and force them into agreeing to British war aims at the peace table without allies on the field of battle. Instead, for military, social, economic and doctrinal reasons, British strategy was subtle, relying on the nation's strengths. An insular position, limited continental European interests (besides the key Low Countries), an economy heavily involved in overseas trade and a powerful navy provided Britain with the advantage in a long-term maritime war of financial strength. Britain therefore fought with 'economic pressure exercised through seapower. This naval body had two arms; one financial, which embraced the subsidising and military provisioning of allies; the other military, which embraced sea-borne expeditions against the enemies vulnerable extremities.' Overseas operations provided Britain with 'a solid commercial base from which to continue the wars'. In the Napoleonic Wars 'whatever was said and hoped by Englishmen who day-dreamed of quick victories, the method pursued in the end was *financial attrition*'. While the cost of the war spiralled from £29 million in 1804 to over £70 million in 1813, 'Britain was able to sustain a level of expenditure that far outstripped that of every other country in Europe'. How could Britain manage this level of expenditure?[5]

The answer was by preserving and increasing revenue, through higher and wider taxation and expanding and increasing duties on overseas commerce. This is why Popham and Canning and others were interested in opening up the supposedly lucrative markets of South America. In 1807 British exports to Brazil were valued at £1,200,000 whereas by 1812 they had risen to over £2 million. But it was not direct trade with Brazil that was important, for the crucial factor in combating Napoleon's continental blockade was the transfer of the Portuguese government which allowed Britain to penetrate the more lucrative markets of Spanish America. Although

South America was never as valuable as contemporaries believed, Popham had optimistically estimated that South America shipped $50 million per year to European Spain. The actual value of the trade has to be seen in the context of the struggle between Britain and France. British exports to areas in the Americas outside the USA, valued at £7.8 million in 1805, increased following the arrival of the Portuguese royal family in Brazil from £10,440,000 in 1807 to £16,590,000 in 1808. With the traditional European markets constrained by the continental blockade and exports to the lucrative US markets halving (over £8 million down to £4 million) between 1806 and 1808 Latin America became the crucial region for opening up new markets for British trade. For a few years between 1806 and 1808 South America 'really *was* important to Britain'. South America could be opened up to British trade and denied to France and Spain because of the maritime supremacy obtained at Trafalgar and the ongoing operations to prevent French naval rebuilding and to deny Napoleon access to neutral warships.[6]

The West Indies

On 13 December 1805 the Brest fleet, idle observers of the Trafalgar campaign, broke free while Admiral Cornwallis had been driven off his blockading station. But their object was not to cover an invasion force or to meet the Royal Navy in decisive battle. Instead, recognizing that his attempt to obtain control of the Channel had gone, Napoleon turned to a *guerre de course*; a strategy of raiding British commercial interests. The danger of such raiding squadrons had been evident from events in September 1805 when Admiral Allemand's Rochefort squadron had, after failing to link up with the Combined Fleet under Villeneuve, fallen in with a convoy in the western approaches before heading into the South Atlantic where it attacked a convoy from Gorée. In total during his cruise Allemand seized the 50-gun HMS *Calcutta*, the 18-gun brig *Ranger*, a hired cutter and 43 merchant ships and captured 1,200 seamen, but with limited supplies he was back in Rochefort on 23 December.

Now the Brest fleet of 11 sail of the line, four frigates and three smaller vessels split. One force under Vice Admiral Corentin Urbain Leissègues headed for the West Indies to intercept British trade off Jamaica after dropping off 1,000 troops to bolster the garrison of San Domingo. The other, under Rear Admiral Willaumez, was to raid the South Atlantic before heading to the West Indies. Given the inability of the French navy to mount sustained naval operations, both would return to France. They were spotted on 15 December by the *Arethusa* which passed on the intelligence to Vice Admiral Sir John Duckworth who, acting upon intelligence from the *Lark* which had been escorting the Gorée convoy, had been looking for Allemand. He thought he had found him on 25 December 1805 and pursued to the south, but with his fleet strung out he shied away from bringing him to action. The sails sighted were in fact those of Willaumez. Instead of heading back to his station off Cadiz and much to Collingwood's frustration, Duckworth headed to take on water in the West Indies. In response the Admiralty sent two reinforcing squadrons to hunt down the enemy fleets, one to the West Indies and the other to protect the convoy under Popham heading to retake the Cape.[7]

In the West Indies Duckworth received intelligence of a French force headed for San Domingo and on 6 February brought Leissègues to action. Leissègues, flying his flag in the massive 130-gun *Impérial*, had with him the 80-gun *Alexandre*, the 74s *Diomède*, *Jupiter* and *Brave* and two frigates and a corvette. Duckworth attacked headlong in two columns, one to starboard with the 74s *Superb*, *Northumberland*, *Spencer* and the 64-gun *Agamemnon*, the other to port with the 80-gun *Canopus*, and the 74s *Atlas* and *Donegal*, to cut off the French van. Duckworth also had two frigates and two sloops. Fought in light winds, the *Spencer* succeeded in raking the leading French ship *Alexandre* which was in turn attacked by the port column.

As the action became general around 11:10 the *Alexandre* struck; shortly after the *Brave*, having received a devastating raking broadside from the *Donegal*, followed suit; *Donegal* then went on to seize the *Jupiter*. Duckworth's *Superb*, with a picture of Nelson displayed on the mizzen and with her band playing 'God Save the King', together with the *Northumberland* and the *Atlas*, tackled Leissègues' *Impérial*, dismasting her and forcing her aground, a fate also shared by the *Diomède*. Both were later burnt by the British. The French frigates and the corvette escaped the carnage. It was a decisive victory, with all five French sail of the line either burnt or taken. The French lost 1,500 killed and wounded compared to 338 killed and wounded in Duckworth's fleet. Yet Duckworth, having abandoned his station to win a victory, recognized he had some explaining to do, but did so in a rather gauche manner. Nevertheless, his victory, so the outgoing Barham thought, was crucial, for it 'puts us out of all fear from another predatory war in the West Indies'.[8]

With the Cape in British hands, supplies running low and his crew suffering from scurvy, Willaumez headed across the Atlantic to Brazil before appearing in the West Indies in July. He then headed for neutral America where he put into the Chesapeake before returning to France in early 1807, having failed to achieve anything more than the capture of a few prizes. On 25 September 1806 Commodore Samuel Hood intercepted a French frigate squadron from Rochefort bound for the West Indies, capturing four fine 40-gun frigates, all of which were added to the Royal Navy.[9]

On New Year's Day 1807 the Dutch West Indies island of Curaçao was retaken by a force of frigates under Captain Charles Brisbane in the 38-gun *Arethusa*. Brisbane led his force in a daring attack which seized the shipping in the harbour at St Anne, including a Dutch frigate and corvette, and stormed Fort Amsterdam before taking possession of the town. With the Dutch Fort Republiek also silenced, in just one morning Brisbane had taken the island for the loss of just three killed and wounded compared to nearly 200 Dutch casualties.

Following the attack on Copenhagen in December 1807 the now hostile Danish islands of St Thomas and St Croix were seized by an expedition under Rear Admiral Alexander Cochrane flying his flag in the Trafalgar veteran *Belleisle*. Chasing down French squadrons ensured that the islands of Guadeloupe, Martinique and Guiana were virtually cut off from Europe and under a state of siege. The odd single French ship did appear in Caribbean waters but they were hunted down; for example, the French corvette *Lynx* was taken

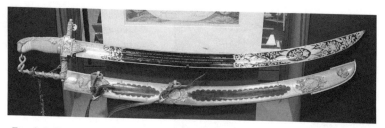

Fig. 8.2. Lieutenant William Coombe's presentation sword for a boat action on 21 January 1807 which captured the French corvette *Lynx* off the Saintes. Coombe, of the *Galatea*, had already lost a leg in a previous action and was wounded in the stump. An aggressive commander, he was killed on 29 November 1808 at Guadeloupe cutting out French vessels sheltering under shore batteries.

by the *Galatea* in January 1807. Such was the fate of the *Diligente*, *Sylphe* and *Espiègle* corvettes, sent to resupply Martinique, the latter two taken in August 1808 by the *Comet* sloop (*Sylphe*) and the *Sibylle* (*Espiègle*) with only the *Diligente* making it to the beleaguered island. Further French attempts to supply Martinique in December 1808 were intercepted by the Royal Navy's blockade of the island. Aggressive tactics and ethos, with promotion and prize money in mind, led to the death of the 12-gun brig *Maria*'s commanding officer, Lieutenant Bennett, in a fight with the far heavier 22-gun *Département de Landes*. The French did score the odd success, such as the capture of the 18-gun *Carnation* by the 16-gun *Palinure*, following the death of *Carnation*'s commanding officer and the incapacitation of her other officers. Despite such setbacks, it was only a matter of time before superior British seapower led to the capture of the remaining French islands and in 1809 that was the object of British policy in the West Indies.

With Sir Sidney Smith now commanding the Royal Navy's forces off the coast of South America, and falling in with Brazilian plans to expand their territory, he detached a British–Portuguese–Brazilian force to seize French Guiana. With British and Portuguese seamen and marines using canoes to navigate the surrounding waterways, the British commander, Captain James Lucas Yeo, led an assault on the forts defending the capital town of Cayenne. But in the

Fig. 8.3. 1847 Naval General Service Medal for the *Galatea*'s boat action with the *Lynx*.

heavy surf many overturned and it was left to the second wave of a Portuguese brig and two cutters to re-embark Yeo's force before depositing them ashore. Following further assaults, on 14 January 1809 Cayenne surrendered with Guiana handed over to Brazil.

The situation of Martinique was so important that the orders to take it arrived from London in January 1809. The force devoted to the operation was considerable: 10,000 troops conveyed by just about everything the Royal Navy had afloat in the theatre – six ships of the line including Cochrane's flagship the 98-gun *Neptune*, a 44-gun ship, seven frigates and 28 smaller vessels, plus the troop-ships. With the Navy fulfilling its usual role of landing seamen, marines and guns, and with ships battering land defences, the French started to burn their naval assets, the *Amphitrite*, and captured *Carnation*, while the *Diligente* was seized. Port Royal had fallen on 10 February, with further reduction of the island's defences. On 24 February Martinique surrendered.

The task now for Cochrane was to remove any other islands that the French could use as raiding bases while attacking any French ships that might appear; indeed a number of French warships were taken during the remainder of 1809. In dealing with the remaining French islands, Cochrane worked with a Spanish force to capture San Domingo on 6 June, leaving only Guadeloupe in French hands. With the naval blockade strangling the island's lifeline back to France, by 27 December Cochrane was ready with 7,000 troops to assault and on 6 February 1810 the last French island fell. With the Dutch islands of St Martin, St Eustatias and Saba mopped up, the only West Indies possession not in British or Spanish hands was Haiti. Not only had Britain removed lucrative sugar islands from the French economy but had now added their revenue to her own coffers.[10]

East Indies

In the east Rear Admiral the Comte de Linois had sailed from Brest as early as March 1803 and over the next few years was loose in the Indian Ocean. He missed the most valuable convoys and on 14 February was deterred by the actions of a convoy of East Indiamen led by Commodore Nathaniel Dance. The convoy was valued at £8 million and its loss would have been keenly felt, but over the course of his entire cruise Linois only managed to take a number of isolated merchant ships. In the meantime a major spat had erupted over command of the Royal Navy forces in the Indian Ocean. Sir Edward Pellew was sent out to replace Peter Rainier, arriving at Madras in December 1804. As ever with the Indian Ocean command, his resources, five 74s, a 64, one 50-gun ship, ten frigates and six sloops, did not match the demands of escorting convoys and other duties. As if this was not bad enough, the Admiralty, acting under pressure from Pitt, split the command, appointing Rear Admiral Sir Thomas Troubridge to the more lucrative Eastern station. Pellew ignored the direct Admiralty order and considered Troubridge to be under his command. Relations between the two men degenerated to the point that when Troubridge, one of the most gifted officers

of his generation, was appointed to command at the Cape, he petu-
lantly insisted that he sail in the unseaworthy *Blenheim* which was
lost at sea with all hands in early February 1807. By this time Vice
Admiral Warren had destroyed Linois' squadron on 13 March 1806.
While French raiding cruises did pose a danger to British trade and
had to be dealt with, which tied up Royal Navy resources, in isola-
tion their effects lacked the potency of a sustained campaign to
undermine British trade.

French possession of Île de France offered great opportunity
for a war on British commerce in the East Indies. With the Cape
secured and Pellew now in sole command of his station again, one
of his first objects for 1807 had been negating two Dutch sail of the
line at Java, which had been achieved in December 1807. His next
priority was to deal with French warships and privateers attacking
British trade, and in March 1808 the *Terpsichore* fought the *Sémillante*
to a standstill, the latter returning to France for repairs. Privateers
were indeed troublesome, and while the most famous, Robert
Surcouf, had made his name in 1800, by 1807 he was back in Indian
waters and in the course of a year took 30 British merchant ships,
much to the outrage of British merchants in India who wrote to the
Admiralty demanding something be done.[11]

That something, as Pellew had already realized, was taking Île
de France and its sister island Bourbon, denying French warships
and privateers a base for action. In the meantime, however, there
were Portuguese colonies to deal with. Given Lisbon's alliance with
Britain and Portugal falling under French control, colonies such
as Madeira would be kept out of French hands by British occupation. Portuguese trade had been under Royal Navy convoy protection since 1797; now an expedition was sent to bring Macao under
British control, but it was a disaster and an Anglo-Sino conflict only
averted by a British withdrawal. The commander of this expedition,
Rear Admiral William O'Bryen Drury, succeeded Pellew to the
command of the East Indies station in January 1809.

This still left the major problem of Île de France. Given the
strong winds and its exposed situation, it had always been difficult
to mount an effective blockade of the island. Following the capture

Fig. 8.4. Île de France. View from the deck of the *Upton Castle*,
transport, of the British army landing.

of the Cape, the blockading force was transferred to that command,
and attempts were made to tighten the noose in the autumn of 1808
with the 64-gun *Raisonnable*, 50-gun *Grampus*, *Nereide* frigate, two
brigs and two sloops. Like all British blockades, it was proactive, the
squadron trying to chase down escaping and incoming French ships
and engaging in a number of cutting-out actions and raids. With the
porous blockade continuing into 1810, the decision was made by the
Governor General of India, Lord Minto, and Drury that the islands
must be taken and a force was organized to sail from Madras. The
two-stage assault began with an attack on Bourbon, which provided
vital food to Île de France, and after a short campaign the island
fell on 8 July 1810. Sparring between the rival naval forces continued, with prizes such as the Indiamen *Windham* taken and retaken,
culminating in a foolhardy attack on a small anchored French
squadron, protected by coral reefs, on the afternoon of 23 August.
Led by Captain Nesbit Willoughby's *Nereide*, followed by the *Sirius*
under Captain Samuel Pym, the *Sirius* and the third British frigate
Magicienne ran aground, leaving the *Nereide* and the final British frigate *Iphigenia* to engage the four French frigates. The battle of Grand
Port was a debacle for the Royal Navy, with *Sirius* and *Magicienne*

being burnt by their crews, and the *Nereide*, rendered unmanageable and being raked by her opponent, turned into a wreck and struck. *Iphigenia* escaped only to be taken four days later. Only *Nereide* had put up a real fight, and at a stroke the British frigate force off Île de France had been reduced from five to a lone ship, the French now possessing six. Over 2,000 British seamen were killed, wounded or captured, more than the losses sustained at Trafalgar. Grand Port was the only French victory of the years 1803–15 but as tactically decisive as it was it did not save Île de France.[12]

The island of Rodrigues, 350 miles to the east of Île de France, had been seized by the British in 1808 to supply the blockading squadron with wood, food and water. It now served as the assembly point for an amphibious assault, drawing warships from the Cape and nearly 7,000 troops from India embarked in transports. Meticulously planned, with landing places at Mapou Bay in the north of the island reconnoitred and channels buoyed, the mechanics of landing had been placed, as was usual by now, under an amphibious expert, Captain Philip Beaver of the *Nisus*. Crucially an overwhelming naval force was brought to bear to prevent any French attempt to interfere with the expedition reaching Rodrigues or the actual landing on Île de France. Admiral Sir Albemarle Bertie's fleet consisted of the 74-gun *Illustrious*, 44-gun *Cornwallis*, the 38-gun frigates *Boadicea*, *Nisus*, *Clorinde*, *Menelaus*, *Nereide* (ex-*Vénus*, taken from the French), along with *Phoebe*, *Doris*, *Cornelia*, *Psyche* and *Ceylon*, plus four sloops, an armed transport, a gunbrig and three hired merchantmen. All the preparation paid off, and in fine weather on 29 November the attack was carried out with such expertise that it surprised the French who had not believed landing at Mapou Bay was possible. This ensured that the 50 ships' boats containing 1,555 men of the assault wave landed unopposed. One eyewitness recalled:

> The division moved towards the shore, presenting a magnificent and interesting spectacle. While pulling to the beach, we could not but feel the most lively anxiety for the event, and continued gazing intently till we saw the troops land, form and advance without a musket being fired.

The landings were covered by ships' boats equipped with carron-ades, 6pdrs and howitzers manned by seamen from the fleet.[13]

Once the British force was landed it moved towards the capital of Port Louis, driving off French outposts, and on 1 December drove off a defensive force of 3,000 outside the city with minimal loss. During the advance supplies were landed from the *Nisus*. On 3 December Île de France, a constant thorn in the British side during the wars, surrendered. Importantly the French frigate squadron was seized along with 24 French merchant ships and several captured British Indiamen were retaken. Also freed from captivity was the navigator and explorer Commander Matthew Flinders, imprisoned on the island when war broke out in 1803.

Such had been the perceived ease of the operation that Beaver complained that the French had only put up a cursory resistance: 'Will anyone be found to rise in the Commons and move a vote of thanks on this occasion?' Bertie, discussing the wider effects of the operation, believed it amounted to the 'extirpation of the Naval Force of the enemy in these seas and the subjugation of the last remaining colonial territory of France'. He was mistaken, for a small French garrison held a post at Tamatave, Madagascar. Taken on 12 February 1811 by the 18-gun sloop *Eclipse*, it was retaken on 19 May by a French force of three frigates that had escaped from Brest in February to reinforce Île de France but had been driven off the now British-occupied island. In a running action between 20 and 25 May the three frigates were taken and Tamatave reoccupied by the British. This finally was the end for France east of the Cape.[14]

Following the French annexation of the Batavian Republic in July 1810 Minto had been keen to seize any remaining Dutch posses-sions, so in December 1810 a British force of the 40-gun *Cornwallis*, 38-gun *Dover* and 18-gun *Samarang* arrived off the heavily fortified island of Amboyna, in modern-day Indonesia. A *ruse de guerre* by the commander Captain Tucker, who embarked seamen and marines in boats hidden by the hulls of his ships and made to leave before launching a swift assault, captured a key Dutch battery. The island swiftly surrendered, as did other Dutch possessions. Further east at Banda Neira on 8 August the *Caroline*, captained by Christopher

Fig. 8.5. Banda Neira Silver Vase. This vase was presented to Captain Christopher Cole by Captains Foote and Kenah who fought with him at the battle of Banda Neira. Made by Makepeace and Harker in 1812, the rich decoration includes war trophies similar to those of the Roman era.

Cole, and *Samarang* launched a daring attack led by Cole. Undaunted by the Dutch guns and outnumbered by the garrison, Cole stormed Fort Belgica, taking it by surprise and sweeping through its open gates. By the morning of 9 August the island had surrendered. For his actions in the Dutch East Indies Cole was knighted in 1812 and, partly owing to his fame for the capture of Banda Neira, became a member of parliament. On the last day of August 1810 the last Dutch island in the Moluccas, Ternate, surrendered.

The final major conquest of the wars was Java, captured by a major expedition assembled at Penang comprising 11,900 troops, over half of which were Sepoys, and escorted by four British frigates and seven sloops, accompanied by eight ships from the Bombay Marine. The force arrived off Java on 4 August, with naval reinforcements arriving next day under Rear Admiral Robert Stopford, including his 74-gun flagship *Scipion*, the 64-gun *Lion*, *Akbar* of 44 guns and six frigates. The campaign was hard, costing the British around a thousand casualties, with sickness ravaging the forces more than action, but Java was finally conquered on 18 September 1811.

During the Java campaign, Captain Edward Stopford of HMS *Otter* lost his right arm serving ashore and, as compensation, was awarded a Lloyd's Patriotic Fund sword. The fund had been set up in July 1803 to provide assistance to British seamen and soldiers who were wounded while serving their country, but also made 'pecuniary awards or honourable badges of distinction for successful exertions of valour or merit'. By 1804 it had raised £174,000 to pay for the awards of a sword, or a piece of plate or cash. As a captain, Stopford received a £100 sword, the value also presented to commanders. Lieutenants and Royal Marine captains would receive a £50 sword and marine lieutenants, masters' mates and midshipmen a £30 sword. The swords were highly decorated and inscribed and housed in a mahogany case.[15]

With the capture of Île de France and the seizure of the remaining Dutch islands the war for the Indian Ocean had been won. British trade was safe and Napoleon's continental blockade and his attempts to undermine British trade by the use of raiding squadrons had been defeated. 'By the end of 1811 every colonial possession of France and her dependencies was in British hands — the most complete ascendancy ever achieved in 250 years of imperial warfare.' That success was down to the Royal Navy.[16]

CHAPTER 9

'A complete stop to all trade and intercourse by Sea'

The War of 1812

The 'War of 1812' between the United States and Britain was a maritime war, which at first appearances had its origins in tensions over trade and the impressment of American sailors. To some it was a war to redress perceived British 'interference' in the rights of United States' merchant ships at sea. Sourcing experienced seamen for the Royal Navy was a constant task and men had always been taken out of British merchantmen. Here differences between the concepts of nationality, British by birth and American by residency, created problems with pressing British nationals from American ships. Between 1800 and 1812 the American merchant fleet expanded to become the second largest in the world, filling the gap left by the British war on enemy merchantmen. With calculations in Washington that up to half of the US merchant fleet was made up of British sailors, the American reluctance to give them up is understandable. Moreover, by serving on American ships for better pay and conditions, British-born sailors were considered to be US nationals. There were Americans on board HMS *Victory* at Trafalgar, and on 18 October 1807 Collingwood found that in one part of his Mediterranean Fleet alone there were 217 Americans. All told, during the wars the Royal Navy contained around 6,500 Americans, with about 3,800 of these later released.[1]

In fact the issue was a minor one until thrust into the limelight by the *Leopard–Chesapeake* affair of June 1807. Sailors on British ships stationed off Chesapeake Bay had been deserting and joining American warships. One, the frigate USS *Chesapeake*, put to sea and on 22 July was challenged by the 50-gun *Leopard*, acting under direct orders from the station commander, Vice Admiral George Berkeley, to search American warships for deserters. On the *Chesapeake* Commodore James Barron, expecting an uninterrupted voyage to the Mediterranean, had not prepared the ship for action but still refused, whereupon *Leopard* opened fire until the badly damaged *Chesapeake* struck with three men killed and 16 wounded. Four men identified as British deserters were taken out. Not only did this add to anti-British feeling along the American seaboard but the incident gave added impetus to the War Hawks' belief that conflict with Britain was desirable and placed impressment on the political agenda. It also highlighted the fact that expansion of American shipping had not been matched by necessary investment in the naval assets to protect that trade.[2]

Given the problems over impressment, war was not inevitable and the American response, the December 1807 Embargo Act, which attempted to stop all American commerce with foreign nations, was a huge own goal, leading to 55,000 American seamen losing their jobs and Treasury receipts from duties nose-diving. This was replaced by the 1809 Non-Intercourse Act which only forbade American trade with Britain and France. But with the 1807 British Orders in Council and Napoleon's continental blockade, the fate of Denmark and Portugal had shown that in this global conflict there was simply no room for neutrals. Yet despite Washington's policies, there remained close economic links between America and Britain, particularly the British colonies in the West Indies, in the years up to 1812. Moreover, there was the American grain supply to Wellington's army in Iberia to be taken into consideration (see Chapter 7).

With the British focused on the extant war with France, American policy was very much opportunistic and expansionist, and by the summer of 1812, with Napoleon ready to crush Russia leading to a probable British defeat, American President James Madison wanted a war to fulfil grandiose American imperial dreams. The Louisiana Purchase of 1804 had opened up the west and there were still possessions held by the crumbling Spanish Empire to take advantage of, as well as diminishing British influence amongst the Native American tribes. Madison and the War Hawks believed Britain was entirely reliant upon American grain and trade. Finally there was British North America, a tempting and easy, so it was believed, prize much eyed by Washington. So while America portrayed itself as the aggrieved belligerent, in fact conflict with the British offered much opportunity.

In 1812 Britain did not want a war with America. The focus was on combating the threat of Napoleonic Europe, and London repealed the Orders in Council which forbade neutrals to trade with France and which President James Madison regarded as a *casus belli*. But it came too late; America declared war on 18 June 1812. Unfortunately for Madison he did not know the character of his own country, never mind the character of the war he was embarking upon.

Early American victories

The young US Navy could only muster 14 warships for active service, did not possess a single dock and had a small, quarrelsome but self-confident officer corps. However, they held an ace card over the Royal Navy. Undisputed masters of the sea since 1805, the Royal Navy had been busy building large numbers of cruisers to increase the pressure on France. In comparison, the US Navy had built a small number of very powerful frigates. While there were ambiguities as to how each side defined tonnage, rate and broadside, it is clear that with a continuous spar deck allowing for a full secondary battery, American frigates possessed a significant advantage in overall firepower. This was particularly evident in the famous 44-gun *Constitution*, *United States* and *President*, armed with 30 24pdrs and a battery of either 32pdr or 42pdr carronades on the spar deck. Their originator, Joshua Humphreys, thought, 'From the construction of those ships, it is expected the commanders of them will have it in their power to engage, or not, any ship they may think proper.'[3]

Captures were made by both sides in the first couple of months as the Royal Navy tried to blockade key American ports while convoying valuable British trade. On 16 July the 14-gun brig USS *Nautilus* was taken by the superior 38-gun *Shannon*; in turn on 13 August the 32-gun USS *Essex* took just eight minutes to defeat her much smaller opponent, the sloop *Alert*. Other captures were made by both sides but the defining moment of the first year of war occurred on 19 August. Captain James Dacres of HMS *Guerriere* managed to loose off three broadsides to every two that came from Captain Isaac Hull's USS *Constitution*, but it was to no avail. Outgunned in weight of shot by three to two, the 38-gun *Guerriere*, with her main armament of 30 18pdrs, was battered into submission in around 35 minutes by the 30 24pdrs and 24 32pdr carronades of the *Constitution*. Dacres lost 15 dead and 63 wounded out of a crew of 244 compared with just seven killed and seven wounded from the 463 men aboard *Constitution*. While *Guerriere* certainly had problems with her masts, which were in a poor state, it was the 50 per cent heavier American firepower which was vital. Hull's victory instantly made him a national hero and gave the American government a much needed victory.[4]

Even worse, it was not just the big frigates that were causing problems. In October the 18-gun USS *Wasp* took the 18-gun *Frolic* in a contest so hard fought and close that *Frolic* was dismasted and the *Wasp*, unable to flee, was taken by a British ship of the line two hours after the fight. *Frolic* had been convoying merchantmen, all of which escaped; her sacrifice had not been in vain. The record of the big American frigates beating inferior-gunned British frigates continued: 25 October saw the notoriously poor-sailing USS *United States* outmanoeuvre, dismast and take the *Macedonian*. Samuel Leech, a 15-year-old powder boy on the *Macedonian*, left a graphic account of the effect of American gunnery on his crew. While they 'fought like tigers',

> Grape and canister shot were pouring thorough our port-holes like leaden rain, carrying death in their trail. The large shot came against

the ship's side like iron hail, shaking her to the very keel, or passing through her timbers and scattering terrific splinters, which did a more appalling work then even their own death giving blows.

Among the horrors, Leech witnessed the ship's boys supplying powder to the guns next to him wounded, one struck by a ball in the leg, which necessitated amputation, the other having his foot amputated after his ankle was struck by a grape or canister shot. Following this Leech had to serve three or four guns himself. He was told that two Portuguese boys serving guns on the quarterdeck had been killed: one suffered appalling burns when the powder he was carrying caught fire: 'the agonized boy lifted up both hands, as if imploring relief, when a passing shot instantly cut him in two'. Leech saw one man have his hand taken off, then, almost immediately, his bowels torn out by a second shot; suffering such a mortal wound he was thrown overboard.[5]

An officer fell, struck in the chest, and later died. Guns were thrown off their carriages. The boatswain had his head 'smashed to pieces by a cannon-ball'. 'So terrible had been the work of destruction round us,' Leech recalled, 'it was termed the slaughterhouse.' 'Even a poor goat [...] did not escape the general carnage; her hind legs were shot off and poor Nan was thrown overboard.' The *United States* 'could sail without difficulty; while we were so cut up that we lay utterly helpless'. *Macedonian* lost 36 killed and 68 wounded out of a crew of 290 compared with seven killed and five wounded out of 478 on board the American frigate. The *United States*'s commander, Captain Stephen Decatur, taking advantage of the incomplete British blockade, towed his prize into New York to predictably joyous scenes. While the *Guerriere* had been taken about 400 miles south-east of Halifax, the range of the American frigates was shown by the fact that *Macedonian* was taken in the Atlantic, around 500 miles south of the Azores.[6]

Worse was to come, for the next victory took place off the Brazilian coast. The *Constitution* and sloop *Hornet* were blockading the port of Bahia where the sloop HMS *Bonne Citoyenne* had sheltered. Unsurprisingly, given that she was carrying £500,000-worth of specie, *Bonne Citoyenne* declined to come out and face the *Hornet* in a single-ship challenge – the needs of war took precedence over affairs of honour. USS *Constitution* then sailed and on 29 December engaged in a three-and-a-half-hour fight – notable for skilled seamanship on both sides – with HMS *Java*. *Java* scored an early success by shooting away the *Constitution*'s wheel and raking her opponent. Steered by the tiller, Commodore Bainbridge, now commanding the *Constitution*, in turn managed to damage *Java* aloft, severely hampering her manoeuvrability and allowing him to rake her stern. After two and a half hours of action, *Java* was at Bainbridge's mercy; he hauled off to repair, before closing to deliver a *coup de grâce*, at which point *Java* struck. Again, losses were disproportionate, with 22 killed and 102 wounded on the British side compared to 14 killed and 20 wounded in the *Constitution*. *Hornet* was driven into Bahia when the 74-gun *Montagu* turned up.

American success in all three frigate fights was, as made clear by Leech, down to the inability of the British 18pdrs to inflict damage on the sturdy American hulls, leading to *Constitution* earning the name 'Old Ironsides'. A secondary issue was that the *Guerriere* and *Macedonian*, both faced with superior opponents, tried to engage at long range and fire high to damage their opponents aloft. This failed to damage American ships sufficiently to prevent them closing, which was where the American spar deck carronades really made the difference. In return the heavier American broadsides wreaked havoc on British masts and rigging, disabling the British ships and giving the Americans freedom to manoeuvre before they closed to batter the British hulls. Given their condition before and after their captures, *Guerriere* and *Java* were destroyed. Clearly, by 1812 many ships in the Royal Navy were suffering from wear and tear, the needs of war leading to ships remaining in service when their better days were behind them. Moreover, the experiences of the American ships *Hornet* and the *Wasp* had shown that while individual success might be achieved, there were bigger beasts that roamed the seas: British ships of the line. When they could be brought to bear they tipped the balance back towards the Royal Navy. *Hornet* in fact escaped from Bahia and went on to take the

British sloop *Peacock* off Demerara on 24 February 1813, *Peacock* sinking shortly after striking.[7]

Clearly, something needed to be done. British frigates and smaller ships were not only outgunned by their opponents but now serious questions were being asked about the effectiveness of gunnery. Officers had, it appears, become complacent. On the *Peacock* more time was spent on her appearance than her gunnery — the court martial following her loss declared that there had been no gunnery practice on board for three years. This led to an Admiralty order to the British commander in American waters, Admiral Sir John Borlase Warren, to ensure gunnery practice was held regularly. In contrast to the *Peacock*, some officers on the American station, such as Captain Philip Broke of the *Shannon*, approached gunnery with much zeal. Broke made numerous modifications to his guns and gunnery methods to increase the accuracy and effectiveness of his fire.[8]

If in the early months of the war the Royal Navy had been unprepared, physically and mentally, for conflict with the United States, by 1813 it was starting to get its act together. Broke, for example, blockaded an American frigate in Boston. This was not one of the three heavies, but the 38-gun *Chesapeake*, still a formidable opponent given her 28 18pdrs and 20 32pdr carronades and commanded by the aggressive and now, perhaps, overconfident Captain James Lawrence, formerly of the *Hornet*. In fact the fight on 1 June 1813 was the closest to an equal fight so far. As Broke stood out to sea he gave precise orders to his crew: 'Don't try to dismast her. Fire into her quarter; maindeck into maindeck; quarterdeck into quarterdeck. Kill the men and the ship is yours.' As Lawrence closed in, the *Chesapeake*'s topsail yard was brought down and she luffed up, allowing the crew of the *Shannon* to do exactly what Broke had told them. During six minutes of intense gunnery *Shannon* raked her opponent with devastating accuracy. Lawrence was hit twice, famously extolling his men, 'Don't give up the ship!', as the *Chesapeake* smashed into the *Shannon*. Broke, wearing his customary top hat, led the *Shannon*'s boarders in a short and bloody mêlée. As the ships separated American morale had been shattered and, having lost most of

Fig. 9.1. Captain Philip Broke's HMS *Shannon* taking the
USS *Chesapeake* in just 11 minutes, 1 June 1813.

her officers, the *Chesapeake* struck 11 minutes after the first shot had
been fired.

Casualties were high, given the brevity of the fight. Out of 330
men on the *Shannon*, 34 were killed or mortally wounded, with
a further 49 injured, including Broke – he would recover but not
long enough to see action again. On the *Chesapeake*, 69 were dead
with 77 wounded out of 395 men. It was *Shannon*'s gunnery that had
shocked the Americans: she had scored 54 roundshot hits, of which
80–90 per cent were against the *Chesepeake*'s main deck where the
American crew were concentrated, and 306 grape or canister hits.
In return *Chesapeake* inflicted 25 roundshot hits on Broke's ship, of
which perhaps half were against *Shannon*'s gundecks, and 130 grape
or canister hits. The boarding, though bloody, was the *coup de grâce*.
Broke had shown that after a year of failure the Americans could be
beaten by better rather than heavier gunnery.[9]

In the early months of the war the Americans had managed to
get small cruising squadrons to sea, such as the *Constitution* and

Hornet that had appeared off Brazil. By 1813 the heavy frigates could not get to sea; only smaller warships slipped past the blockade and were hunted down. This was the fate of the 32-gun USS *Essex*, which had been attacking British whalers in the South Atlantic and then in the Pacific. She was caught by the *Phoebe*, which engaged the *Essex* at long range; the latter, armed solely with carronades, was unable to close and make them count.

Far more numerous than American warships were privateers, 526 of which put to sea during the conflict. While rich pickings could be had close to home during the early months of the war, once Royal Navy numbers increased, privateers had to look further afield, such as the Bay of Biscay (to Wellington's chagrin), the Baltic (causing problems for Saumarez), the lucrative East Indies and of course the busiest shipping lanes in the world, those around the British Isles. In February 1813 the Baltimore privateer *Dolphin* took two British ships in the waters off southern Spain, the convergence of Atlantic, Mediterranean and East Indies trade routes. In five privateer cruises the Salem brig *Grand Turk* took around 30 British ships while the Baltimore *Comet* took 27 in her career.

Moreover, while their potential for attacking British trade increased in range during the war, because of this need to operate farther afield, and with privateers increasing in hull size, armament and manpower, their actual numbers declined. Crucially, however, their chances of evading Royal Navy warships also diminished. In April 1813 the *Dolphin* was one of four ships taken by the British blockade of American ports. The lengths that the Royal Navy would go to in negating privateers is shown by an attack by boats from the 74-gun *Plantagenet*, the *Rota* frigate and a sloop against the *General Armstrong* in the Azores. This was a dangerous operation, for the *General Armstrong* succeeded in beating off the attack, killing 34 and wounding a further 86 out of an attacking force of 180 men. But despite this tactical failure for the Royal Navy, the *General Armstrong* was unable to escape and was burnt by her crew. The ultimate object of the attack – removing her capacity to endanger British trade – had been achieved.[10]

There were a number of reasons why the American challenge

at sea was defeated, of which improvements in British gunnery, as evidenced by Broke and by the fate of the USS *Essex*, was only one factor. Furthermore, as a stop-gap, the Admiralty had sent out orders for 18pdr frigates to avoid the three American heavies. A more long-term solution, however, was the tightening of the Royal Navy's blockade. Without a battlefleet to break the British blockade, American ships became increasingly useless, bottled up in their ports and unable to take to sea.

Blockades

While defeating the American raiding strategy was very much a defensive measure, the question remained of how Britain could defeat a power like the United States. The answer to the latter was the reason for the former: blockades. The use of the plural here is intentional, for the Royal Navy implemented two types of blockade during the war against America. The first was a naval blockade to bottle up the nascent US Navy and American privateers in port; which in turn would allow the effective implementation of a second, economic, blockade designed to ruin American trade and thereby the American economy.

Fundamentally the war in North America was directly related to the war in Europe. Napoleon's war with Russia undermined one of the foundations of American policy, namely that Britain was reliant on American grain for its campaign in Iberia. With Russia now an ally of Britain, the enormous grain and flour supplies from Northern Europe were once again available to Britain for domestic consumption and for shipping on to Iberia. The value of British Baltic trade had slumped to £2.3 million in 1811 but doubled to £5.4 million in 1812. While Napoleon's invasion of Russia might have given Madison an opportunity, not only did it free up British naval forces from the Baltic but with Russia sending 15 ships of the line to the North Sea to work with the Royal Navy, it freed up Royal Navy ships for the North American station in early 1813.[11]

The marked increase of Royal Navy warships in American waters bore fruit in 1813–14, allowing for more effective convoy escorts and for Admiral Warren to tighten the blockade. In March the Admiralty impressed upon him the need for most 'active and vigorous prosecution of the war', to place 'all the Enemy's Ports in a state of close and permanent blockade'. What they had in mind was 'a complete stop to all trade and intercourse by Sea'. On 7 August the command had consisted of 33 warships, the 74-gun *St Domingo*, the 64-gun *Africa*, the 44-gun *Acasta*, eight frigates, 13 sloops, six gunbrigs and two store ships. Clearly this was not enough to block-ade the entire American coastline.

By 26 July 1814, the entire coast from Halifax to New Orleans had been broken down into distinct commands, allowing for the blockade to be tightened and the creation of a central reserve force with the admiral commanding. This latter force comprised *Tonnant*, *Dragon*, *Ramillies* and *Royal Oak*, all 74s, three frigates, four sloops and three bomb-vessels. In addition, there was a 50-gun, six frig-ates, three brigs and three sloops on their way and expected to arrive on the station. Between Halifax and Nantucket were the 74s *Bulwark* and *Spencer*, the 50s *Leander* and *Majestic*, four frigates and 13 sloops, the workhorses of a blockade, a small 4-gun cutter, and two bomb-vessels. From Nantucket to Delaware was the 74-gun *Superb*, the 50-gun *Ventura*, three 40-gun ships, five 38-gun frigates and three sloops, plus a schooner and a further two sloops to be added to the force. Off the Chesapeake were the 74s *Albion* and *Asia*, a 40-gun ship, a frigate, four sloops and a bomb-vessel. A frigate and four sloops, with a further frigate and two sloops to be added, were stationed off Cape Hatteras. Completing the blockade were a frig-ate, a brig, three sloops and a 4-gun cutter around the Bahamas and patrolling the Gulf of Mexico. That made a total of 78 warships on station with 13 more expected. The Admiralty ensured that these ships would be led by some of the best officers available, includ-ing Rear Admiral George Cockburn and captains Robert Dudley, Thomas Hardy and John Beresford.[12]

While the ships of the line were deployed to watch over the heavy American frigates, the number of brig-rigged sloops and other small vessels deployed was crucial. Swift vessels, with a shallow draft, good sea-keeping qualities and armed with carronades to pack a punch, they were the workhorses of trade protection and blockade, roles at which the brig-rigged sloop excelled. In 1804 there were only 33 brig sloops, but with the need to enforce the blockade of Europe, then the United States, their numbers grew to 155 in 1814. They saw service in the Baltic, fighting Danish gunboats, in the Mediterranean, where they escorted convoys to Wellington's army in Iberia, and extensive service in the War of 1812. Of particular note was the 18-gun *Cruizer* class, of which 110 were eventually built, the most numerous of any class of ship in the Royal Navy during the wars.

While this aggrandizement of naval force had a defensive aspect, protecting British trade, which in turn was the lifeblood of the overall British war effort, the naval blockade provided a working control of the sea in the North American theatre, which could then be exploited by the implementation of a wider economic blockade of American ports to hit Washington in the pocket. So while events in Europe had a positive effect on Britain's ability to bring naval and economic pressure to bear, in Washington after mid-1813 American policy-makers were starting to come to the conclusion that, with their ships penned in port, further victories over isolated Royal Navy warships were becoming increasing remote and their *guerre de course* against British trade, based on warships and privateers, could be no more than an irritant to British maritime dominance.

It seems that Madison and Congress really did not understand what a maritime war with Britain might entail. As off Brest, Toulon, in the West and East Indies, the Royal Navy, thanks to its highly organized administrative structure, in-theatre bases, and its maritime supremacy, could operate with a sustained presence on the enemy's coast, blockading fleets in port and chasing them down when they escaped. It was not infallible, and the strategy off North America took a little while to be implemented effectively, but once established it had two effects. It protected British trade, for, despite the attempts of the US Navy's cruisers and privateers, British merchant tonnage had actually increased from 20,637 ships totalling 2,263,000 tonnage in 1812 to 21,449 vessels and 2,414,000 tonnage in 1814.[13]

The second effect was offensive: to strangle American trade and thereby bankrupt the American economy, which was, 'fiscally dependent on the continuation of normal trade relations with Britain, its major trading partner'. In 1807, before the Embargo Act, American imports had totalled $144,740,342, which fell to $78,788,540 in 1812 and then plummeted to $12,967,859 in the crucial year of 1814. The reason was the blockade, for when it was lifted at the conclusion of hostilities, American imports leapt back up to $85,356,680 in 1815. At the start of the war Washington received 92.3 per cent of its tax revenue from import duties. With revenues denied and increased expenditure on the war, American debt, which had been declining from $86,400,000 in 1805 to $48,000,000 in 1812 grew to $63,545,831 in 1814 and nearly double again to a whopping $119,635,831 in 1815. Again, the effect of the blockade can be seen in total American foreign trade figures which in 1812 were valued at $117,316,236, going down to $19,895,441 in 1814, and, as the peace dividend kicked in, shot up to $137,914,753 in 1815. More evidence comes from the numbers of US vessels on the global trade routes: in 1812 the tonnage of ships in foreign trade was 667,999, falling to 56,626 tons in 1814 before rising to 700,000 in 1815. Moreover, the British blockade also destroyed American coastal shipping, a vital aspect of domestic trade and supplies, and it was impossible to replace waterborne traffic with land transport. The rise of American shipping up to 1812 had been destroyed by 1814. It was the Royal Navy's blockade which allowed Britain to shape the course of the war and to dictate the outcome, by bleeding the US economy white to the point where the country was bankrupt by the end of 1814.[14]

The Great Lakes

While Britain had been winning the war against American raiders at sea and was steadily strangling American trade and revenues, there was another theatre that was crucial to the outcome of the conflict. With Washington bent on an aggressive imperial war to add British North America to US territory, defending against attacks in the north was a key element of British strategy. Given the nature of the operating environment, with just a few population centres and numerous forts, logistics would be crucial. But the region had a poor road network and the primary mode of communication and transport was the Great Lakes and rivers of the American–Canadian border. Effective use of naval power would again be critical.

When war commenced, the Great Lakes were controlled by British naval power in the form of the Provincial Marine. Based at the head of the St Lawrence, the Lake Ontario Division consisted of the 20-gun ship-corvette *Royal George*, launched in 1809, and two older vessels – the 14-gun *Earl of Moira* and the 6-gun schooner *Duke of Gloucester* – as well as the most recent addition, the 10-gun schooner *Prince Regent*. On Lake Erie were the 20-gun *Queen Charlotte* and the 6-gun *General Hunter* and a new schooner launched in June 1812, the 12-gun *Lady Prevost*, all based out of Amherstburg. The Governor-in-Chief Sir George Prevost very much envisaged that these vessels would be employed in a purely defensive role, primarily transporting troops and supplies of the army. That, as Lieutenant James Richardson noted, was what the Ontario Squadron did during 1812, managing to 'keep open the communication between the Eastern and Western divisions of the Army [...] The importance of such services in the then uninhabited state of the country, and the lack of land conveyance owing to the badness of the roads must be obvious.' [15]

Despite Prevost's intentions, on 19 July 1812 the Master and Commander Hugh Earl, in charge of the Ontario Division, staged a bombardment of the American position at Sackets Harbor, which contained the sole US ship on the lake, the *Oneida*, but to little effect. There were further small-scale skirmishes but, again, little damage was caused by either side. With the British maintaining a 'fleet in being', denying the Americans freedom to use the lakes, and the presence of British regular troops on land, two major American assaults collapsed: at Detroit on 16 August 1812 and at the Niagara river on 13 October. Clearly, if the Americans were to make headway they needed to wrest control of the lakes and rivers from the British.

Realizing that an invasion of Canada required control of the lakes, an American navy captain, Isaac Chauncey, was appointed to increase American naval strength on Lakes Ontario and Erie. Concentrating on the former, he took the conflict to the British and by winter he had, by pushing the British back into Kingston, assumed command of Lake Ontario. Alarmed, Prevost asked for assistance. In return he received from Admiral Warren three commanders to bring the Provincial Marine under naval command. Meanwhile a force was being made ready in England for service on the lakes to be commanded by Commodore James Yeo.

Along with changes in command, both sides added ships to their fleets. The Americans launched a 24-gun corvette, the *Madison*, while the British laid down a 30-gun frigate and two corvettes. Through taking prizes and hiring American merchantmen on the lakes, overall between 1812 and 1813 the Americans managed to add more vessels to their Ontario fleet than the British. This allowed them to take a more aggressive stance, using 13 ships of various sizes, from the 24-gun *Madison* to the 1-gun *Raven*, to transport and land a force which attacked York on 27 April 1813, forcing the British to withdraw. American forces sacked the town, burnt the new 30-gun frigate still under construction, seized the timbers of the *Duke of Gloucester*, which had been broken up, and looted naval stores. The British *Prince Regent* escaped to Kingston. The next American target was to be Fort George, at the mouth of the Niagara river.

While they paused to regroup, on 15 May, Yeo and 456 Royal Navy personnel arrived at Kingston, effectively abolishing the Provincial Marine and bringing its activities under Royal Navy command. By 27 May Yeo was in a position to launch his own attack: the American frigate *General Pike*, on the stocks at Sackets Harbor, was the target to distract the American invasion already under way. The newly built 22-gun *Wolfe*, 20-gun *Royal George*, 18-gun *Earl of Moira*, 12-gun *Lord Beresford* and *Sir Sidney Smith*, plus the *Black Snake*, *Glengarry* and *Quebec*, all gunboats, and the merchantman *Lady Murray* arrived off Sackets Harbor on 29 May with 800 soldiers. Despite a successful landing and with a fire started in the dockyard, Prevost ordered the troops withdrawn. It was, however, tactically unsuccessful, leading to recriminations between Prevost and Yeo, for the *General Pike* was unharmed and launched in June.[16]

It did, however, leave the Americans very wary of further attacks on their base, and Yeo used this to much wider effect, continuing to provide crucial support to British land forces which blunted the American assault on Upper Canada in 1813. Clearly, in order to get their campaign going again, the Americans would have to challenge Yeo's freedom of action and that would require a decisive naval engagement. In the ensuing naval campaigns in 1813 and 1814, both sides strived to engage on terms advantageous to them and detrimental to the enemy and, as a consequence, while there were a number of skirmishes and long-range actions, wind and weather intervened. All that Yeo had to do was keep his 'fleet in being', thereby supporting army operations ashore. This would deny the Americans freedom of the lake necessary for land operations to attack his bases and hence lead to a British victory.

In fact the decisive aspect had already shifted from action on the lake to action in the dockyards in a naval arms race that witnessed ever larger ships as each side strived for material and numerical advantage. This all culminated in April 1814 with the British laying the keel for a 102-gun first rate, the *St Lawrence*. This remarkable ship was specially designed to sail in the shallow inland waters of Lake Ontario and incorporated a number of important design features. Operating close to land required a shallow hull, and that was achievable because unlike an ocean-going ship she would not need to be provisioned for months of sea service. She was short and lacked a poop deck, yet carried more firepower than the *Victory*, and was the only freshwater ship of the line built by the Royal Navy. With construction of the *St Lawrence* under way, in the summer of 1814 Thomas Strickland, a master builder specially sent out from England by the Navy Board, arrived to oversee construction in the Kingston navy yard. Building her had been a mammoth task, and some of the necessities of her fitting out – guns, rigging and sails – had been cannibalized from warships at Quebec, giving some indication as to how important she was to British strategy by this

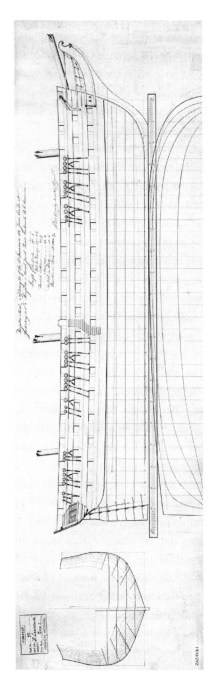

Fig. 9.2. The shallow draft of the 102-gun first rate HMS *St. Lawrence*.

time. Moreover, some supplies had to be shipped from Halifax to Montreal and Quebec and then transported on to Kingston. *St Lawrence* was launched on 10 September 1814 and took to the lake on 16 October. The Americans retreated into Sackets Harbor, giving the Royal Navy supremacy of the lake. The American response, the 130-gun *New Orleans*, was laid down in December 1814 but was still on the stocks when peace came.

On 25 December the Royal Navy's *Psyche*, a 56-gun frigate, was launched (though she was not fitted out until after the war). Cut at Chatham Dockyard from fir, then shipped across the Atlantic in what might be termed 'flat packed' form, *Psyche* was assembled at Kingston. She came with her own shipwrights and crew. This was not a new idea, for several gunboats had been sent in similar fashion during 1776, but it is a remarkable testimony to the supremacy of British naval administration which was crucial to the Royal Navy's effectiveness in successfully defending this part of Canada from American invasion. One of the reasons why the Admiralty sent out ships such as the *Psyche* was to make good the losses suffered further west on Lake Erie. There events had taken a different turn.[17]

While Chauncey and Yeo were concentrating on Lake Ontario, the British land defences around Lake Erie were in the hands of Major General Isaac Brock. He had been busy spectacularly blunting American attacks, though losing his life in the process at Queenston Heights on 13 October 1813. The American campaign on Lake Erie was kick-started in early 1813 with the arrival of Master Commandant Oliver Hazard Perry. By the end of July 1813 American forces totalled 11 vessels, with the 20-gun brigs *Lawrence* and *Niagara* of particular concern for the British. In turn, Yeo sent Commander Robert Barclay along with a small number of officers and seamen to galvanize the Royal Navy's presence on Lake Erie. Barclay arrived at Amherstburg in June 1813 and found a number of vessels in an unsatisfactory state and the 19-gun *Detroit* still on the stocks. Stores for the *Detroit* were to be shipped from Yeo, so maintaining his links with Kingston were crucial, but here Perry intervened. He used his force to prevent supplies reaching Barclay by water; instead they had to go overland. Although launched in July, the *Detroit* had to be armed with guns from the squadron owing to the blockade and the fact that her 24pdr carronades had been captured by the Americans during the sack of York.

With the majority of his crews consisting of Provincial Marine personnel or soldiers, Barclay only had around 60 Royal Navy officers and men. He was also outnumbered in terms of ships and outgunned in weight of shot. His squadron was still not ready, but Barclay understood the necessity of wresting control of the lake from Perry, and sailed to force an action. He initially found the Americans in Presque Isle Bay and, feeling unable to meet them in action, mounted a short blockade, which was curtailed by a lack of supplies. On 10 September the fleets finally clashed in a three-hour, hard-fought action. Initially the action went well for Barclay, his long-range guns on *Detroit* and *Queen Charlotte* wreaking havoc on Perry's flagship the *Lawrence*. Perry shifted his flag to the *Niagara* and bore down on the British line, now falling into some disorder due to heavy casualties amongst the squadron's officers. *Niagara* broke the line, and with most of its officers dead or wounded the entire British squadron surrendered. This effectively won the struggle for Lake Erie for the Americans but they could not turn the crushing tactical victory into a wider strategic effect.[18]

With the British focus on Lake Ontario, Lake Champlain had seen little naval activity; by 1813 there was a small flotilla of gunboats. On 2 June 1813 an ill-judged American attack by two schooners led to their capture and transfer to British service as the *Broke* and *Shannon*, named in honour of the famous frigate and her commander. With more naval personnel available, including Commander Daniel Pring appointed to command the squadron and Captain Thomas Everard of the *Wasp* who joined in with 80 officers and men, on 31 July an attack was launched. This was in line with Lieutenant Colonel John Murray's plan to use the flotilla to transport his thousand men to attack American positions on Lake Champlain, where he raided Plattsburg, seized stores, and captured several American merchant ships.

Further raids were conducted in 1813 and both sides spent the winter building new vessels. Pring was superseded by Captain

Peter Fisher, who oversaw the building of a new frigate, the 37-gun *Confiance*, launched on 25 August 1814. This was a key part of Prevost's planning, for Napoleon's abdication had freed up British troops for service in North America, 10,000 men arriving from Europe, allowing Prevost to mount an offensive into New York state. With the land part of the invasion under way on 1 September, Prevost required the British flotilla to assist and the *Confiance* was sent into action without a full complement or sufficient training. By now Fisher had been replaced by Captain George Downie who, with his flag flying in *Confiance*, ordered the squadron to sail and defeat the American squadron on the lake. On 11 September the British attacked, Downie's plan being to close with the American ships and break their line, the *Confiance* taking up a raking position between the largest American ships, *Saratoga* and *Eagle*. In light airs Downie could not reach the enemy line and, with his ships being raked as they advanced, he anchored 300 yards short and entered into a gunnery duel in which he was killed. The British gunboats failed to enter the action. After about two hours the *Confiance*, holed between 250 and 300 times between wind and water, and the 16-gun *Linnet* surrendered, as did the *Broke* and *Shannon*. It was a disaster: American gunnery had been far more accurate, inflicting 170 British casualties. Prevost, watching from the shore, felt that the Navy's failure to obtain command of the lake undermined his assault and he retreated to Canada.[19]

Washington in flames

While the British invasion of New York state had been a disaster, it was not the only army–navy operation in 1814. Between 1812 and 1813 much of the Royal Navy's attention focused on first dealing with the American naval and privateer raiders, then implementing the blockades. Not only were American warships largely confined to ports, allowing the British freedom of navigation, but American coastal defences were, apart from a few key ports such as New York, underdeveloped and largely reliant on decrepit gunboats. So while increased British warship numbers allowed the tightening of the blockades, they also provided scope for more offensive action — to take the blockade ashore through amphibious raids. Warren and Cockburn agreed that the Chesapeake Bay area offered the most scope for British activity, especially with the frigate USS *Constellation*, moored near Norfolk, proving a tempting target.

With channels sounded and buoyed, Cockburn moved three 74-gun ships of the line, *Dragon*, *Marlborough* and *Victorious*, into Hampton Roads, seized American merchantmen and prepared to mount a fireship attack on the American frigate. Locals implored Cockburn not to attack their trade and towns, giving some indication that the blockade was starting to bite. In fact the blockade 'caused an entire and complete stagnation of all commerce [...] there was now only to be heard from one end of the country to the other lamentations of individuals who were now beginning to suffer from the effects of war'. Cockburn continued his harassing campaign, taking American armed schooners, cutting out American merchantmen and burning a US army depot.[20]

The small-scale raiding was turning nasty, and Cockburn complained of sneaky attacks by local citizens on his men 'whenever they thought they could get a mischievous shot at any of our people without being seen or exposed to personal risk'. Retribution for such attacks came in the form of burning houses where shots had come from and homes that had been abandoned, the inhabitants, Cockburn thought, having fled to join the militia in the woods. When in early May he approached Fredericktown and Georgetown and was fired upon, Cockburn burnt every unoccupied house. Other places had heeded his warnings and sent delegations to assert that they would not oppose his searches for American war stores; in turn Cockburn kept his word, leaving them untouched. With Warren receiving two marine regiments as reinforcements, an attempted amphibious landing in June at Norfolk started well but, when boats became stuck on mudflats under fire, the attack was called off. The next attack, on Hampton, was more successful: troops were landed, defences destroyed and the force re-embarked. With the campaigning season winding down, Cockburn, with the Americans placing a price on his head, left for Bermuda, convinced

Fig. 9.3. Rear Admiral George Cockburn was the man who burned the White House and most of the other public buildings in Washington on 24 August 1814.

that American defences and local forces would crumble in the face of determined attack.[21]

With command of the Royal Navy in North American passing from Warren to Vice Admiral Alexander Cochrane, greater emphasis would be placed on the amphibious war in 1814. Cockburn persuaded him to send reinforcements arriving from Europe to the Chesapeake for an attack on Baltimore, Philadelphia or Washington. Weighing up the possibilities, Cockburn settled on the latter, a target that Cochrane himself had discussed in London before taking command. Also implemented was a plan to tempt slaves to flee their American masters and enrol as free men under British military command, which had some success. Nevertheless, the main effort was devoted to the attack on Washington, and Cockburn undertook nine raids in 25 days during June 1814 to divert attention from his true object. On 29 July further reinforcements from Europe arrived, the force available to Cochrane now totalling 3,700 men under the command of Sir Pulteney Malcolm. After a meeting on 14 August between Cochrane, Major General Robert Ross and Cockburn, the latter convinced his superior and the land commander that even with just 4,000 men Washington could be attacked 'for greater political effect' than Baltimore or Philadelphia.

On 19 August the most famous British expedition of the War of 1812 landed, covered by gunboats, at Benedict. Cockburn, with a flotilla of barges, boats and cutters, kept abreast of the army's advance until on 24 August an American force of 8,000 men was defeated at Bladensburg and that evening British troops were in Washington, now abandoned by American forces. After the Americans set fire to the dockyard, the British burned the Capitol, Treasury, War Office, the Arsenal and the Presidential residence. A total of $1.5 million worth of government property went up in flames: a 'great fire in the direction of Washington', one eyewitness recalled. Within 24 hours the British had gone, leaving a smouldering Washington behind them. It was more than revenge for the sack of York, it was 'an exploit which for morale effect both in America and in England has never been excelled'.[22]

An attack on Baltimore in September began with the death of Ross but was followed by the rout of American forces until the British expedition found superior numbers defending the city. It was now the Navy's turn to reduce Fort McHenry which defended Baltimore harbour; this could not be done – the city was out of reach. Often seen as a defeat, one which provided the American nation with their national anthem, the raid had led to the Americans burning shipping, stores and buildings. This had an impact, bringing the war directly ashore and influencing the American delegation

Fig. 9.4. Sword presented to Captain John Richard Lumley of the 38-gun frigate *Pomone* for his part in the capture of the USS *President*.

discussing peace at Ghent. Those discussions culminated in the 24 December Treaty of Ghent which brought an end to the war, though it was not ratified until February 1815. Territorially and diplomatically it was a return to the status quo of 1812 and thus represented the achievement of British war aims. Britain had won and the reason was that 'Unlike the United States, Britain had the means to protect its foreign trade, which in turn provided the wealth which could be efficiently taxed and borrowed to finance wars to successful conclusions, both in Europe and in North America.'

With their attack on Canada blunted, their navy bottled up in port and their economy bankrupt, the failed British attack on New Orleans on 8 January 1815, before news of Ghent arrived, provided Madison with a tactical victory out of which a wider 'victory' narrative could be constructed. Events of 15 January 1815 were, perhaps, more reflective of the true course of the war when the USS *President* was taken by the frigate *Endymion*, with a little assistance from the *Pomone* and *Tenedos*.[23]

'That will do [...] Fire, my fine fellows'

Algiers, 1816

With Napoleon exiled to Elba and Europe at peace, the Treaty of Ghent marked the formal end of hostilities between Britain and America, actual hostilities ceasing with the American ratification on 18 February 1815. There was, of course, one further act to play out: Napoleon's escape from Elba, return to France and defeat at Waterloo on 18 June. There were a few clashes between Royal Navy and French ships but the Navy was to play a highly public role in Napoleon's ultimate fate, as noted in the Introduction, when on 15 July 1815, after a failed attempt to sail for America, he gave himself up to *Bellerophon* and Captain Frederick Lewis Maitland. *Bellerophon* first went to Torbay, then anchored in Plymouth Sound where the deposed emperor became the number one attraction for sightseers. St Helena was selected for Napoleon's internment, and he was transferred to the *Northumberland*, under the command of Sir George Cockburn, for the journey.

There was one further role for the Royal Navy during the Napoleonic Wars. The slave trade, but not slavery itself, had been abolished in the British Empire in 1807. During the wars there had been many instances of sailors of all nationalities being seized by North African states and sold into slavery. With the war now fought and won by Britain, something had to be done to free Christian slaves held by the Dey of Algiers. The problem for the Royal Navy was finding sailors who, after many years of conflict, were unwilling to risk their lives again in time of peace. They wanted to be paid and go home. The commander of the force destined for Algiers, Sir Edward Pellew, now Baron Exmouth, found his flagship, the 100-gun *Queen Charlotte*, short of 200 men. Impressment had been abolished, so a bounty of an extra two months' pay was offered up for volunteers.

Exmouth sailed from Portsmouth on 24 July 1816, put into Gibraltar on 14 August and arrived off Algiers on the 27th of the month. With his flagship were four other ships of the line, the 98-gun *Impregnable*, and the 74-gun *Superb*, *Minden* and *Albion*, ten frigates, four sloops, four bomb-vessels and eight ships' boats equipped with Congreve's rockets. The fleet was to sail into the confined waters of Algiers harbour, nullify the formidable land defences and destroy the Algerine fleet of nine frigates and 36 gunboats in the harbour. With steely nerve, *Queen Charlotte* anchored 80 yards from the head of the mole. Exmouth had clearly been inspired by Nelson's tactics at Copenhagen and ordered his fleet to anchor by the stern to keep their fire concentrated on specific targets, in *Queen Charlotte*'s case, the heavily defended mole. Exmouth would not fire the first shot, nor was the Dey willing to attack until the British ships were close in where they would be vulnerable to swarms of flotilla craft which would board and overpower the British sailors. Lack of discipline led to a gun firing from the town, at which point Exmouth declared, 'That will do [...] Fire, my fine fellows', and his fleet opened up.

Also, in a nod to Nelson, the ships following the flagship were to pass ahead and anchor, bringing to bear their broadsides. But, as in 1801, the plan went awry. The three 74s anchored short of their positions while the *Impregnable* anchored about 450 yards out and started an uneven duel with the land batteries which kept up a telling fire, inflicting more than 200 casualties on her crew. Instead it fell to the smaller vessels to support their commander, particularly the 50-gun *Leander* and the frigate *Severn*. On board the latter 'even British women served at the same guns with their husbands' while the bomb-vessels and rocket boats rained fiery death upon defenders. Two hours into the action, the defenders' fire started to slacken

Fig. E.1.Presentation sword of Sir Edward Pellew, Lord Exmouth, for his action against the Dey of Algiers, 27 August 1816, with inset showing the *Queen Charlotte* bombarding the mole.

and a fire from the mole spread to the Algerine fleet. By dusk, the town was ablaze and at around 23:00 Exmouth withdrew his ships. *Queen Charlotte*'s crew had sustained 139 casualties.

The next day Algiers was a scene of hellish destruction, blackened and smouldering, 'shattered, and crumbled to ruins'. The Dey, clearly defeated, relented, agreeing to give up enslaved Christians, and over the course of the next few weeks released 1,211 slaves. Their freedom had cost, in total, the lives of 141 British sailors and 742 wounded, many of whom would die, increasing the initial death toll. That was a casualty rate of 16 per cent, far in excess of the Nile (11 per cent), Copenhagen (12.5 per cent) and Trafalgar (9 per cent).

The great wars with France had been over for more than a year and Britain, through the Royal Navy, was keen to use her maritime supremacy as a force for good – to build a better world than had existed before. As *Albion*'s Captain John Coode poignantly wrote: 'We did not combat for kings or governments, but for our suffering fellow creatures.'[1]

'Lords of the sea'

In the course of 22 years of conflict the Royal Navy fought and won six major battlefleet actions (all between 1794 and 1805), fought a dozen or so squadron-sized actions, numerous smaller or single-ship actions, had cut out enemy vessels in boat actions, convoyed thousands of British merchant ships, attacked enemy commerce, implemented blockades of enemy ports, facilitated at least 68 major amphibious assaults, hauled guns, supplies and ammunition ashore and provided boots on the ground. The Royal Navy lost around 6,500 lives in combat, 13,000 men to shipwreck and fire, and somewhere between 70,000 and 80,000 men to sickness, disease, accidents on board and natural wastage. Accidental loss accounted for 101 Royal Navy warships during the wars.[1]

With regard to the naval situation, in 1815 the Royal Navy simply had no rival. In that year there were 884 Royal Navy warships, though some were old and would soon be decommissioned as part of the peace dividend. Translating that into tonnage (warships above 500 tons), the Royal Navy possessed 609,300 tons, more than the rest of the world's warship tonnage added together. Between 1793 and 1815 the Royal Navy had lost 166 warships to enemy action but in return had captured or destroyed 712 French, 196 Spanish, 172 Dutch, 85 Danish, 17 American, 15 Turkish and four Russian, in total 1,201 enemy warships. Dundas's strategy of dealing a death blow to enemy naval power had been realized by fleet battle and blockade.[2]

As Dundas intended, winning the naval war provided security in home waters, allowing British trade access to the world's markets and the Royal Navy the means to support trade and diplomacy in the Baltic, the Mediterranean and overseas. So not only were naval rivals destroyed but British commercial rivals as well. In 1793 official British imports were valued at £19.3 million while exports and re-exports totalled £20.4 million. By 1814 those figures had grown to £80.8 million and £70.3 million. Trade with the British West Indies doubled between 1793 and 1814, and particularly noteworthy was the new Latin American market during the crucial 1807–12 period. Attacks on British shipping had led to the loss of just over 2 per cent of British merchant ships during the wars. Although isolated incidents caused alarm, there is no greater testimony to the failure of Britain's enemies to mount a sustained attack than the actual growth of the British merchant fleet, which had expanded to become the world's carrier of choice, as Canning had intended. In 1803 there were 18,068 ships registered of 1,986,000 tons and that had grown to 21,869 ships of 2,478,000 tons in 1815. British dominance of global shipping in the nineteenth century to the point where she would possess more registered shipping than the rest of the world combined, was founded on the head start given by the Royal Navy's activities during 1793–1815.[3]

Britain handed back most of her colonial conquests in 1815 but, as the carrier of global trade, it was crucial that she retain the strategically vital nodes in the global trade network. These included existing possessions such as Gibraltar, but also Malta, the Cape of Good Hope, Ceylon and Mauritius – advance bases to protect global trade routes. The great British maritime theorist Sir Julian Corbett summed this up rather well:

> the result of our long war experience had been rather to enhance than diminish the strategic importance of such naval positions. The men who knew what naval war was were dominated by the idea that though battles might place in our hands the command of the sea, the exercise of that command was impossible, without advance bases rightly distributed.[4]

So by 1815 the British Empire was not a territorial empire but a maritime trading empire based on free access to global trade routes,

Fig. C.1. 'Nappy in tow' by Cruickshank, 24 August 1803. With John Bull brandishing a club and threatening to hang Napoleon, a country magistrate pronounces sentence on Napoleon's failure to mount an effective challenge to British maritime supremacy.

guaranteed by strategic positions and the Royal Navy. As Nicholas Rodger has concluded: 'Trade, not territory, was the key to Britain's prosperity: seaborne trade secured by naval power.'[5]

But we must not ignore the key British war aim: an independent Low Countries. In 1813 Castlereagh wrote that to leave Antwerp in the hands of the French 'is little short of imposing upon Great Britain the charge of a perpetual war establishment'. Yet it took victory at the battle of Waterloo, fought on the road to Antwerp, to give Britain a greater voice at the Congress of Vienna to shape the post-war European situation to her benefit, primarily the creation of the United Kingdom of the Netherlands. But crucial here was Britain's economic position which, despite spiralling war costs, allowed her to bankroll the alliances of 1814 and 1815 to decisively defeat Napoleonic France. Britain sent £60 million in total to her allies during the wars, just over £10 million in 1814 and £8,649,725 in 1815. Crucial in this latter figure was the £2 million to Russia and the £2,156,513 to Prussia: it was British money that kept Blücher's army in the field, ready to appear at Waterloo in timely fashion.[6]

Britain could only manage this level of overall expenditure by preserving and enhancing her maritime security. There were, of course, limits to British seapower, as shown in the Baltic and at the Dardanelles for instance. But what was crucial was the sustained campaign to destroy enemy naval power which allowed Britain to protect her overseas trade and colonies and attack those of her enemies. That was the situation up to 1805. After Trafalgar, when faced with Napoleon's economic warfare and attempts to rebuild his naval forces, British efforts were designed to deny her enemies naval assets while expanding into untapped markets. This provided increased revenue through higher and wider taxation and expanded and increased duties on overseas commerce, thereby providing a fiscal stimulus to the British economy. It also paid for the expansion of the Royal Navy to protect such investments and the financing of allies to help achieve British aims in Europe. So after 1805 British strategy was directed towards achieving a peace that would not only bring the war against Napoleonic France to a close but would shape the post-war world in a manner that was most beneficial to British interests. The role of the Royal Navy was vital, and, given the importance of events of 1815, perhaps the final word is best left to the Prussian Field Marshal August Graf Niedhardt von Gneisenau, Blücher's chief of staff, who wrote of Britain after the battle of Waterloo: 'they are the Lords of the sea, and neither in this dominion nor in world trade have they any rivals left to fear'.[7]

Notes

Preface. 'The ever to be lamented death of Vice Admiral Lord Viscount Nelson'

1. Collingwood to Marsden, 22 October 1805, G.L.N. Collingwood (ed.), *A Selection from the Public and Private Correspondence of Vice-Admiral Lord Collingwood* (London: James Ridgway, 1829), pp. 119–23; A. Lambert, *Nelson: Britannia's God of War* (London: Faber and Faber, 2004), p. 311. See also S. Willis, *In the Hour of Victory: The Royal Navy at War in the Age of Nelson* (London: Atlantic Books, 2013), pp. 257–60.
2. Log of HMS *Victory*, 22 October 1805, TNA ADM 51/4514.

Introduction. 'Wherever there is water to float a ship, we are sure to find you in our way'

1. D. Cordingly, *Billy Ruffian: The Bellerophon and the Downfall of Napoleon: The Biography of a Ship of the Line, 1782–1836* (London: Bloomsbury Publishing, 2004), p. 249; A Lambert, 'Nelson, Trafalgar and the Meaning of Victory', *History Today*, vol. 54, issue 11 (2004).
2. C.D. Hall, *British Strategy in the Napoleonic War, 1803–15* (Manchester: MUP, 1992), pp. 83–5; C. Esdaile, *Napoleon's Wars: An International History, 1803–1815* (London: Allen Lane, 2008), p. 77; J.W. Fortescue, *A History of The British Army*, 13 vols (London: Macmillan, 1899–1930), vol. 4, part 1, p. 74; M. Howard, *The Causes of Wars and Other Essays* (London: Temple Smith, 1983), p. 179.
3. T. Blanning, *The Pursuit of Glory: Europe 1648–1815* (London: Penguin Books, 2007), p. 105; C. Emsley, *The Longman Companion to Napoleonic Europe* (London: Longman, 1993), p. 132.
4. P. Mackesy, *The War in the Mediterranean, 1803–1810* (Cambridge, MA: Harvard University Press, 1957), p. ix; M. Duffy, 'World-Wide War and British Expansion, 1793–1815', in P.J. Marshall (ed.), *The Oxford History of the British Empire: Volume Two, The Eighteenth Century* (Oxford: OUP, 2001), pp. 190–1; R. Muir, *Britain and the Defeat of Napoleon,*

1807–1815 (New Haven and London: Yale University Press, 1996), p. 191.

5. P. Schroeder, *The Transformation of European Politics, 1763–1848* (Oxford: Clarendon Press, 1994), p. 298; Duffy, 'World-Wide War', pp. 184–207; J.S. Corbett, 'Napoleon and the British Navy after Trafalgar', *Quarterly Review* (1922), pp. 243–43.

6. R. Morriss (ed.), *The Channel Fleet and the Blockade of Brest, 1793–1801* (Navy Records Society, no. 141, 2001), pp. 1–6; M. Duffy, 'The establishment of the Western Squadron as the linchpin of British Naval Strategy', in M. Duffy (ed.), *Parameters of British Naval Power 1650–1850* (Exeter: EUP, 1992), pp. 60–81.

7. J.S. Corbett, *Some Principles of Maritime Strategy* (London: Brassey's, 1988), p. 9.

8. J. Black, *Britain as a Military Power, 1688–1815* (London: Routledge, 1999), p. 221.

Chapter 1. 'Never was a more hard fought action in the Seas': Home Waters, 1793–1802

1. Auckland to Grenville, 15 February 1793, 28 February 1793, *Historical Manuscripts Commission Reports on the Manuscripts of J. B. Fortescue Preserved at Dropmore, 1892–1927* (London: HMSO, 1912), vol. 2, pp. 379–80, 381–2; W. James, *The Naval History of Great Britain from the Declaration of War by France in 1793 to the Accession of George IV*, 6 vols (London: Macmillan, 1837), vol. 1, p. 89; Fortescue, *A History of The British Army*, vol. 4, part 1, pp. 66, 112.

2. List of Storeships sent with Ordnance and Stores to Flanders. 4 Aug.–18 Sept. 1793, TNA FO 95/5/3 Folio 289, Buckingham to Grenville, 2 September 1793, 13 September 1793, *Dropmore*, 2, pp. 420, 423.

3. Fortescue, *British Army*, vol. 4, p. 125; Dundas to Grenville, 12 October 1793, *Dropmore*, vol. 2, p. 444; James, *Naval History*, vol. 1, p. 90; Murray to Popham, 9 November 1793, NMM ADM 359/13/191.

4. H. Popham, *A Damned Cunning Fellow: The Eventful Life of Rear-Admiral Sir Home Popham 1762–1820* (Tywardreath: The Old Ferry Press, 1991), pp. 44–6; Report by Philip Stephens, 28 December 1793, NMM ADM 359/13/212.

5. P.H. Stanhope *Notes of Conversations with the Duke of Wellington, 1831–1851* (London, 1938), p. 182; Popham, *A Damned Cunning Fellow*, pp. 46–52.

6. *Ibid.*, pp. 48–52.

7. Morriss (ed.), *The Channel Fleet*, p. 3.

8. Morriss (ed.), *The Channel Fleet*, p. 3; see R. Gardiner, *Fleet Battle and Blockade: The French Revolutionary War, 1793–1797* (London: Chatham Publishing, 1996), p. 14.

9. R. Harding, 'Sir Charles Henry Knowles', in R. Harding and P. Le Fevre (eds), *British Admirals of the Napoleonic Wars* (London: Chatham Publishing, 2005) p. 129.

10. Admiralty to Howe, 17 April 1794, TNA ADM 1/1347.

11. D. King (ed.), *Every Man Will Do his Duty: An Anthology of First-Hand Accounts from the Age of Nelson* (London: Conway, 1997), pp. 22–4; Willis, *Hour of Victory*, pp. 74–5.

12. Willis, *Hour of Victory*, pp. 75–6.

13. M. Duffy and R. Morriss, *The Glorious First of June, 1794: A Naval Battle and its Aftermath* (Exeter: UEP, 2001), p. 5.

14. Morriss, *The Channel Fleet*, pp. 26–9.

15. M. Rae, 'Sir Edward Pellew', in Harding and Le Fevre (eds), *British Admirals of the Napoleonic Wars*, pp. 278–9; S. Taylor, *Commander: The Life and Exploits of Britain's Greatest Frigate Captain* (London: Faber and Faber, 2012), chapter 4; N.A.M. Rodger, *The Command of the Ocean: A Naval History of Britain, 1649–1815* (London: Penguin, 2004), p. 433; Gardiner, *Fleet Battle and Blockade*, pp. 51–5; Powlett to Colpoys, 14 April 1795, Smith to Spencer, 21 July 1795; Morriss, *The Channel Fleet*, pp. 59–60, 96–7.

16. Spencer to Bridport, 5 December 1796, Morriss, *The Channel Fleet*, p. 159.

17. Rodger, *The Command of the Ocean*, p. 437.

18. Morriss, *The Channel Fleet*, p. 164.

19. Gardiner, *Fleet Battle and Blockade*, pp. 158–9; T. Grocott, *Shipwrecks of the Revolutionary & Napoleonic Eras* (London: Chatham Publishing, 1997), p. 47.

20. Willis, *Hour of Victory*, p. 125.

21. *Ibid.*, pp. 130–1.

22. Popham, *A Damned Cunning Fellow*, ch. 6.

23. D.W. Mitchell, *A History of Russian and Soviet Sea Power* (London: Macmillan, 1974), p. 105; R. Gardiner, *Nelson against Napoleon: From the Nile to Copenhagen, 1798–1801* (London: Chatham Publishing, 1997), pp. 120–3.

24. Morriss, *The Channel Fleet*, chs 10 and 11.

25. J. Davey, *The Transformation of British Naval Strategy: Seapower and Supply in Northern Europe, 1808–1812* (Woodbridge: Boydell Press, 2012), pp. 20, 28; Hall, *British Strategy in the Napoleonic War*, p. 89.

26. Mitchell, *Russian and Soviet Sea Power*, p. 111.

27. S. Howarth, *Battle of Copenhagen, 1801: 200 Years* (Shelton: The 1805 Club, 2003), p. 15.

28. N. Tracy, *Nelson's Battles* (London: Chatham Publishing, 1996), pp. 141–4.

29. O. Feldbaek, 'The Battle of the King's Deep, 2 April 1801: The Danish Perspective', in Howarth, *Battle of Copenhagen*, p. 37.

30. C. White, 'The View from Nelson's Quarterdeck', in Howarth, *Battle of Copenhagen*, p. 53.

31. Willis, *Hour of Victory*, p. 238; Feldbaek, *Copenhagen*, p. 153.

32. Willis, *Hour of Victory*, pp. 235–8.

33. Mitchell, *Russian and Soviet Sea Power*, pp. 112–13.

Chapter 2. 'Nelson's Patent Bridge for Boarding First Rates': The Mediterranean, 1793–1802

1.   Rodger, *The Command of the Ocean*, p. 427.

2.   Lord Russell, *Knight of the Sword: The Life and Letters of Admiral Sir William Sidney Smith* (London: Victor Gollancz Ltd, 1964), pp. 30–1.

3.   James, *Naval History*, vol. 1, pp. 69–75; Gardiner, *Fleet Battle and Blockade*, pp. 94–5.

4.   Russell, *Knight of the Sword*, pp. 32–7; James, *Naval History*, vol. 1, pp. 76–9.

5.   James, *Naval History*, vol. 1, pp. 80–3. Rodger, *The Command of the Ocean*, p. 427.

6.   Hood to Dundas, 22 February 1794; *The London Gazette*, 15 March 1794.

7.   Nelson to Frances, 20 May 1794, N.H. Nicolas (ed.), *The Dispatches and Letters of Vice Admiral Lord Viscount Nelson*, 7 vols (London: Chatham Publishing, 1997), vol. 1, p. 397.

8.   Nelson to Frances, 27 June 1794; Nelson to Hood, 12 July 1794; Nelson to Hood, 20 July 1794, in Nicolas (ed.), *The Dispatches and Letters of Vice Admiral Lord Viscount Nelson*, vol. 1, pp. 415, 432–3, 448–9; P. Goodwin, *Nelson's Ships: A Comprehensive History of the Vessels in which He Served* (London: Conway, 2002), p. 121; Gardiner, *Fleet Battle and Blockade*, p. 112.

9.   Rodger, *The Command of the Ocean*, p. 433; A. Lambert, 'William, Lord Hotham', in Harding and Le Fevre (eds), *British Admirals of the Napoleonic Wars*, pp. 26–9.

10. Lambert, 'Hotham', pp. 32–3, 37; R. Knight, *The Pursuit of Victory: The Life and Achievement of Horatio Nelson* (London: Penguin, 2006), p. 177; Nelson to Frances, 1 April 1795, in Nicolas (ed.), *The Dispatches and Letters of Vice Admiral Lord Viscount Nelson*, vol. 2, pp. 27–9; Rodger, *The Command of the Ocean*, pp. 433–4. James, *Naval History*, vol. 1, pp. 290–2.

11. Nelson to his brother, 29 July 1795; Nelson to Hotham, 27 August 1795, in Nicolas (ed.), *The Dispatches and Letters of Vice Admiral Lord Viscount Nelson*, vol. 2, pp. 63–4, 73–4.

12. Lambert, 'Hotham', pp. 42–3.

13. Spencer to Dundas, 31 October 1796, in J.S. Corbett (ed.), *The Private Papers of George, Second Earl Spencer, First Lord of the Admiralty, 1794–1801*, 4 vols (London: Navy Records Society, 1913–1924), vol. 1, pp. 323, 325, 327–8.

14. Spencer to Jervis, 10 December 1796, in Corbett (ed.), *Spencer Papers*, vol. 2, p. 76; Jervis to Admiralty, 2 December 1796; Jervis to Nepean, 2 December 1796, TNA ADM 1/395; Nelson to de Burgh, 29 December 1796, 30 December 1796, in Nicolas (ed.), *The Dispatches and Letters of Vice Admiral Lord Viscount Nelson*, vol. 2, pp. 322–4; James, *Naval History*, vol. 1, p. 314; B. Lavery (ed.), *Shipboard Life and Organisation, 1731–1815* (Navy Records Society, no. 138, 1998), p. 590. For the victualling efforts see M. Robson, '"A considerable portion of the defence of the Empire": Lisbon and victualling the Royal Navy during the French Revolutionary War, 1793–1802', *Historical Research* (forthcoming, summer 2014).

15. James, *Naval History*, vol. 1, p. 318; Goodwin, *Nelson's Ships*, p. 245; Jervis to Nepean, 22 December 1796, TNA ADM 1/395; Jervis to Spencer, 29 December 1796, 30 December 1796, in 1796, in Corbett (ed.), *Spencer Papers*, vol. 2, pp. 82–5; W. James, *Old Oak: The Life of John Jervis, Earl of St. Vincent* (London: Longmans Green, 1950), p. 88.

16. Rodger, *The Command of the Ocean*, p. 439.

17. J.S. Tucker, *Memoirs of Admiral the Right Hon The Earl of St Vincent*, 2 vols (London: Richard Bentley, 1844), vol. 1, p. 255.

18. Gardiner, *Fleet Battle and Blockade*, pp. 89–90.

19. Nicolas (ed.), *The Dispatches and Letters of Vice Admiral Lord Viscount Nelson*, vol. 2, pp. 344–7.

20. Willis, *Hour of Victory*, pp. 104–5.

21. Knight, *Pursuit of Victory*, pp. 228–30.

22. Rodger, *The Command of the Ocean*, p. 451; James, *Old Oak*, p. 115.

23. Knight, *Pursuit of Victory*, pp. 244–6.

24. *Ibid.*, p. 252.

25. St Vincent to Spencer, 10 January 1798; Spencer to St Vincent, 29 April 1798, in Corbett (ed.), *Spencer Papers*, vol. 2, pp. 429–30, 438.

26. B. Lavery, *Nelson and the Nile: The Naval War against Bonaparte 1798* (London: Chatham Publishing, 1998), ch. 4.

27. St Vincent to Spencer, 19 May 1798, in Corbett (ed.), *Spencer Papers*, vol. 2, pp. 446–7; Willis, *Hour of Victory*, p. 165; Lavery, *Nelson and the Nile*, ch. 8.

28. Tracy, *Nelson's Battles*, pp. 109–10; Lavery, *Nelson and the Nile*, ch. 10.

29. Knight, *Pursuit of Victory*, p. 286; Nelson to Howe, 8 January 1799, in Nicolas (ed.), *The Dispatches and Letters of Vice Admiral Lord Viscount Nelson*,

vol. 3, p. 230

30. Lavery, *Nelson and the Nile*, p. 170.

31. Knight, *Pursuit of Victory*, pp. 290–2.

32. Gardiner, *Nelson against Napoleon*, pp. 36–9.

33. Knight, *Pursuit of Victory*, ch. 19.

34. Russell, *Knight of the Sword*, ch. 5.

35. James, *Naval History*, vol. 2, pp. 283–6.

36. Knight, *Pursuit of Victory*, chs. 19, 20.

37. *Ibid.*, p. 336.

38. Gardiner, *Nelson against Napoleon*, pp. 88–93.

39. Mackesy, *British Victory*, p. 24.

40. Mackesy, *British Victory*, passim; Gardiner, *Nelson against Napoleon*, pp. 78–84.

41. Victualling Board Letters to Army, 15 March 1801, TNA ADM 109/104.

Chapter 3. 'The first point to make perfectly certain': The Global War, 1793–1802

1. P. Deane and W.A. Cole, *British Economic Growth, 1688–1959: Trends and Structure* (Cambridge: CUP, 1962), p. 34. Monetary figures are from M. Duffy, *Soldiers, Sugar and Seapower: The British Expeditions to the West Indies and the War Against Revolutionary France* (Oxford: Clarendon Press, 1987), pp. 7, 17, 18.

2. Duffy, 'World-Wide War, p. 187; Duffy, *Soldiers, Sugar and Seapower*, p. 7.

3. Duffy, 'World-Wide War', p. 186; J. Ehrman, *The Younger Pitt, Volume Two: The Reluctant Transition* (London: Constable, 1983), pp. 262–4; Schroeder, *Transformation of European Politics*, pp. 118, 127; Duffy, *Soldiers, Sugar and Seapower*, p. 5.

4. Duffy, 'World-Wide War', pp. 186–7; Ehrman, *The Younger Pitt, Volume Two: Reluctant Transition*, pp. 262–4; Schroeder, *Transformation of European Politics*, pp. 118, 127; Black, *Britain as a Military Power*, pp. 241–3.

5. James, *Naval History*, vol. 1, pp. 114–16; B. Collins, *War and Empire: The Expansion of Britain, 1790–1830: The Projection of British Power, 1775–1830* (London: Longman, 2010), pp. 91–2.

6. James, *Naval History*, vol. 1, pp. 114–16.

7. Duffy, *Soldiers, Sugar and Seapower*, pp. 41–52.

8. M. Duffy, '"Science and Labour": The Naval Contribution to Operations ashore in the Great Wars with France, 1793–1815', in P. Hore (ed.), *Seapower Ashore, 200 Years of Royal Navy Operations on Land* (London: Chatham Publishing, 2001), p. 43, Duffy, *Soldiers, Sugar and Seapower*, ch. 3.

9. *Ibid.*

10. *Ibid.*, pp. 59–88.

11. Fortescue, *A History of The British Army*, vol. 4, part 1, pp. 425–38.

12. R. Morriss, *The Foundations of British Maritime Ascendancy: Resources, Logistics and the State, 1755–1815* (Cambridge: CUP, 2010), pp. 335–48; Collins, *War and Empire*, p. 91.

13. Morriss, *Foundations of British Maritime Ascendancy*, p. 341.

14. W.S. Hathaway (ed.), *The Speeches of the Right Honourable William Pitt in the House of Commons*, 4 vols (London: Longman, 1806), vol. 2, p. 429.

15. Duffy, *Soldiers, Sugar and Seapower*, ch. 12.

16. *Ibid.*, p. 291; J. Ehrman, *The Younger Pitt, Volume Three: The Consuming Struggle* (London: Constable, 1997), pp. 424–5.

17. Gardiner, *Nelson against Napoleon*, pp. 144–5.

18. Fortescue, *British Army*, vol. 4, part 1, pp. 384–5, 565. Rodger, *The Command of the Ocean*, p. 436.

19. Fortescue, *British Army*, vol. 4, part 1, p. 325; Esdaile, *Napoleon's Wars*, p. 156; Duffy, 'World-Wide War', pp. 188–9; Schroeder, *Transformation of European Politics*, p. 127.

20. Morriss, *Foundations of British Maritime Ascendancy*, p. 84; Duffy, *Soldiers, Sugar and Seapower*, p. 379.

21. James, *Naval History*, vol. 1, pp. 118–20.

22. C. Wilkinson, 'Peter Rainier', in Harding and Le Fevre, *British Admirals of the Napoleonic Wars*, pp. 95–7.

23. Morriss, *Foundations of British Maritime Ascendancy*, p. 84; Wilkinson, 'Rainier', *passim*.

24. Wilkinson, 'Rainier', p. 104.

25. Rodger, *The Command of the Ocean*, p. 436; Baring to Dundas, 4 January 1795, in W.G. Perrin, *The Letters and Papers of Admiral Viscount Keith*, Navy Records Society, vol. 62 (1926), vol. 1, pp. 209–10.

26. James, *Naval History*, vol. 1, pp. 300–2; Collins, *War and Empire*, pp. 100–1; Perrin, *Keith Papers*, vol. 1, p. 344.

27. Gardiner, *Nelson against Napoleon*, p. 161.

28. Wilkinson, 'Rainier', pp. 106–9.

29. Popham, *A Damned Cunning Fellow*, ch. 9.

30. Gardiner, *Nelson against Napoleon*, p. 12.

31. Morriss, *Foundations of British Maritime Ascendancy*, pp. 132, 227; Gardiner, *Nelson against Napoleon*, p. 12.

32. Morriss, *Foundations of British Maritime Ascendancy*, pp. 87, 97–8; Gardiner, *Nelson against Napoleon*, p. 12.

33. Rodger, *The Command of the Ocean*, p. 477; Morriss, *Foundations of British Maritime Ascendancy*, pp. 176–7.

34. Morriss, *Foundations of British Maritime Ascendancy*, pp. 154–5.

Chapter 4. 'I do not say they cannot come, I merely say they cannot come by sea': The Invasion Threat, 1802–05

1. R. Morriss, *Cockburn and the British Navy in Transition: Admiral Sir George Cockburn 1772–1853* (Exeter: EUP, 1997), pp. 53–7.

2. R. Woodman, *The Victory of Seapower: Winning the Napoleonic War, 1806–1814* (London: Chatham Publishing, 1998), pp. 14–15.

3. A. Schom, *Trafalgar: Countdown to Battle 1803–1805* (London: Michael Joseph Ltd, 1990), p. 77.

4. A.T. Mahan, *The Influence of Seapower upon the French Revolution and Empire, 1793–1812*, 2 vols (London: Sampson Low and Co., 1892), vol. 2, pp. 116–17.

5. *Ibid.*, pp. 131–3; M. Robson, *The Battle of Trafalgar* (London: Conway, 2005), pp. 11–23.

6. Schom, *Trafalgar*, p. 60; B. Lavery, *Nelson's Fleet at Trafalgar* (London: NMM, 2004), p. 39.

7. R. Gardiner, *The Campaign of Trafalgar, 1803–1805* (London: Chatham Publishing, 1997), pp. 69–70; Mahan, *The Influence of Seapower*, vol. 2, p. 119; B. Lavery, *We Shall Fight on the Beaches: Defying Napoleon and Hitler, 1805 and 1940* (London: Conway, 2009), ch. 8.

8. Pellew's Speech, 15 March 1804, in H.W. Hodges and E.A. Hughes (eds), *Select Naval Documents* (Cambridge: CUP, 1936), pp. 210–11; R. Andidora, *Iron Admirals: Naval Leadership in the Twentieth Century* (Westport, CT: Greenwood Press, 2000), p. 4; Mahan, *The Influence of Seapower*, vol. 2, p. 118.

9. N. Tracy (ed.), *The Naval Chronicle: The Contemporary Record of the Royal Navy at War* (London: Chatham Publishing, 1999), vol. 3, pp. 59–61. See also Popham, *A Damned Cunning Fellow*, pp. 117–19.

10. J. Robb-Webb, 'Corbett and the Campaign of Trafalgar', *Defence Studies*, vol. 8, no.2 (June 2008), p. 165.

11. Nelson to the Lord Mayor, 1 August 1804, in Nicolas (ed.), *The Dispatches and Letters of Vice Admiral Lord Viscount Nelson*, vol. 6, pp. 124–5; Nelson to Elliot and Nelson to Acton, 30 January 1804, in Nicolas (ed.), *The Dispatches and Letters of Vice Admiral Lord Viscount Nelson*, vol. 5, pp. 395–6.

12. Nelson to Sidmouth, 11 May 1805, in Nicolas (ed.), *The Dispatches and Letters of Vice Admiral Lord Viscount Nelson*, vol. 6, p. 436.

13. Collingwood to Carlyle, 2 July 1805, in E. Hughes (ed.), *The Private Correspondence of Admiral Lord Collingwood* (Navy Records Society, no. 98, 1956–57), p. 159; Nelson to Davison, 7 May 1805; Nelson to Simon Taylor, 10 June 1805, in Nicolas (ed.), *The Dispatches and Letters of Vice Admiral Lord Viscount Nelson*, vol. 6, pp. 427, 450–1; Duffy, *Soldiers, Sugar*

and Seapower, p. 19; Corbett, *The Campaign of Trafalgar*, pp. 4–23, et seq.

14. G.T. Eggleston and V. Stuart, *His Majesty's Sloop of War* Diamond Rock (London: Robert Hale, 1978), passim.

15. Nelson to Marsden, 12 June 1805, 20 July 1805, in Nicolas (ed.), *The Dispatches and Letters of Vice Admiral Lord Viscount Nelson*, vol. 6, pp. 452–3, 473.

16. James, *Naval History*, vol. 4, pp. 6, 359; Tracy, *Naval Chronicle*, vol. 3, p. 162; Robson, *Trafalgar*, pp. 48–61.

17. Tracy, *Naval Chronicle*, vol. 3, p. 166. James, *Naval History*, vol. 4, p. 359.

18. Tracy, *Naval Chronicle*, pp. 157–8.

19. Nelson to Fremantle, 16 August 1805, in Nicolas (ed.), *The Dispatches and Letters of Vice Admiral Lord Viscount Nelson*, vol. 7, p. 5; *The Times*, 6 August 1805; Schom, *Trafalgar*, p. 243; Knight, *The Pursuit of Victory*, p. 495; Robson, *Trafalgar*, pp. 48–61; Tracy, *Naval Chronicle*, vol. 3, pp. 169–70.

20. Tracy, *Nelson's Battles*, p. 163; E. Desbrière, *The Campaign of Trafalgar*, 2 vols (Oxford: OUP, 1933), vol. 2, pp. 90–4; N. Tracy, 'Sir Robert Calder's Action', *The Mariner's Mirror*, vol. 77 (1991).

21. www.hms-victory.com/index.php?option=com_content&view=categor ies&id=81&Itemid=486.

Chapter 5. 'Engage the Enemy more closely': The Battle of Trafalgar, 1805

1. British Library, Add MS 36,747 f.55; Tracy, *Nelson's Battles*, p. 207; James, *Naval History*, vol. 3, pp. 371–2; Nicolas (ed.), *The Dispatches and Letters of Vice Admiral Lord Viscount Nelson*, vol. 6, pp. 443–4, vol. 7, p. 67, n.3; C. White, *The Nelson Encyclopædia* (London: Chatham Publishing, 2002), pp. 236–7, see also C. White, 'Nelson's 1805 Battle Plan', *Journal of Maritime Research* (2002).

2. White, *Nelson Encyclopaedia*, p. 271; Nicolas (ed.), *The Dispatches and Letters of Vice Admiral Lord Viscount Nelson*, vol. 7, p. 60; Duff to his wife, 10 October 1805, in Tracy (ed.), *Naval Chronicle*, vol. 3, pp. 191–2.

3. Hodges and Hughes (eds), *Select Naval Documents*, pp. 219–23; Nicolas (ed.), *The Dispatches and Letters of Vice Admiral Lord Viscount Nelson*, vol. 7, pp. 89–92, Tracy, *Nelson's Battles*, p. 208.

4. Collingwood (ed.), *Correspondence*, p. 124.

5. Goodwin, *Nelson's Ships*, p. 257; Letter written by Captain Pryce Cumby, 30 October 1805, NMM JON/7.

6. King (ed.), *Every Man Will Do His Duty*, p. 160.

7. Nicolas (ed.), *The Dispatches and Letters of Vice Admiral Lord Viscount Nelson*, vol. 7, p. 150.

8. Collingwood (ed.), *Correspondence*, p. 127.

9. Collingwood to Lord Radstock, Collingwood to Duke of Clarence, 12 December 1805, in Collingwood (ed.), *Correspondence*, pp. 163–5; E. Fraser, *The Enemy at Trafalgar* (London: Chatham Publishing, 2004), p. 256; Lavery, *Nelson's Fleet at Trafalgar*, p. 179.

10. Letter written by Captain Pryce Cumby, 30 October 1805, NMM JON/7.

11. King, *Every Man Will Do His Duty*, p. 162.

12. Gardiner, *The Campaign of Trafalgar*, p. 159.

13. Goodwin, *Nelson's Ships*, p. 259; W. Beatty, *The Authentic Narrative of the Death of Lord Nelson* (London: Davison for Cadell and Davies, 1807), pp. 28–9.

14. K. Fenwick, *HMS Victory* (London: Cassell, 1959), p. 274.

15. Fraser, *The Enemy at Trafalgar*, pp. 158–73.

16. E. Fraser, *The Sailors Whom Nelson Led* (London: Methuen & Co. Ltd, 1913), pp. 301–2; Gardiner, *The Campaign of Trafalgar*, p. 153.

17. Codrington to his wife, 31 October 1805, in J. Bourchier, *Memoir of The Life of Admiral Sir Edward Codrington*, 2 vols (London, 1873), vol. 1, pp. 64–6; Lavery, *Nelson's Fleet at Trafalgar*, p. 174; Willis, *Hour of Victory*, p. 278.

18. Nicolas (ed.), *The Dispatches and Letters of Vice Admiral Lord Viscount Nelson*, vol. 7, pp. 168–9.

19. Scott to Mr Rose, 22 December 1805, in Nicolas (ed.), *The Dispatches and Letters of Vice Admiral Lord Viscount Nelson*, vol. 7, p. 246; Collingwood to Marsden, 22 October 1805, in Collingwood, *Correspondence*, p. 123.

20. King, *Every Man Will Do His Duty*, pp. 163–4.

21. Tracy, *Naval Chronicle*, vol. 3, p. 231.

22. Lavery, *We Shall Fight on the Beaches*, p. 410.

23. Rodger, *The Command of the Ocean*, p. 543.

Chapter 6. 'I cannot too much lament not to have arrived a few days sooner': Home Waters and the Baltic, 1805–15

1. P.H. Stanhope, *Life of the Right Honourable William Pitt*, 4 vols (London: John Murray, 1867), vol. 4, p. 382; Ehrman, *The Younger Pitt, Volume Three: The Consuming Struggle*, p. 829.

2. R. Harding, *Seapower and Naval Warfare, 1650–1830* (London: UCL Press, 1999), p. 270, table 10.1; S. Marthinsen, 'French Sail-of-the-Line in the Napoleonic Wars (1792–1815)', *Warship 1994* (London: Conway, 1994), pp. 15–21; James, *Naval History*, vol. 4, p. 283; J. Glete, *Navies and Nations: Warships, Navies and State Building in Europe and America, 1500–1860*, 2 vols (Stockholm: Almqvist and Wiksell International,

1993), vol. 2, pp. 386–7.

3. James, *Naval History*, vol. 4, pp. 283–4; Glete, *Navies and Nations*, vol. 2, pp. 384–5, 389.

4. Hall, *British Strategy*, pp. 157–63; A.N. Ryan (ed.), *The Saumarez Papers: Selections from the Baltic Correspondence of Vice-Admiral Sir James Saumarez* (Navy Records Society, no. 110, 1968). See also Ryan, 'The Navy at Copenhagen in 1807', and 'Documents Relating to the Copenhagen Operation, 1807', in N.A.M. Rodger (ed.), *The Naval Miscellany Volume 5* (The Navy Records Society, no. 125, 1984); T. Munch-Petersen, 'Lord Cathcart, Sir Arthur Wellesley and the British attack on Copenhagen in 1807', in C.M. Woolgar (ed.), *Wellington Studies 2* (Southampton: University Press, 1999); and T. Munch-Petersen, *Defying Napoleon: How Britain Bombarded Copenhagen and Seized the Danish Fleet in 1807* (London: The History Press, 2007).

5. Davey, *Transformation of British Naval Strategy*, p. 20.

6. Mulgrave to Saumarez, 20 February 1808, in Ryan (ed.), *Saumarez Papers*, p. 7; T. Voelker, *Admiral Saumarez Versus Napoleon: The Baltic, 1807–12* (Woodbridge: Boydell Press, 2009) ch. 2 and pp. 34–5.

7. Castlereagh to the King, 17 April 1808, in A.A. Aspinall (ed.), *The Later Correspondence of George III*, 5 vols (Cambridge: University Press, 1962–70), vol. 5, pp. 65–6; Admiralty to Saumarez, 16 April 1808, 22 April 1808, in Ryan (ed.), *Saumarez Papers*, pp. 11–14; Hall, *British Strategy*, pp. 163–4; Voelker, *Saumarez*, pp. 45–6; Davey, *Transformation of British Naval Strategy*, p. 33; Rodger, *The Command of the Ocean*, p. 559.

8. Voelker, *Saumarez*, pp. 54–6.

9. Voelker, *Saumarez*, pp. 56–63; R.V. Hamilton (ed.), *Letters and Papers of Admiral of the Fleet Sir Thos. Byam Martin*, vol. 2 (Navy Records Society, no. 12, 1897–98).

10. Woodman, *Victory of Seapower*, pp. 119–21.

11. Voelker, *Saumarez*, pp. 107–17.

12. Saumarez to Byam Martin, 15 July 1812, in Ryan (ed.), *Saumarez Papers*, p. 237.

13. Mitchell, *A History of Russian and Soviet Sea Power*, pp. 131–3; Morris to Saumarez, 28 August 1812, in Ryan (ed.), *Saumarez Papers*, p. 251.

14. Woodman, *Victory of Seapower*, pp. 44–7; B. Vale, *The Audacious Admiral Cochrane: The True Life of a Naval Legend* (London: Conway, 2004), ch. 5.

15. Hall, *British Strategy*, p. 9; Marthinsen 'French Sail-of-the-Line', pp. 15–21; James, *Naval History*, vol. 4, p. 283; Woodman, *Victory of Seapower*, pp. 136–7.

16. Rodger, *The Command of the Ocean*, p. 562.

17. Woodman, *Victory of Seapower*, pp. 136–40.

18. M. Duffy, 'World-Wide War and British Expansion', p. 205.

Chapter 7. 'Our maritime superiority': The Mediterranean and the Peninsular War, 1805–15

1. Woodman, *Victory of Seapower*, pp. 144–7.
2. Rodger, *The Command of the Ocean*, pp. 522–4; R. Hill, *The Prizes of War: The Naval Prize System in the Napoleonic Wars, 1793–1815* (Sutton: Sutton, 1998); R. Miller, *Britain and Latin America in the Nineteenth and Twentieth Centuries* (London: Longman, 1993), p. 32. C.R. Boxer, *The Portuguese Seaborne Empire, 1415–1825* (Manchester: Carcanet, 1991), p. 173.
3. Convention of 22 October between Britain and Portugal, TNA FO 93/77 [1B]; Canning to Leveson Gower, 5 November 1807, TNA PRO 30/29 8/4, ff.183.
4. Journal of Sir W.S. Smith, TNA ADM 50/50; Return of Smith's squadron 1st Dec 1807, TNA ADM 8/94; Smith to Pole, 22 November 1807, TNA ADM 1/19; K. Light, 'Britain and the Portuguese Navy, 1760–1810', *The British Historical Society of Portugal, Twenty Second Annual Report and Review*, 1995, p. 43; James, *Naval History*, vol. 4, p. 316.
5. N. Macaulay, *Dom Pedro: The Struggle for Liberty in Brazil and Portugal, 1798–1834* (Durham: Duke University Press, 1986), p. 19; Aspinall (ed.), *The Later Correspondence of George III*, vol. 4, p. 661 n. 1.
6. Smith to Moore, 5 December 1807, in G.S. Graham and R.A. Humphreys (eds), *The Navy and South America, 1807–1823* (Navy Records Society, vol. 104, 1962), pp. 3–4; see also K. Light, *The Migration of the Royal Family of Portugal to Brazil in 1807/08* (Rio de Janeiro: Kenneth Light, 1995), pp. 48, 54–5; James, *Naval History*, vol. 4, p. 318; Macaulay, *Dom Pedro*, pp. 21–3.
7. Beresford to Castlereagh, 29 December 1807, TNA WO 1/354, pp. 29–31, 37–40; Hall, *British Strategy*, p. 168; James, *Naval History*, vol. 4, p. 350.
8. James, *Naval History*, vol. 5, pp. 3–5; Collingwood to his wife, 15 May 1808, in Collingwood (ed.), *Correspondence*, p. 355; P. Mackesy, *The War in the Mediterranean, 1803–1810* (Cambridge, MA: Harvard University Press, 1957), ch. 9.
9. Mackesy, *The War in the Mediterranean*, p. 256; James, *Naval History*, vol. 5, p. 10; Hall, *British Strategy*, p. 408; C.D. Hall, *Wellington's Navy: Sea Power and the Peninsular War, 1807–1814* (London: Chatham Publishing, 2004), pp. 8–11; Cotton to Pole, 16 January 1808, TNA ADM 1/339.
10. Yeo to Cotton, 14 February 1808, Cotton to Pole, 17 February 1808, TNA ADM 1/339; W.L. Clowes, *The Royal Navy: A History from the Earliest Times to the Present*, 7 vols (London: Sampson, Low Marston and Company Ltd, 1897–1903), vol. 5, p. 407; D.D. Horward, 'Portugal and the Anglo-Russian Naval Crisis (1808)', *Naval War College Review*, no.

34 (1981), p. 53; P.C. Krajeski, *In the Shadow of Nelson: The Naval Leadership of Admiral Sir Charles Cotton, 1753–1812* (London: Greenwood Press, 2000), pp. 63–8; Cotton to Pole, 23 April 1808, TNA ADM 1/339; James, *Naval History*, vol. 5, pp. 20–1, 38–40.

11. Cotton to Pole, 4 July 1808, 14 July 1808, TNA ADM 1/340; Horward, 'Portugal and the Anglo-Russian Naval Crisis', p. 59.

12. Wellesley to Cotton, 30 July 1808, Wellesley to Castlereagh, 25, 26 July 1808, 1 August 1808, in J. Gurwood (ed.), *The Dispatches of Field Marshal the Duke of Wellington, during his various campaigns in India, Denmark, Portugal, Spain, the Low Countries, and France*, 8 vols (London: Parker Furnival and Parker, 1844), vol. 4, pp. 30–9.

13. Convention between Cotton and Seniavin, 3 September 1808, Cotton Naval Papers 588/041A/74, 588/041A/46; Hall, *Wellington's Navy*, p. 33; Hall, *British Strategy*, pp. 171–2; Mackesy, *The War in the Mediterranean*, p. 227.

14. Hall, *Wellington's Navy*, ch. 2.

15. Woodman, *Victory of Seapower*, pp. 158–64.

16. B.M. de Toy, 'Commanders-in-Chief: Wellington, Berkeley and Victory in the Peninsula', in C.M. Woolgar (ed.), *Wellington Studies II* (Southampton: University of Southampton, Hartley Institute, 1999), pp. 197–8; C.D. Hall, 'The Royal Navy and the Peninsular War', *The Mariner's Mirror*, vol. 79, no. 4 (November 1993).

17. De Toy, 'Commanders-in-Chief', pp. 204–7; Lavery, *Nelson's Navy*, p. 152; Hall, 'Peninsular War', pp. 410–11; J. Grehan, *The Lines of Torres Vedras: The Cornerstone of Wellington's Strategy in the Peninsular War, 1809–1812* (Staplehurst: Spellmount, 2000), pp. 56, 63.

18. De Toy, 'Commanders-in-Chief', pp. 203–11; D.D. Horward, 'British Seapower and its Influence upon the Peninsular War', *Naval War College Review*, no. 31 (1978), p. 63, Hall, 'Peninsular War', p. 410; Grehan, *Torres Vedras*, pp. 12, 36–8.

19. Hall, *British Strategy*, p. 32. W. Freeman Galpin, 'The American Grain Trade to the Spanish Peninsula, 1810–1814', *American Historical Review*, XXVIII (1923), pp. 24–5; R. Knight and M. Wilcox, *Sustaining the Fleet, 1793–1815: War, the British Navy and the Contractor State* (Woodbridge: Boydell Press, 2010), p. 10, 54; Morriss, *The Foundations of British Maritime Ascendancy*, p. 389.

20. Horward, 'British Seapower', p. 59; de Toy, 'Commanders-in-Chief', pp. 188–9, 208; Hall, 'Peninsular War', p. 416; Rodger, *The Command of the Ocean*, p. 564.

21. Hall, 'Peninsular War', p. 403.

22. P. Padfield, *Maritime Power and the Struggle for Freedom: Naval Campaigns That Shaped the Modern World 1788–1851* (London: John Murray, 2004), p. 309.

23. Martin to Lord Keith, 21 September 1813, in Hamilton (ed.), *Letters and Papers of Byam Martin*, vol. 2, p. 409; H. Davies, *Wellington's Wars: The Making of a Military Genius* (Yale: YUP, 2012), p. 178.

24. Padfield, *Maritime Power and the Struggle for Freedom*, p. 305.

25. T. Pocock, *Remember Nelson: The Life of Captain Sir William Hoste* (London: HarperCollins, 1977), p. 174.

26. M. Duffy, 'Science and Labour': The Naval Contribution to Operations ashore in the Great Wars with France, 1793–1815', in Hore (ed.), *Seapower Ashore*, pp. 48–9.

Chapter 8. 'The carrier of the commerce of the continent of Europe': Economic warfare, 1805–15

1. Schroeder, *The Transformation of European Politics*, pp. 311–31; L.E. Davis and S.L. Engerman, *Naval Blockades in Peace and War: An Economic History since 1750* (Cambridge: CUP, 2012), pp. 328–31.

2. Memorandum by Canning, 2 April 1808, HAR GC, 46a.

3. Woodman, *Victory of Seapower*, pp. 64–5; James, *Naval History*, vol. 4, pp. 272–3.

4. M. Robson, 'Sir Arthur Wellesley as a "Special Adviser": Politics and Strategic Planning, 1806–1808', in C.M. Woolgar (ed.), *Wellington Studies V* (Southampton: Hartley Institute, University of Southampton, 2013); Rodger, *The Command of the Ocean*, pp. 548–9.

5. Howard, *The Causes of Wars*, pp. 173, 184–6; B.H. Liddell Hart, 'Economic Pressures or Continental Victories', *Journal of the Royal United Services Institute*, no. 76 (1931), pp. 495–500 and *The British Way in Warfare* (London: Faber and Faber, 1932), p. 7; D.A. Baugh, 'British Strategy during the First World War in the Context of Four Centuries: Blue-Water versus Continental Commitment', in D.M. Masterson (ed.), *The Sixth Symposium of the U.S. Naval Academy* (Delaware: Scholarly Resources Inc, 1987), p. 87 and 'Great Britain's "Blue-Water" Policy, 1689–1815', *International History Review*, vol. 10 (1988), p. 56; C. Esdaile, *The Wars of Napoleon* (London: Longman, 1995), p. 156.

6. Blanning, *The Pursuit of Glory*, p. 111; Emsley, *The Longman Companion to Napoleonic Europe*, p. 132; Hall, *British Strategy*, pp. 97–8, 112–13; W.W. Kaufmann, *British Policy and the Independence of Latin America, 1804–1828* (Hamden: Archon Books, 1967), pp. 10–13; Popham, *A Damned Cunning Fellow*, pp. 133–4, D.C.M. Platt, *Latin America and British Trade, 1806–1914* (London: Adam and Charles Black, 1972), pp. 4–7, 28, table 1.

7. Woodman, *Victory of Seapower*, pp. 17–19, James, *Naval History*, vol. 4, pp. 183–203.

8. Willis, *Hour of Victory*, pp. 316–19; Woodman, *Victory of Seapower*, p. 24.

9.   James, *Naval History*, vol. 4, p. 264.

10. Woodman, *Victory of Seapower*, pp. 72–80.

11. S. Taylor, *Storm and Conquest: The Battle for the Indian Ocean, 1808–10* (London: Faber and Faber, 2008), ch. 1, p. 12.

12. Woodman, *Victory of Seapower*, pp. 92–6, Taylor, *Storm and Conquest*, pp. 290–300.

13. Taylor, *Storm and Conquest*, p. 329.

14. *Ibid.*, pp. 317–33; Woodman, *Victory of Seapower*, pp. 92–7.

15. www.lloydsswords.com/background.php.

16. Duffy, 'World-Wide War and British Expansion', p. 205.

Chapter 9. 'A complete stop to all trade and intercourse by Sea': The War of 1812

1.   Rodger, *The Command of the Ocean*, pp. 565–6; Padfield, *Maritime Power and the Struggle for Freedom*, p. 297; A. Lambert, *The Challenge: Britain Against America in the Naval War of 1812* (London: Faber and Faber, 2012), Kindle, loc 403.

2.   B. Arthur, *How Britain Won the War of 1812: The Royal Navy's Blockades of the United States, 1812–1815* (Woodbridge: Boydell Press, 2011), p. xxi.

3.   R. Gardiner, *The Naval War of 1812* (London: Chatham Publishing, 1999), pp. 31–2.

4.   Padfield, *Maritime Power and the Struggle for Freedom*, p. 316.

5.   King, *Every Man Will Do His Duty*, pp. 307–10.

6.   *Ibid.*, pp. 307–10; Gardiner, *The Naval War of 1812*, p. 46–8.

7.   Rodger, *The Command of the Ocean*, p. 568; Lambert, *The Challenge*, Kindle loc 1919.

8.   Rodger, *The Command of the Ocean*, p. 568; Padfield, *Maritime Power and the Struggle for Freedom*, p. 320; Lambert, *The Challenge*, Kindle loc 978, 989.

9.   Padfield, *Maritime Power and the Struggle for Freedom*, pp. 328–9.

10. Gardiner, *The Naval War of 1812*, pp. 65–9.

11. Knight and Wilcox, *Sustaining the Fleet, 1793–1815*, p. 54. Mitchell, *A History of Russian and Soviet Sea Power*, p. 134; Padfield, *Maritime Power and the Struggle for Freedom*, p. 300; Lambert, *The Challenge*, Kindle loc 1111.

12. Arthur, *How Britain Won the War of 1812*, pp. 91, 222–6; Lambert, *The Challenge*, Kindle loc 1697.

13. Arthur, *How Britain Won the War of 1812*, p. 241.

14. *Ibid.*, pp. 52, 143, 227–31, 241.

15. R. Malcolmson, *Warships of the Great Lakes, 1754–1834* (London: Chatham Publishing, 2003), pp. 45, 63–4.

16. Gardiner, *How Britain Won the War of 1812*, pp. 98–102; Malcolmson,

Warships of the Great Lakes, pp. 77–9.

17. Gardiner, *How Britain Won the War of 1812*, pp. 105–9, 122–3; Malcolmson, *Warships of the Great Lakes*, pp. 100–18.

18. Malcolmson, *Warships of the Great Lakes*, pp. 85–98.

19. *Ibid.*, pp. 119–33.

20. Morriss, *Cockburn and the British Navy in Transition*, p. 91.

21. *Ibid.*, pp. 92–3.

22. *Ibid.*, p. 110.

23. Arthur, *How Britain Won the War of 1812*, p. 63; Lambert, *The Challenge*, ch. 10.

Epilogue. 'That will do [...] Fire, my fine fellows': Algiers, 1816

1. Taylor, *Commander*, chs 13 and 14 and Kindle loc 5634; M. Rae, 'Sir Edward Pellew', in Harding and Le Fevre (eds), *British Admirals of the Napoleonic Wars*, pp. 289–93.

Conclusion. 'Lords of the sea'

1. Figures from Lavery, *Nelson's Navy*, pp. 187, 310.

2. Lavery, *Nelson's Navy*, p. 317; James, *Naval History*, vol. 6, p. 526; Glete, *Navies and Nations*, vol. 2, appendix 2, pp. 553–695.

3. Padfield, *Maritime Power and the Struggle for Freedom*, p. 307; Morriss, *The Foundations of British Maritime Ascendancy*, p. 83; P. Kennedy, *The Rise and Fall of British Naval Mastery* (London: Fontana, 1991), p. 178.

4. Corbett (ed.), *The Private Papers of George, Second Earl Spencer*, vol. 2, p. 367.

5. Rodger, *The Command of the Ocean*, p. 573.

6. Padfield, *Maritime Power and the Struggle for Freedom*, p. 309; Kennedy, *Naval Mastery*, p. 174; Emsley, *The Longman Companion to Napoleonic Europe*, p. 136; Hall, *British Strategy*, p. 86; Esdaile, *The Wars of Napoleon*, p. 156.

7. Rodger, *The Command of the Ocean*, p. 574; Muir, *Britain and the Defeat of Napoleon, 1807–1815*, pp. 374–81.

Bibliography

The National Archives: ADM 1/19, ADM 1/339, ADM 1/340, ADM 1/1347, ADM 8/94, ADM 50/50, ADM 51/4514, ADM 109/104, WO 1/354, FO 95/5/3, FO 93/77 [1B], PRO 30/29 8/4

Cambridge County Record Office: Cotton Naval Papers, 588/041A/74

Harewood Collection: George Canning Papers, HAR GC, 46a

National Maritime Museum: ADM 359/13/212, NMM JON/7

British Library: Add MS 36,747

Andidora, R., *Iron Admirals: Naval Leadership in the Twentieth Century* (Westport, CT: Greenwood Press, 2000)

Arthur, B., *How Britain Won the War of 1812: The Royal Navy's Blockades of the United States, 1812–1815* (Woodbridge: Boydell Press, 2011)

Aspinall, A.A. (ed.), *The Later Correspondence of George III*, 5 vols (Cambridge: University Press, 1962–70)

Baugh, D.A., 'British Strategy during the First World War in the Context of Four Centuries: Blue-Water versus Continental Commitment', in D.M. Masterson (ed.), *The Sixth Symposium of the U S. Naval Academy* (Delaware: Scholarly Resources Inc, 1987)

——, 'Great Britain's "Blue-Water" Policy, 1689–1815', *International History Review*, vol. 10 (1988)

Beatty, W., *The Authentic Narrative of the Death of Lord Nelson* (London: Davison for Cadell and Davies, 1807)

Black, J., *Britain as a Military Power, 1688–1815* (London: Routledge, 1999)

Blanning, T., *The Pursuit of Glory: Europe 1648–1815* (London: Penguin Books, 2007)

Bourchier, J., *Memoir of the Life of Admiral Sir Edward Codrington*, 2 vols (London, 1873)

Boxer, C.R., *The Portuguese Seaborne Empire, 1415–1825* (Manchester: Carcarnet, 1991)

Clowes, W.L., *The Royal Navy: A History from the Earliest Times to the Present*, 7 vols (London: Sampson, Low Marston and Company Ltd, 1897–1903)

Collingwood, G.L.N. (ed.), *A Selection from the Public and Private Correspondence of Vice-Admiral Lord Collingwood* (London: James Ridgway, 1829)

Collins, B., *War and Empire: The Expansion of Britain, 1790–1830: The Projection of British Power, 1775–1830* (London: Longman, 2010)

Corbett, J.S., *The Campaign of Trafalgar* (London: Longmans, 1910)

——, 'Napoleon and the British Navy after Trafalgar', *Quarterly Review* (1922)

——, *Some Principles of Maritime Strategy* (London: Brassey's, 1988)

—— (ed.), *The Private Papers of George, Second Earl Spencer, First Lord of the Admiralty, 1794–1801*, 4 vols (London: Navy Records Society, 1913–24)

Cordingly, D., *Billy Ruffian: The Bellerophon and the Downfall of Napoleon: The Biography of a Ship of the Line, 1782–1836* (London: Bloomsbury Publishing, 2004)

Davey, J., *The Transformation of British Naval Strategy: Seapower and Supply in Northern Europe, 1808–1812* (Woodbridge: Boydell Press, 2012)

Davies, H., *Wellington's Wars: The Making of a Military Genius* (Yale: YUP, 2012)

Davis, L.E. and Engerman, S.L., *Naval Blockades in Peace and War: An Economic History since 1750* (Cambridge: CUP, 2012)

de Toy, B.M., 'Commanders-in-Chief: Wellington, Berkeley and Victory in the Peninsula', in C.M. Woolgar (ed.), *Wellington Studies II* (Southamton: University of Southampton, Hartley Institute, 1999)

Deane, P. and Cole, W.A., *British Economic Growth, 1688–1959: Trends and Structure* (Cambridge: CUP, 1962)

Desbrière, E., *The Campaign of Trafalgar*, 2 vols (Oxford: OUP, 1933)

Duffy, M., *Soldiers, Sugar and Seapower: The British Expeditions to the West Indies and the War Against Revolutionary France* (Oxford: Clarendon Press, 1987)

——, 'The establishment of the Western Squadron as the linchpin of British Naval Strategy', in M. Duffy (ed.), *Parameters of British Naval Power 1650–1850* (Exeter: EUP, 1992)

——, 'World-Wide War and British Expansion, 1793–1815', in P.J. Marshall (ed.), *The Oxford History of the British Empire: Volume Two, The Eighteenth Century* (Oxford: OUP, 2001)

—— and Morriss, R., *The Glorious First of June, 1794: A Naval Battle and its Aftermath* (Exeter: UEP, 2001)

Eggleston, G.T. and Stuart, V., *His Majesty's Sloop of War Diamond Rock* (London: Robert Hale, 1978)

Ehrman, J., *The Younger Pitt, Volume Two: The Reluctant Transition* (London: Constable, 1983)

——, *The Younger Pitt, Volume Three: The Consuming Struggle* (London: Constable, 1997)

Emsley, C., *The Longman Companion to Napoleonic Europe* (London: Longman, 1993)

Esdaile, C., *The Wars of Napoleon* (London: Longman, 1995)

——, *Napoleon's Wars: An International History, 1803*–1815 (London: Allen Lane, 2008)

Fenwick, K., *HMS* Victory (London: Cassell, 1959)

Fortescue, J.W., *A History of the British Army*, 13 vols (London: Macmillan, 1899–1930)

Fraser, E., *The Sailors Whom Nelson Led* (London: Methuen & Co. Ltd, 1913)

——, *The Enemy at Trafalgar* (London: Chatham Publishing, 2004)

Freeman Galpin, W., 'The American Grain Trade to the Spanish Peninsula, 1810–1814', *American Historical Review*, XXVIII (1923)

Gardiner, R., *Fleet Battle and Blockade: The French Revolutionary War, 1793–1797* (London: Chatham Publishing, 1996)

——, *The Campaign of Trafalgar, 1803–1805* (London: Chatham Publishing, 1997)

——, *Nelson against Napoleon: From the Nile to Copenhagen, 1798–1801* (London: Chatham Publishing, 1997)

——, *The Naval War of 1812* (London: Chatham Publishing, 1999)

Glete, J., *Navies and Nations: Warships, Navies and State Building in Europe and America, 1500–1860*, 2 vols (Stockholm: Almqvist and Wiksell International, 1993)

Goodwin, P., *Nelson's Ships: A Comprehensive History of the Vessels in which He Served* (London: Conway, 2002)

Graham, G.S. and Humphreys, R.A. (eds), *The Navy and South America, 1807–1823* (Navy Records Society, vol. 104, 1962)

Grehan, J., *The Lines of Torres Vedras: The Cornerstone of Wellington's Strategy in the Peninsular War, 1809–1812* (Staplehurst: Spellmount, 2000)

Grocott, T., *Shipwrecks of the Revolutionary & Napoleonic Eras* (London: Chatham Publishing, 1997)

Gurwood, J. (ed.), *The Dispatches of Field Marshal the Duke of Wellington, during his various campaigns in India, Denmark, Portugal, Spain, the Low Countries, and France*, 8 vols (London: Parker Furnival and Parker, 1844)

Hall, C.D., *British Strategy in the Napoleonic War, 1803–15* (Manchester: MUP, 1992)

——, 'The Royal Navy and the Peninsular War', *The Mariner's Mirror*, vol. 79, no. 4 (November 1993)

——, *Wellington's Navy: Sea Power and the Peninsular War, 1807–1814* (London: Chatham Publishing, 2004)

Hamilton, R.V. (ed.), *Letters and Papers of Admiral of the Fleet Sir Thos. Byam Martin* (Navy Records Society, no. 12, 1897–98)

Harding, R., *Seapower and Naval Warfare, 1650–1830* (London: UCL Press, 1999)

—— and Le Fevre, P. (eds), *British Admirals of the Napoleonic Wars* (London: Chatham Publishing, 2005)

Hathaway, W.S. (ed.), *The Speeches of the Right Honourable William Pitt in the House of Commons*, 4 vols (London: Longman, 1806)

Hill, R., *The Prizes of War: The Naval Prize System in the Napoleonic Wars, 1793–1815* (Sutton: Sutton, 1998)

Historical Manuscripts Commission Reports on the Manuscripts of J. B. Fortescue Preserved at Dropmore, 1892–1927 (London: HMSO, 1912)

Hodges, H.W. and Hughes E.A. (eds), *Select Naval Documents* (Cambridge: CUP, 1936)

Hore, P. (ed.), *Seapower Ashore: 200 Years of Royal Navy Operations on Land* (London: Chatham Publishing, 2001)

Horward, D.D., 'British Seapower and its Influence upon the Peninsular War', *Naval War College Review*, no. 31 (1978)

——, 'Portugal and the Anglo-Russian Naval Crisis (1808)', *Naval War College Review*, no. 34 (1981)

Howard, M., *The Causes of Wars and Other Essays* (London: Temple Smith, 1983)

Howarth, S., *Battle of Copenhagen, 1801: 200 Years* (Shelton: The 1805 Club, 2003)

Hughes, E. (ed.), *The Private Correspondence of Admiral Lord Collingwood* (Navy Records Society, no. 98, 1956–57)

James, W., *The Naval History of Great Britain from the Declaration of War by France in 1793 to the Accession of George IV*, 6 vols (London: Macmillan, 1837)

James, W., *Old Oak: The Life of John Jervis, Earl of St. Vincent* (London: Longmans Green, 1950)

Kaufmann, W.W., *British Policy and the Independence of Latin America, 1804–1828* (Hamden: Archon Books, 1967)

Kennedy, P., *The Rise and Fall of British Naval Mastery* (London: Fontana, 1991)

King, D. (ed.), *Every Man Will Do His Duty: An Anthology of First-Hand Accounts from the Age of Nelson* (London: Conway, 1997)

Knight, R., *The Pursuit of Victory: The Life and Achievement of Horatio Nelson* (London: Penguin, 2006)

—— and Wilcox, M., *Sustaining the Fleet, 1793–1815: War, the British Navy and the Contractor State* (Woodbridge: Boydell Press, 2010)

Krajeski, P.C., *In the Shadow of Nelson: The Naval Leadership of Admiral Sir Charles Cotton, 1753–1812* (London: Greenwood Press, 2000)

Lambert, A., *Nelson: Britannia's God of War* (London: Faber and Faber, 2004)

——, 'Nelson, Trafalgar and the Meaning of Victory', *History Today*, vol. 54, issue 11 (2004)

——, *The Challenge: Britain Against America in the Naval War of 1812* (London: Faber and Faber, 2012)

Lavery, B., *Nelson's Navy: The Ships, Men and Organisation 1793–1805* (London: Conway, 1989)

——, *Nelson and the Nile: The Naval War against Bonaparte 1798* (London: Chatham Publishing, 1998)

——, *Nelson's Fleet at Trafalgar* (London: NMM, 2004)

——, *We Shall Fight on the Beaches: Defying Napoleon and Hitler, 1805 and 1940* (London: Conway, 2009)

—— (ed.), *Shipboard Life and Organisation, 1731–1815* (The Navy Records Society, no. 138, 1998)

Liddell Hart, B.H., 'Economic Pressures or Continental Victories', *Journal of the Royal United Services Institute*, no. 76 (1931)

——, *The British Way in Warfare* (London: Faber and Faber, 1932)

Light, K., 'Britain and the Portuguese Navy, 1760–1810', *The British Historical Society of Portugal, Twenty Second Annual Report and Review*, 1995

——, *The Migration of the Royal Family of Portugal to Brazil in 1807/08* (Rio de Janeiro: Kenneth Light, 1995)

Macaulay, N., *Dom Pedro: The Struggle for Liberty in Brazil and Portugal, 1798–1834* (Durham: Duke University Press, 1986)

Mackesy, P., *The War in the Mediterranean, 1803–1810* (Cambridge, MA: Harvard University Press, 1957)

Mahan, A.T., *The Influence of Seapower upon the French Revolution and Empire, 1793–1812* (London: Sampson Low and Co., 1892)

Malcolmson, R., *Warships of the Great Lakes, 1754–1834* (London: Chatham Publishing, 2003)

Marthinsen, S., 'French Sail-of-the-Line in the Napoleonic Wars (1792–1815)', *Warship 1994* (London: Conway, 1994)

Miller, R., *Britain and Latin America in the Nineteenth and Twentieth Centuries* (London: Longman, 1993)

Mitchell, D.W., *A History of Russian and Soviet Sea Power* (London: Macmillan, 1974)

Morriss, R., *Cockburn and the British Navy in Transition: Admiral Sir George Cockburn 1772–1853* (Exeter: EUP, 1997)

——, *The Foundations of British Maritime Ascendancy: Resources, Logistics and the State, 1755–1815* (Cambridge: CUP, 2011)

—— (ed.), *The Channel Fleet and the Blockade of Brest, 1793–1801* (Navy Records Society, no. 141, 2001)

Muir, R., *Britain and the Defeat of Napoleon, 1807–1815* (New Haven and London: Yale University Press, 1996)

Munch-Petersen, T., 'Lord Cathcart, Sir Arthur Wellesley and the British attack on Copenhagen in 1807', in C.M. Woolgar (ed.), *Wellington Studies 2* (Southampton: University Press, 1999)

——, *Defying Napoleon: How Britain Bombarded Copenhagen and Seized the Danish Fleet in 1807* (London: The History Press, 2007)

Nicolas, N.H. (ed.), *The Dispatches and Letters of Vice Admiral Lord Viscount Nelson*

(London: Chatham Publishing, 1997)

Padfield, P., *Maritime Power and the Struggle for Freedom: Naval Campaigns That Shaped the Modern World 1788–1851* (London: John Murray, 2004)

Perrin, W.G., *The Letters and Papers of Admiral Viscount Keith* (Navy Records Society, vol. 62, 1926)

Platt, D.C.M., *Latin America and British Trade, 1806–1914* (London: Adam and Charles Black, 1972)

Pocock, T., *Remember Nelson: The Life of Captain Sir William Hoste* (London: HarperCollins, 1977)

Popham, H., *A Damned Cunning Fellow: The Eventful Life of Rear-Admiral Sir Home Popham 1762–1820* (Tywardreath: The Old Ferry Press, 1991)

Robb-Webb, J., 'Corbett and the Campaign of Trafalgar', *Defence Studies*, vol. 8, no. 2 (June 2008)

Robson, M., *The Battle of Trafalgar* (London: Conway, 2005)

——, *Britain, Portugal and South America in the Napoleonic Wars: Alliances and Diplomacy in Economic Maritime Conflict* (London: I.B.Tauris, 2010)

——, 'Sir Arthur Wellesley as a "Special Adviser": Politics and Strategic Planning, 1806–1808', in C.M. Woolgar (ed.), *Wellington Studies V* (Southampton: University of Southampton, Hartley Institute, 2013)

Rodger, N.A.M., *The Command of the Ocean: A Naval History of Britain, 1649–1815* (London: Penguin, 2004)

Russell, Lord, *Knight of the Sword: The Life and Letters of Admiral Sir William Sidney Smith* (London: Victor Gollancz Ltd, 1964)

Ryan, A.N., 'The Navy at Copenhagen in 1807', *The Mariner's Mirror*, no. 39 (1953)

——, 'Documents Relating to the Copenhagen Operation, 1807', in N.A.M. Rodger (ed.), *The Naval Miscellany Volume 5* (Navy Records Society, no. 125, 1984)

—— (ed.), *The Saumarez Papers: Selections from the Baltic Correspondence of Vice-Admiral Sir James Saumarez* (Navy Records Society, no. 110, 1968)

Schom, A., *Trafalgar: Countdown to Battle 1803–1805* (London: Michael Joseph Ltd, 1990)

Schroeder, P., *The Transformation of European Politics, 1763–1848* (Oxford: Clarendon Press, 1994)

Stanhope, P.H., *Life of the Right Honourable William Pitt*, 4 vols (London: John Murray, 1867)

——, *Notes of Conversations with the Duke of Wellington, 1831–1851* (London, 1938)

Taylor, S., *Storm and Conquest: The Battle for the Indian Ocean, 1808–10* (London: Faber and Faber, 2008)

——, *Commander: The Life and Exploits of Britain's Greatest Frigate Captain* (London: Faber and Faber, 2012)

Tracy, N., 'Sir Robert Calder's Action', *The Mariner's Mirror*, vol. 77 (1991)

——, *Nelson's Battles* (London: Chatham Publishing, 1996)

—— (ed.), *The Naval Chronicle: The Contemporary Record of the Royal Navy at War* (London: Chatham Publishing, 1999)

Tucker, J.S., *Memoirs of Admiral the Right Hon The Earl of St Vincent*, 2 vols (London: Richard Bentley, 1844)

Vale, B., *The Audacious Admiral Cochrane: The True Life of a Naval Legend* (London: Conway, 2004)

Voelker, T., *Admiral Saumarez Versus Napoleon: The Baltic, 1807–12* (Woodbridge: Boydell Press, 2009)

White, C., 'Nelson's 1805 Battle Plan', *Journal of Maritime Research* (2002)

——, *The Nelson Encyclopædia* (London: Chatham Publishing, 2002)

Willis, S., *In the Hour of Victory: The Royal Navy at War in the Age of Nelson* (London: Atlantic Books, 2013)

Woodman, R., *The Victory of Seapower: Winning the Napoleonic War, 1806–1814* (London: Chatham Publishing, 1998)

Websites

www.hms-victory.com

www.lloydsswords.com

Index

Numbers in *italics* refer to illustrations.

Abercromby, Lieutenant General Ralph, 27, 69–72, 82, 84–6, 95
Aboukir Castle, 72
Acasta, HMS, 211
Achille, French ship, 129–30, 132, 139
Achille, HMS, 130–1
Acre, siege of, 63–5
Active, HMS, 164
Adair, Captain Charles (RM), 133–5, *134*
Aden, 95
Admiralty
  gunnery orders, 207
  publication of Calder's dispatch, 116
  Royal Dockyards, 98
  Transport Board, 82, 98, 174
  Victualling, 97, 98, 117, 119, 175
  Victualling Board, 175
  Wellesley's criticisms of, 178
Africa, HMS, 137, 138, 150, 211
Africaine, HMS, 168
Agamemnon, HMS, 34, 43, 115, 116, 130, 139, 189
Aggershus, Danish ship, 34
Agincourt, HMS, 26

Aigle, French ship, 129–32
Akbar, HMS, 199
Alarm, HMS, 84
Albatross, HMS, 95
Albion, HMS, 211, 228, 230
Alceste, HMS, 168
Alert, HM sloop, 204
Alexander, Captain James, 93
Alexander, HMS, 16, 21, 55–7, 59, 60, 66
Alexander I, Tsar, 36, 158
Alexandre, French ship, 189
Alexandria, 55, 56, 65, 71, 95, 166
Alfred, HMS, 170
Algeciras, French ship, 129
Allemand, Admiral Zacharie, 168, 188–9
Amazon, HMS, 23, 32, 35
Amboyna, 90–1, 95, 197
America, HMS, 92
Amherstburg, 214, 218
Amiens, Peace of, 95–9, 102, 185
Amphion, HMS, 180–1
Angerstein, Julius, 102
Anholt, HMS, 154
Anstruther, Colonel John, 70–2
Antigua, *83*, 148
Antwerp, 2, 3, 147, 161–2, 179, 233
Apollo, HMS, 179
Aquilon, French ship, 59

Ardent, HMS, 26

Arethusa, HMS, 19–20, 84–5, 189–90

Arethuse, French ship, 42

Argonauta, Spanish ship, 115, 129, 130

Argonaute, French ship, 130

Arrogant, HMS, 84, 92–4

Arrogante, Spanish ship, 84

Asia, HMS, 80, 211

Astrea, HMS, 20

Atcherley, Captain James (RM), 137

Athenien, HMS, 163

Atlas, French ship, 115

Atlas, HMS, 189

Audacious, HMS, 12, 59, 66, 68

Babet, French ship, 20

Bahama, Spanish ship, 130

Bainbridge, Commodore William, 206

Baird, Lieutenant General David, 95, 185, 186

Ball, Captain Alexander, 55

Banda Neira expedition, 197, *198*, 199

Bantry Bay, French expedition, 21–2

Barbados, 76–9, 111
    Carlisle Bay, 79, 82

Barclay, Commander Robert, 218–19

Barfleur, HMS, 114–16, 173

Baring, Sir Francis, 91, 102

Barron, Commodore James, 202

Bastia, siege of, 43

Batavia, 93

battles
    Aix Roads, 158–60, *160*
    Algeciras Bay (Saumarez's action), 68, *69*

Algiers, 227–30

Bladensburg, 223

Camperdown, 23–6

Cape St Vincent, 26, 48–52

Copenhagen, 30–6, 230

Cornwallis's Retreat, 20

Glorious First of June, 11–18, 26, 121

Hotham's actions, 45–6

Lissa, 178–82, *182*

New Orleans, 225

Nile and Nile campaign, 54–63, 230

Plattsburg, 220

Sackets Harbor, 214, 215, 218

San Domingo, 189–90

Santa Cruz, 52–4

Trafalgar, 121–43, *138*; Calder's action, 114–19; campaign, 108–19; Nelson's tactics, 121–2, *123*; Strachan's action, 142

Waterloo, 162, 227, 233–4

Bayntum, Captain Henry, 137

Beatty, Surgeon William, xix, *xxi*, 140

Beaver, Captain Philip, 196–7

Bedford, HMS, 167–8

Belize, 86

Belle Isle, 29, 158

Belleisle, HMS (ex-French *Formidable*), 21, 128, 129, 136, 190

Bellerophon, HMS, 1, *2*, 59, 126, 129, 130, 141, 142, 168, 227

Bellona, French ship, 181

Bellona, HMS, 34, 84

Beresford, Captain John, 211

Beresford, General William, 168

Bergen-op-Zoom, British attack on, 162

Berkeley, Admiral George, 173, 174, 202

Bernadotte, Marshal Jean, 155

Berry, Captain Edward, 51, 68, 139

Bertie, Admiral Albemarle, 196–7

Berwick, French ship (ex-Royal Navy), 131

Bienvenue, French ship, 80

Biter, bomb vessel, 27

Black Snake, gunboat, 215

Blackwood, Captain Henry, 119, 127–8

Blankett, Captain John, 91, 95

Blenheim, HMS, 49, 51, 194

Bligh, Captain John, 170

Bligh, Captain William, 26, 35

Blossom, HMS, 169

Boadicea, HMS, 196

Bombay Castle, HMS, 47

Bombay Marine, 199

Bonaparte, Napoleon *see* Napoleon Bonaparte

Bonne Citoyenne, HMS, 55, 205–6

Boulogne, 37, 104, 106, 110, 161

    Stone ships expedition, 107–8

Bowen, Captain James, 173

Bowen, Captain Richard, 53

Boyne, HMS, 79–80

Brave, French ship, 189

Brest, 1, 3, 4, 10–15, 16, 21, 22, 29–30, 65, 66, 102, 179

    difficulty of blockading, 17, 29, 108, 158, 178, 188, 193, 197

Brilliant, HMS, 8

Brisbane, Captain Charles, 190

Britain

    blockade of USA, 210–13

    defence against invasion, 105–8

    economic warfare against USA, 210–13

    grain supplies, 3, 30, 175, 202–3, 210

    Home Defence Force, 105

    Orders in Council, 155, 184, 202–3

    Provincial Marine, 214, 215, 219

    Royal Military Canal, 105

    Sea Fencibles, 106

    subsidies, 3, 4, 77, 102, 143, 150, 166, 184, 187, 233

    war aims, 2–4

    see also British army; British trade; Royal Navy

Britannia, HMS, 138

British army

    9th Regiment of Foot, 78

    38th Regiment of Foot, 185

    60th Regiment of Foot, 78

    69th Regiment of Foot, 50

    78th Regiment of Foot, 92

    93rd Regiment of Foot, 185

British trade, 75–6

    Baltic, 3, 146, 150, 152, 155, 210

    East Indies, 90

    growth, 97–8, 187, 232

    South America, 187–8

    West Indies, 88, 185

Brock, Major General Isaac, 218

Broke, Captain Philip, 207–8, 210

Broke, HM schooner, 219–20

Brueys, Vice Admiral François-Paul, 55, 56, 60, 62

Bruix, Admiral Étienne, 29, 65–6

Brunswick, HMS, 150

Bucentaure, French ship, 125, 132, 133, 137, 139

Buenos Aires expedition, 186

Bulwark, HMS, 211

Burford, HMS, 89

Cadiz, 45, 47, 66, 104, 105, 109, 111, 114, 117, 118, 131–2,

Cadiz (*cont.*)
    139–40
Caesar, HMS, 14, 68
Calcutta, 88, 148
Calcutta, HMS, 188
Calder, Admiral Robert, 48, 51,
    109, 114–18
Calvi, siege of, 44
Cambrian, HMS, 172
Campbell, Rear Admiral Donald,
    109
Canada (British North America), 3,
    215–20, 225
Canning, George, 148, *149*, 166,
    167, 185, 187, 232
Canopus, HMS (ex-French *Franklin*),
    62, 164, 189
Cape of Good Hope expeditions, 89,
    91–3, 95, 148, 185–6
Cape Town, 92, 186
Captain, HMS, 46, 49, 51, 52, 168
Carnation, HMS, 191–2
Carnegie, William, 7th Earl
    Northesk, 138
Caroline, HMS, 197
Carysfort, HMS, 93
Cattaro, siege of, 182
Censeur, HMS, 45
Centaur, HMS, 150, 153, 168
Centurion, HMS, 89, 90, 95
Cerberus, HMS, 180–1
Ceylon, 90, 232
Ceylon, HMS, 196
Chatham, HMS, 162
Chatham Dockyard, 218
Chesapeake, US ship, 202, 207, *208*,
    208
Chesapeake Bay, 190, 202, 211, 221,
    222
Childers, HMS, 1

Christian, Rear Admiral Hugh, 81–2
Clorinde, HMS, 196
Cochrane, Admiral Alexander, 70–
    2, 111, 190, 192, 193, 222–3
Cochrane, Captain Thomas, 158–
    60, 172
Cockburn, Rear Admiral George,
    101, 111, 221, *222*, 222, 223,
    227
Codrington, Captain Edward, 137,
    138, 176
Cole, Captain Christopher, *198*, 199
Collier, Captain George, 177
Collingwood, Admiral Cuthbert,
    xix, 49, 109, 122, 125, 126–32,
    139–42, 163–4, *165*, 169, 172,
    178, 179, 189, 201
Colossus, HMS, 119, 130, 143
Colpoys, Admiral John, 21–2
Comet, HMS (ex-*Sylphe*), 191
Comet, US privateer, 209
Commerce de Marseilles, French ship,
    42, 66
Confiance, HMS, 169
Confiance, HMS (1814), 220
Conquérant, French ship, 59
Conqueror, HMS, 137–8
Constellation, US ship, 221
Constitution, US ship, 202–6, 208
Coode, Captain John, 230
Cooke, Captain John, 129
Coombe, Lieutenant William, *191*
Coote, Major General Eyre, 27
Copenhagen expedition (1807),
    148–9, *149*
Corbett, Sir Julian, 232
Cork, victualling centre, 21
Cornwallis, HMS, 196–7
Cornwallis, Vice Admiral William,
    20, 88, 102, 111, 114, 116, 188

Corona, Venetian ship, 181

Corsican campaign, 43–4

Corunna, evacuation of, 172–3

Cotton, Admiral Charles, 169–71, 173

Courier, French ship, 89

Craig, Major General John, 92

Crescent, HMS, 19

Cressy, HMS, 158

Cruizer class, 212

Culloden, HMS, 17, 48–9, 51, 53, 57, 59

Cumberland, HMS, 179

Cumby, William, 126, 129

Curaçao expedition, 190

Curieux, HMS, 111, 114

Cuyler, Major General Cornelius, 78

Cybèle, French ship, 88, 89, 93

Dacres, Captain James, 204

Daedalus, HMS, 11, 95

Dance, Commodore Nathaniel, 193

Dannebrog, Danish ship, 34–5

Dardanelles expedition, 163–5

Decatur, Captain Stephen, 205

Defence, HMS, 13–14, 59, 119, 131; loss of, 156

Defiance, HMS, 115, 129, 131, 132, 142

Den Helder expedition, 27–8, 30

Denmark
    Mosquito War, 152
    navy, 32, 33–7, 97, 146–9, 167, 231

Département de Landes, French ship, 191

Deptford, stores, 9

Désirée, HMS, 34

Detroit, HMS, 218–19

Diadem, HMS, 185

Diamond, HMS, 18

Diamond Rock, HMS, 110, 111, 154

Dictator, HMS, 150

Digby, Captain Henry, 137

Diligente, French ship, 191–2

Dillon, Midshipman William Henry, 13–14

Diomède, French ship, 189, 190

Diomede, HMS, 89, 90

Director, HMS, 26

Dolphin, US privateer, 209

Donegal, HMS, 119, 141, 189

Doris, HMS, 196

Dover, HMS, 197

Downie, Captain George, 220

Dragon, HMS, 115, 211, 221

Dreadnought, HMS, 131, 142

Droits de l'Homme, French ship, 22, 23

Drury, Rear Admiral William, 194–5

Dubourdieu, Rear Admiral Bernard, 180

Duckworth, Vice Admiral John, 65, 66, 87, 164, 165, 189, 190

Dudley, Captain Robert, 211

Duff, Captain George, 119, 124, 129

Duguay-Trouin, French ship, 139

Duke, HMS, 78

Duke of Gloucester, HMS, 214–15

Dumanoir, Rear Admiral Pierre, 131, 139

Duncan, Vice Admiral Adam, 23, 25–6

Dundas, General David, 43

Dundas, Henry, 8, 16, 40, 75, 76, 77, 79, 81, 82, 83, 84, 86, 87, 88, 91, 99, 107, 143, 145, 231

Dunkirk, 7, 8, 21

Durham, Captain Philip, 131–2

Dutch Republic
  Cape colony, 91–3, 185–6
  East Indies colonies, 90–1, 197,
    199
  fleet, 9, 24–7, 93, 146–7
  fleet losses, 97, 162, 190, 194,
    231
  South American colonies, 82, 86
  West Indies colonies, 86, 190,
    193

Eagle, US ship, 220
Earl, Commodore Hugh, 214
Earl of Moira, HMS, 214–15
East India Company, 88, 91, 93, 95,
    102
East Indies, 3, 77, 88–91, 96, 193–
    9, 209, 212
  local war, 88–9
Echo, HM sloop, 92
Eclipse, HM sloop, 197
Edgar, HMS, 33–5
Egypt, 30, 55–6, 62, 63, 65, 96
Egyptian expedition (1801), 69–72,
    73
  Red Sea expedition, 94–6
  victualling, 70
Egyptian expedition (1807), 166
Elba, 46, 47, 227
Elephant, HMS, 33–6
Elliot, Midshipman George, 57
Elliot, Sir Gilbert, 1st Earl Minto,
    45, 51, 195, 197
Elphinstone, George, 1st Viscount
    Keith, 30, 41, 66, 70, 92, 93,
    95, 106, 107, 111
Emerald, HMS, 53, 55
Endymion, HMS, 20, 225
España, Spanish ship, 115
Espiègle, French ship, 191

Essex, US ship, 204, 209, 210
Europa, HMS, 77
Euryalus, HMS, xx, 128, 139
Everard, Captain Thomas, 219
Excellent, HMS, 49, 51, 163, 172
Experiment, transport, 9

Fane, HMS, 172
Faulkner, Captain Robert, 79, 80,
    81
Favourite, HM sloop, 84
Ferrol
  attack on, 30
  blockade of, 111, 169
Firme, Spanish ship, 115–16
Fisher, Captain Peter, 220
Fishguard, French attack on, 23
Floating Battery No. 1, Danish ship,
    34
Flora, HMS, 19
Flore, French ship, 181
Foley, Captain Thomas, 32, 35, 57,
    59, 62
Ford, Commodore John, 77–8
Formidable, French ship (1794), 21;
    (1795), 68, 139
Forte, French ship, 93, 94
Fortitude, HMS, 43
Foudroyant, HMS, 66, 68, 167
Fougueux, French ship, 127–9, 136
Fox, cutter, 53
Fox, HMS, 95
France
  continental blockade, 143, 152,
    154, 187, 188, 199, 202
  invasion threat, 8, 10, 21, 23, 26,
    27, 37, 45, 54, 83, 102–8, 110,
    114, 117, 118, 143, 161
  navy losses, 42, 62, 97, 141, 142,
    231

navy, rebuilding after Trafalgar, 145–6

Franklin, French ship, 60, 62

Fraternité, French ship, 22

Fremantle, Captain Thomas, 32, 53, 54, 137, 182

French Guiana expedition, 190–2

Frolic, HMS, 204

Fulton, Robert, 107

Galatea, HMS, 191, *191*, *192*,

Gallardo, Spanish ship, 84

Galles, Vice Admiral Morard de, 11, 21, 22

Gambier, Admiral James, 13, 148, 158–60

Ganteaume, Rear Admiral Honoré, 30, 104, 169

Gardner, Admiral Alan, 78

Gardner, Captain Alan, 115

General Armstrong, US privateer, 209

General Hunter, HMS, 214

General Pike, US ship, 215, 216

Généreux, French ship, 62, 68

Gibraltar, 30, 44, 68, 109, 113, 114, 148, 174, 228
    problems as a base, 47
    repair, 140, 142
    victualling, 70, 119

Glatton, HMS, 35

Glengarry, gunboat, 215

Glory, HMS, 114

Goliath, HMS, 56, 57, 59, 150

Goodall, Vice Admiral Samuel, 45

Grampus, HMS, 195

Grand Turk, US privateer, 209

Graves, Admiral Thomas, 32, 35

Gravina, Admiral Federico, 131

Grey, Lieutenant General Charles, 79, 81, 82

Guadeloupe, 80–2, 111, 190, *191*

Guerrier, French ship, 59

Guerriere, HMS, 204–6

Guillaume Tell, French ship, 62, 68

Hallowell, Captain Benjamin, 30, 60, 130, 179

Hamilton, Captain Edward, *84*, *85*

Hannibal, HMS, 68

Hardy, Captain Thomas, 119, 122, 133, 140, 211

Hare, Captain Charles, 41

Hargood, Captain William, 94, 129

Harvey, Admiral Henry, 84

Haswell, Lieutenant John, 82, 84–6

Hecla, bomb vessel, 27

Hector, HMS, 78

Heligoland, 154

Hermione, HMS, *84*, *85*

Hero, HMS, 72, 115, 116, 156

Heroine, HMS, 90

Héros, French ship, 42, 139

Heureux, French ship, 59, 60, 62

Hibernia, HMS, 167

Hind, armed schooner, 78

Hoche, General Lazare, 21–2

Holstein, Danish ship, 36

Hood, Admiral Alexander, 1st Viscount Bridport, 17, 20, 21, 22, 29, 65

Hood, Captain Samuel, 53, 59, 152, 153, 168, 190

Hood, Samuel, 1st Viscount, 39, 40–4, 79

Hornet, US ship, 205–7, 209

Hoste, Captain William, 180–2

Hotham, Vice Admiral William, 44–6

Howe, Admiral Lord Richard, 10–17, *17*, 21, 26, 121

Hull, Captain Isaac, 204

Île de France, 88–90, 93, 94
    expedition, 194–7, *195*, 199
Illustrious, HMS, 196
Impérial, French ship, 189
Imperieuse, HMS, 159, 172
Implacable, HMS, 150, 153
Impregnable, HMS, 228
impressment, 201, 202, 228
Indefatigable, HMS, 21–3
Intrepid, HMS, 94, 163, 168
Intrépide, French ship, 137–9
Invincible, HMS, 84, 86
Iphigenia, HMS, 195, 196
Iris, French ship, 42

Jamaica, 76–8, 86, 109, 110, 189
Java, 89, 93, 194
    expedition, 199
Java, HMS, 206
Jean Bart, French ship, 89, 158
Jervis, John, 1st Earl St Vincent, 26,
    28, 29, 32, 46–9, 51–5, 65, 66,
    79, 81, 82, 107, 124, *149*
    as First Lord, 98, 99
Juno, HMS, 42, 163
Jupiter, French ship, 189
Jylland, Danish ship, 33, 34

Keats, Rear Admiral Richard, 122,
    154
Kingsmill, Admiral Robert, 22
Knowles, Admiral Charles, 11

La Cléopâtre, French ship, 19
La Gloire, French ship, 20
La Minerve, HMS, 48, 88
La Pomone, French ship, 20
La Tapageuse, French ship, *146*

Lady Murray, merchantman, 215
Lady Prevost, HMS, 214
Laforey, Vice Admiral John, 77, 78
Lake Champlain, 219
Lake Erie, 214, 215, 218, 219
Lake Ontario, 214–16, 218, 219
Lángara, Admiral Juan de, 47
Lawrence, Captain James, 207
Lawrence, US ship, 218, 219
League of Armed Neutrality, 31, 32,
    37, 87, 96
Leander, HMS, 60, 211, 228
Leech, Samuel, 204–6
Leissègues, Vice Admiral Corentin,
    189
Lennox, Captain Charles, 93
Leopard, HMS
Leviathan, HMS, 95, 202
Linois, Rear Admiral Charles-
    Alexandre, 193, 194
Lion, HMS, 199
Lloyd's Patriotic Fund, *146*, 199
London, HMS, 167, 168
L'Orient, French ship, 55, 56, 59,
    60, *61*
Louis, Rear Admiral Thomas, 164
Lucas, Captain Jean, 133, 136, 141
Lucifer, bomb vessel, 172
Lynx, French ship, 190, *191*, *192*

MacBride, Admiral John, 8
Macedonian, HMS, 204–6
Madeira expedition, 168
Madison, President James, 202, 203,
    210, 212, 225
Madison, US ship, 215
Madras, 89, 90, 91, 93, 101, 148,
    193, 195
Magicienne, HMS, 195
Maitland, Captain Frederick, 1, 227

Maitland, Lieutenant Colonel
    Frederick, 196
Majestic, HMS, 59, 211
Malcolm, Sir Pulteney, 223
Malta, 30, 31, 55, 63, 66, 70, 72,
    102, 148, 169, 174, 181, 232
    Valetta harbour, 55
Malta, HMS, 116
Manley, Captain John, 7
Maria, HM gunbrig, 191
Marlborough, HMS, 167, 168, 221
Mars, HMS, 119, 124, 129, 136, 150
Martin, Admiral Thomas Byam, *83*,
    153, 157, 179
Martinique, 78, 84, 86, 104, 109,
    110, 158, 190, 191, 192
    expedition, 79–81, *81*
    Fort Louis, 80, *81*
Maurice, Captain James, 154
Medusa, HMS, 37, *37*
Menelaus, HMS, 196
Mercedes, Spanish ship, 105
Mercure, French ship, 60, 62
Merlin, HM sloop, 86
Meteor, bomb vessel, 164, 172
Middleton, Charles, 1st Baron
    Barham, 16, 17, *113*, 114, 117,
    190
Milford, HMS, 182
Miller, Captain Ralph, 50, 59
Minden, HMS, 228
Minerva, HMS, 88
Minorca, 30, 46, 66
    expedition, 65
    Port Mahon, 65, 148
    victualling, 70
Minotaur, HMS, 139
Missiessy, Rear Admiral Édouard de,
    108, 111, 161, 162
Mitchell, Admiral Andrew, 27, 29

Molloy, Captain Anthony, 14
Monarca, Spanish ship, 129, 130, 141
Monarch, HMS, 25, 78, 92, 107, 167,
    168
Montagu, HMS, 206
Montañés, Spanish ship, 129, 130
Mont-Blanc, French ship, 115, 139
Montréal, French ship, 42
Moore, Captain Graham, 167, 168
Moore, Sir John, 150, 152, 154,
    172, 173
Moorsom, Robert, 124, 131
'Mortello' tower, 43
Mucius, French ship, 13
Murray, Lieutenant Colonel John,
    219
Mutine, HMS, 55
mutinies, 16, *84*
    Nore and Spithead, 23–6

Napoleon Bonaparte, 1, *2*, 2, 3, *5*,
    31, 41, 95, 102, *103*, 109, 118,
    143, 145, 149, 152, 154, 155,
    162, 163, 173, *184*, 186, 220,
    233
    and Acre, 63–5
    and Amiens, 96
    Decree of Berlin, 183
    Decree of Milan, 183
    economic warfare, 183, 184, 187,
        188, 199, 202
    and Egypt, 55,
    imprisonment, 227
    invasion of Russia, 156–7, 202,
        210
    invasion plans, 103–6, 117
    naval rebuilding, 145–7, 179, 183
    neutral warships, 188
    surrenders to *Bellerophon*, 1, 227
Narcissus, HMS, 186

Nautilus, HMS sloop, 78

Nautilus, US ship, 204

Naval General Service Medal, *182*, *192*

Nelson, Admiral Lord Horatio, xvii, 30, 46, 47–8, 66, 68, 104, 114, 117, 142, 163, 167, 175, 179, 180

  Band of Brothers, 56, *61*, 122

  and Boulogne, 37

  at Copenhagen, 32–6

  at Cape St Vincent, 48–52

  at Corsica, 43–4

  death xvii–xx, *xviii*, 135, 140

  frustration with Hotham, 45

  leadership legacy, 180, 189

  leadership style, 124

  at Naples, 63, 66, 68

  at Nile, 55–63, *61*

  tactical legacy, 180, 228

  at Tenerife, 52–4

  at Trafalgar, 118, 119, 125–8, 132–3, 135, 137, *138*, 139, 140; chasing of Villeneuve, 108–13; shot, 135; tactics, 121–4, *123*

Neptune, French ship, 129, 137

Neptune, HMS, 133, 136–7, 192

Neptuno, Spanish ship, 139

Nereide, HMS, 86–7, 195–6

New Orleans, US ship, 218

Niagara, US ship, 218–19

Nisus, HMS, 196–7

Northumberland, HMS, *2*, 66, 189, 227

Nymphe, HMS, 19, 169

Océan, French ship, 158

Oneida, US ship, 214

Onslow, Vice Admiral Richard, 25–6

Orde, Admiral John, 109, 111

Orestes, HM sloop, 95

Orion, HMS, 55, 59, 130, 137–9, 141, 142, 150

Orpheus, HMS, 90

Ostend expeditions, 7–9, 108

  Saas lock, 26–7

Otter, HMS, 199

Palinure, French ship, 191

Pallas, HMS, *146*

Parker, Admiral Hyde, 32, 35, 36, 46

Pascoe, Lieutenant John, 126

Paul I, Tsar, 29–31, 36

Peacock, HM sloop, 207

Pellew, Edward, 1st Baron Exmouth, 19–23, 29, 107, 138, 176, 180, 193–4, 228–30, *229*

Pellew, Israel, 138

Peninsular War, 170–8

  Lines of Torres Vedras, 173–6; Royal Navy gunboats, 174; Royal Navy signalling, 174

  Mondego river, British landing at, 170–1

  Royal Navy support, Biscay coast, 177–8

  Royal Navy support, east coast of Spain, 176–7

  specie, 176

  Tagus river, Royal Navy flatboats, 173

  victuals, 175–6

Perle, French ship, 43

Perry, Master Commandant Oliver Hazard, 218–19

Perseverance, HMS, 88

Peuple Sovereign, French ship, 59, 60

Phaeton, HMS, 20, 101

Phipps, Henry, 1st Earl Mulgrave, 158, 159
Phoebe, HMS, 196, 209
Phoenix, HMS, 88
Pitt, John, 2nd Earl Chatham, 8, 44, 162
Pitt, William, 30, 32, 75, 82, 99, 103, 107, 145, 149, 186, 193
Plantagenet, HMS, 209
Pluton, French ship, 115, 129
Plymouth, 11, 98, 227
Polyphemus, HMS, 129, 131
Pomone, HMS, 224, 225
Pompée, French ship, 42
Pondicherry, 88, 95
    siege of, 88
Popham, Rear Admiral Home Riggs, 8–9, 26–8, 95, 96, 107, 108, 160, 177, 185–9
    organizes Sea Fencibles at Ostend, 8
    telegraphic code, 118, 126, 174
Portsmouth, 98, 118, 186, 228
    Spithead anchorage, 10–12, 22, 23, 89, 171
Portugal, navy, 109, 166–8
Powlett, Lord Henry, 20
President, US ship, 203, 224, 225
Prevost, Sir George, 214–16, 220
Prince, HMS, 132, 137, 142
Prince George, HMS, 49
Prince of Wales, HMS, 84, 86, 114–16, 119
Prince Regent, HMS, 214–15
Princess-Royal, merchantman, 89
Príncipe de Asturias, Spanish ship, 48, 131, 132, 139
Pring, Commodore Daniel, 219
Proserpine, HMS, 178
Prøvestenen, Danish ship, 34

Prowse, Captain William, 124
Prudente, French ship, 89
Psyche, HMS (1814), 218
Psyche, HMS (ex-French Psyché), 196
Puissant, French ship, 42
Purvis, Rear Admiral John, 169
Pym, Captain Samuel, 195

Quebec, gunboat, 215
Quebec, HMS, 8
Queen, HMS, 78, 142
Queen Charlotte, HMS (1790), 12, 13, 16, 17
Queen Charlotte, HMS (1810), 214, 219
Queen Charlotte, HM sloop (1812), 228–30, 229
Quiberon Bay expedition, 20, 29

Rainier, Vice Admiral Peter, 89–91, 93–5, 193
Raisonnable, HMS, 195
Ramillies, HMS, 211
Ranger, HM brig, 188
Rattlesnake, HM sloop, 92
Raven, US ship, 215
Rayo, Spanish ship, 139
Real Carlos, Spanish ship, 68
Red Sea expedition, 94–5
Redoubtable, French ship, xix, 133, 136
Régénérée, French ship, 93–4
Resistance, HMS, 90, 94
Résolue, French ship, 88
Retribution, HMS (ex-Hermione), 84
Revenge, HMS, 124, 126, 130, 131, 140, 142, 158
Revolutionaire, HMS, 18
Révolutionnaire, French ship, 12
Reynolds, Admiral Robert, 23, 156

Riou, Captain Edward, 32, 35
Rivoli, French ship, 182, *182*
Robinson, William, 126, 131, 140
Rochefort, 1, 104, 110, 111, 168, 188, 190
Rodney, Admiral George, 16, 121, 124
Rose, HMS, 158
Rosily, Admiral François Étienne de, 118
Ross, Major General Robert, 223
Rota, HMS, 209
Rotely, Lewis, 134, *135*,
Rotherham, Captain Edward, 128, 138
Rothschild, Nathan, 102, 177
Royal George, HMS, 214–15
Royal Navy
  Baltic Fleet, 150–8
  Cadiz, blockade of, 52–5, 119, 124, 164, 169, 174, 189
  Cadiz, raid on (1800), 70
  Channel Fleet, 10–11, 17, 18, 20, 21, 29, 78, 98, 109, 117, 118
  convoys, 11, 12, 45, 83–4, 89, 152, 154–5, 158, 166, 175, 178, 185, 188, 189, 193, 194, 204, 210, 212, 231
  coppering, 98–9, 127, 153
  Mediterranean Fleet, 39, 44, 46, 49, 66, 111, 163, 176, 180, 201
  Royal Marines, xx, 40, 41, 43, 53, 63, 78, 87, 92, 119, 131, 133, 134, 135, 170, 172, 174, 182, 185, 191, 192, 197
  strength, 97, 231
  victualling, 21, 25, 29, 46, 47, 70, 97, 98, 111, 117, 119, 175
  Western Squadron, 10, 16, 17
Royal Oak, HMS, 211

Royal Sovereign, HMS, xx, 20, 125, 127, 128, 138, 142
Russell, HMS, 34
Russia, navy, 27, 147, 157, 163, 171, 178, 231
  Baltic Fleet, 32, 36, 146, 152–4, 158
  Mediterranean Fleet, 31, 166, 167, 169, 171

St Antoine, French ship, 68
St Domingo, HMS, 211
Saint-Domingue, 78, 80, 86
St George, HMS, 33, 156
St Lawrence, HMS, 216, *217*, 218
Saint Martin, 87
Salvador del Mundo, Spanish ship, 49
Samarang, HMS, 197, 199
San Agustín, Spanish ship, 137
San Damaso, Spanish ship, 84–5
San Francisco de Asís, Spanish ship, 139
San Hermenegildo, Spanish ship, 68
San Idelfonso, Spanish ship, 131, 132
San Isidro, Spanish ship, 49
San José, Spanish ship, 49, 51
San Juan Nepomuceno, Spanish ship, 131, 132
San Nicolás, Spanish ship, 49–51
San Rafael, Spanish ship, 115, 116
San Vicente, Spanish ship, 84
Santa Ana, Spanish ship, 128, 129, 139
Santa Cecilia, Spanish ship, 84
Santander, capture of, 177
Santísima Trinidad, Spanish ship, xx, 49, 51, 137, 139
Saratoga, US ship, 220
Saumarez, James, 19, 55, 59
  action off Algeciras, 68, *69*

and Baltic, 150–8, *151*, 209
Scipio, HMS, 84
Scipion, French ship, 139
Scipion, HMS, 199
Scott, Alexander, xix, 140
Scott, John, 133
scurvy, 17, 190
   use of lemon juice in Channel
     Fleet, 17, 29
Seahorse, HMS, 53
Séduisant, French ship, 22
Seine, French ship, 93, 94
Sémillante, French ship, 194
Sercey, Rear Admiral Pierre, 93–4
Sevelod, Russian ship, 153
Severn, HMS, 228
Seymour, Vice Admiral Hugh, 86–7
Shannon, HM schooner, 219, 220
Shannon, HMS, 168, 204, 207–8,
   208
Shipley, Captain Conway, 169
Sibylle, HMS (ex-*Espiègle*), 191
Sir Edward Hughes, East Indiaman,
   101
Sir Sidney Smith, HMS, 215
Sirius, HMS, 114, 115, 124, 163, 195
slavery, 227
Smith, Admiral Sidney, 18, 66, 95,
   108
   at Acre, 63–5, *64*
   and Dardanelles, 163–4
   at Lisbon, 167, 169
   in South America, 191
   at Toulon, 41–2
Snape, Captain Andrew, 20
Spain, navy, 30, 47, 48, 49–52, 66,
   68, *69*, 84, 86, 94, 105, 109,
   110, 111, 125, 114–17, 128–31,
   137, 139, 141, 147, 169, 193
   losses, 97, 141, 142, 231

   at Toulon, 40–2
Spartiate, French ship, 59, 60
Spartiate, HMS, 62, 139
Spencer, HMS, 68, 189, 211
Spencer, George, 19, 22, 32, 42, 47,
   51, 54
Standard, HMS, 164
Stately, HMS, 92
States General, Dutch ship, 26
Stewart, Lieutenant Colonel
   William, 34
Stockham, Captain John, 131
Stopford, Captain Edward, 199
Stopford, Admiral Robert, 158, 199
Strachan, Admiral Sir Richard, 142,
   161
Stuart, Lieutenant General Charles,
   44
Success, HMS, 168
Suffolk, HMS, 89, 90
Superb, HMS, 68, 122, 150, 189,
   211, 228
Surcouf, Robert, 194
Surprise, HMS, *84*
Swallow, HMS, 41, 42
Sweden, navy, 146, 147, 152, 153,
   155
Swift, HM sloop, 89, 90
Swiftsure, French ship (ex-Royal Navy
   Swiftsure), 130, 138
Swiftsure, HMS (1787), 30, 56–60
Swiftsure, HMS (1804), 129, 130, 142
Sylphe, French ship, 191
Syren, HMS, 7

Tamatave expedition, 197
Tartarus, bomb vessel, 27
Tate, Admiral George, 157
Temeraire, HMS, 128, 133, 136, 139,
   142, 179

Tenedos, HMS, 225

Tenerife expedition, 52–4

Terpsichore, HMS, 53, 194

Terrible, gunboat, 42

Terror, bomb vessel, 84

Thémistocle, French ship, 42

Theseus, HMS, 53, 54, 59, 63, 65

Thompson, Vice Admiral Charles, 49

Thorn, HM sloop, 84

Thornton, Richard, 102

Thouars, Captain Aristide Du Petit, 60

Thunderer, HMS, 131, 142, 164

Tigre, French ship, 21

Tigre, HMS, 63, 65, 179

Timoléan, French ship, 62

Tonnant, French ship, 43, 59, 60, 62

Tonnant, HMS (ex-French), 62, 129, 142, 211

Topaze, French ship, 42

Topaze, HMS, 179

Toulon, 3, 11, 18, 30, 39–47, 54, 55, 66, 79, 104, 108, 109, 111, 169, 178, 179, 180, 212
    counter-revolution, 11, 39
    occupation of, 41–2

Tourville, French ship, 13

Trieste, attack on, 182

Trincomalee, 90, 95, 148

Trist, Lieutenant Robert, 169

Triumph, HMS, 26, 115, 116

Troubridge, Rear Admiral Thomas, 53, 193

Trusty, HMS, 77, 78

Turkey, navy, 55, 163–6, 231

Tyler, Captain Charles, 129

Ulysses, armed transport, 84

Union, gunboat, 42

Unité, French ship, *18*

United States
    decline in trade, 213
    Embargo Act (1807), 202
    impressed sailors, 202
    navy, 202, 203–12, 215–20, 221, 225; losses, 231
    Non-Intercourse Act (1809), 202
    privateers, 177–8;

Upton Castle, transport, *195*

Ushant, 10, 12, 21, 22, 29

Vanguard, HMS, 55–7, 59, 60, 63, 150

Venerable, HMS, 25–6, 68, 160

Vengeance, HMS, 84

Ventura, HMS, 211

Vertu, French ship, 93, 94

Vesuvius, bomb vessel, 80

Victorieuse, HM sloop, 84

Victorious, HMS, 92, 93, 182, 221

Victory, HMS, xvii, xix, xx, *xxi*, 40, 44, 46, 118
    in Baltic, 150
    at Cape St Vincent, 49
    at Corunna, 173
    crew, 118–19, 201
    at Lisbon, 175, *176*
    and Nelson, 118–19, 122
    at Trafalgar, 124–6, 127, 128, 132–6, *135*, 139, 142

Villaret-Joyeuse, Rear Admiral Louis-Thomas, 11, 12, 20

Ville de Paris, HMS, 52, *165*, 173, 179

Villeneuve, Admiral Pierre-Charles, 62, 104, 108–19, 125, 126, 132, 133, 137–9, 141, 142, 154, 188

Virgine, HMS, 94

Volage, HM sloop, 180–1
Volontaire, HMS, 179, 186
Vrijheid, Dutch ship, 26
Vulcan, fireship, 41

Walcheren expedition, 160–2
Walker, Midshipman Henry, 141
Waller, Captain John, 53
War on the Great Lakes, 213–20
Warren, Admiral John Borlase, 19,
    20, 30, 194, 207, 211, 215, 221,
    222
Washington, attack on, 220–3
Wasp, HMS, 219
Wasp, US ship, 204, 206
Watkins, Captain Frederick, 86–7
Weazel, HM sloop, 182
Wellesley, Sir Arthur, 162, 170, 171,
    173–8, 186, 187, 202, 209, 212
West Indies
    Abercromby–Christian
        expedition, 81–2
    Abercromby–Hervey expedition,
        82–6
    British strategy, 3, 4, 75–7
    British trade with, 75–6

Grey–Jervis expedition, 79–80
    local war, 78–9
    losses, 87–8
West, Captain John, 172
Western, Lieutenant John, 7
Willaumez, Admiral Jean-Baptiste,
    158, 159, 189–90
Williamson, Captain John, 26
Willoughby, Captain Nesbit, 195
Windsor Castle, HMS, 114–16, 165
Winter, Admiral Jan Willem de,
    24–6
Wolfe, HMS, 215
Woodford, East India Company ship,
    93
Woodlark, HMS, 158

Yeo, Captain James, 191, 192, 215,
    216, 218
York, Duke of, Prince Frederick, 8,
    9, 10, 28
York, HMS, 168

Zealous, HMS, 53, 56, 57, 59
Zebra, HM sloop, 84
Zebra, HMS, 79–80, *81*